Paradiso Seasons

Paradiso

DENIS COTTER

PHOTOGRAPHY BY JÖRG KÖSTER

DESIGN AND ART DIRECTION BY JOHN FOLEY

First published in 2003 by

Atrium

(an imprint of Attic Press Ltd)

Crawford Business Park

Crosses Green

Cork

Ireland

Photographs © Jörg Köster 2002–2003

Designed by John Foley at Bite, Cork
Set in Adobe Minion

Cover illustration by Eoin Kelly

Repro by The Scanning Shop, Dublin
Printed in Spain by Estudios Gráficos Zure - E48950 Erandio (Bizkaia)

9 8 7 6 5 4 3 2 1

British Library Cataloguing in Publication data
A CIP catalogue record for this book is available from the British Library.

ISBN 0-9535353-4-7
A CIP record for this publication is available from the Library of Congress.

For all Atrium books visit www.corkuniversitypress.com

Visit Café Paradiso on the internet at www.cafeparadiso.ie

Introduction

At some time during the writing of this book, I took a computer and a pile of notes to a hotel that I love for its peaceful atmosphere and beautiful setting. I was looking forward to mixing writing with a little calm idleness. The first morning I had a breakfast that shocked me so much I had to repeat the order next day to see if it was true, a culinary pinch in the arm. The dish was poached eggs and grilled tomatoes, simple, classic and well-cooked in the technical sense. The egg was the palest I had ever seen and had so little flavour it was a weird and disturbing thing to have in my mouth; and the tomato, which was in the process of changing from green to orange, had been grown in such a way that it would never have tasted of much if it had been left to ripen for another month. In a blind tasting I would have been hard pushed to guess their species. Both items were probably purchased with price as the main, or indeed only, criteria. I have no doubt that the eggs were the cheapest available, probably produced in appalling conditions that could only be improved by adding a penny or two to the price, something neither the producer nor his clients would be willing to do. This thinking is endemic in the catering industry and, unfortunately, in the wider food business too, where these hopelessly diluted versions of foods become accepted as the standard. Foods which were once loved for their extraordinary individuality, preciousness and vibrant flavours have been turned into dull everyday fodder.

The most fundamental truths are often almost impossibly simple. Despite a persistent tendency for cooking to be seen as an obscure and complicated art form, available only to a few eccentric and angry geniuses, the basic 'food truths' keep surfacing time and again. To eat well, you need good food; good food, as distinct from pretty food, requires good ingredients; good ingredients are grown and produced with respect and care and in a balance with their time and place; to cook good food with these ingredients you need to work with the same respect and care, to find the same balance. This is the underlying principle of eating seasonally, the source of an holistic and immeasurable pleasure of food in perfect balance. There is nothing complex in this principle; it is simple, and ancient.

Cooking vegetables at their best and with foods that are natural partners gives us the pleasure of feasting on the abundant. Does anything make more perfect sense than eating foods whose seasonal curves cross each other or rise and fall together? It is no accident that our senses take watercress and the soft sheep's-milk cheese of spring to be a perfect match; or tomatoes and basil, peas and mint, pumpkins and chestnuts, peaches and lavender.

In Café Paradiso, I try to make the best seasonal produce the focus of our cooking. Most dishes are based on one or two vegetables that I want to highlight, though they use other vegetables and ingredients in supporting roles. Everything, from the careful buying to the careful preparation, focused on a vegetable's best characteristics, is done to draw attention to the vegetable, to simply make it a pleasure to eat, so that it will be noticed in a way that may or may not have been expected.

I get more of a kick from people saying that they just ate the best beetroot, pumpkin, spring cabbage, asparagus or whatever, than to be told that the cooking is smart. Good cooking helps us to enjoy good food, it is not an end in itself. Clever cooking applied to poor ingredients often makes for depressing eating, a point which is often lost on expensive restaurants.

Sometimes people discover and like flavours they were afraid of or thought they didn't care much for. For others, it is more about re-discovering tastes, and enjoying the double pleasure of the present and remembered meals. As a cook, I find this rediscovering hugely rewarding. It is not so much about forgotten tastes as ones that people have stopped noticing. Awareness, paying attention, noticing is the first and most important step to enjoying food. There is an enormous gulf between the pleasure of consciously eating a ripe organic tomato that you have carefully chosen from a market stall in late summer, and mindlessly slicing one, grabbed from a shop shelf, into a sandwich on a cold winter's afternoon. One is the most delicious thing you can eat at the time, the other is little more than a habit. A stew of sun-ripened peppers, garlic and basil in rich olive oil can make you wonder why you never loved peppers so much before – but only if the peppers are indeed very good.

Peaches, tomatoes, avocados, asparagus, broad beans, sugar snaps, parsnips, leeks, aubergines, sweet peppers, apples and pears… these are extraordinary foods that can give us unique pleasure. Ironically, the more poor imitations we eat, the less pleasure we take. For many of us, the pleasure associated with these wonderful foods has been gradually replaced in our minds by a dull, nagging ordinariness bordering on disappointment, and ultimately we forget they were ever wonderful. When the foods have finally been reduced to ordinariness, we can pass them in the supermarket aisles without even noticing them.

How did we get to a stage where we can pass a peach without giving it a glance, and not think that biting into its lusciously juicy flesh would brighten our day, maybe our week? The exotic beauty of a peach has been replaced with an ever-present imitation that leaves us lukewarm, and, in the gradual process of that replacement, our affection for the peach has been distorted. In the furious drive to provide secure supplies of cheap and plentiful food that dominated food production in the second half of the twentieth century, a compromise was made to sacrifice taste and quality for volume and cheapness. Where the guiding principles are cheapness and year-round availability, the first sacrifice is taste. This is not a small matter. With taste goes the pleasure we look for in food and, when the pleasure is gone or reduced to dullness, our relationship with food is altered. The result is an excess of food that can't quite seem to satisfy the complex longing we call our hunger.

Where do we look for the pleasure in food when so much of it is insipid? To the fast-food section? The freezers of upmarket chain stores which prepare almost-decent imitations of ethnic foods? Or do we search out the artisan growers, cheese-makers, bakers and so on; the people who produce food with taste as the first priority because they couldn't bear to do it any other way. Only one way has the capacity to give us food that satisfies our complex hunger, to feed all the needs we have from food, conscious and subconscious. There is an holistic sense of well-being we enjoy when our hunger is truly satisfied that can only be had from eating good food cooked with great care. We have forgotten that the balance we often have such difficulty maintaining in our relationship with food is present in the natural seasonal order. Asparagus is useful to look at because it is traditionally seen as expensive, rare and very desirable. Those who love it become twitchily excited when it finally shows up with the first warm days and feast themselves on it for its short season. Eaten in late spring when it is fresh, plentiful, bursting with life and utterly of its time, asparagus can be

an exhilarating pleasure. The shortness of the season and the arrival and passing of it are part of that pleasure. Asparagus is in fact admirably and resolutely seasonal and so can only be had out of season by importing it from the opposite hemisphere. The recent development of ever-present cheap and bland asparagus in supermarkets allows us to have inferior asparagus more often, but its very ubiquity makes it ordinary and diminishes its elusive beauty. I believe this is as true of, say, leeks, tomatoes and mangetout as it is of asparagus. We are the poorer for it and I believe that we would derive more pleasure from asparagus by eating it only at its best and in its place and time.

As much as I love asparagus, and as much as it dominates my menus during its peak season, I happily let it go when the time comes. (Well, no, actually I don't. I kick and scream a bit at the first sign of waning, but I pull myself together and get on with it.) A few weeks later it always amazes me how much wonderful food there is and I can't remember where I found the time or space for all that asparagus. Later, in the autumn, pumpkins and leeks gradually sneak onto the menus and a few weeks later they're all over the place. Being a fretful kind of person, I soon wonder how we'll survive when they're gone. But we do, and the next bit is always better, the excitement in the new vegetables coming on stream always more than makes up for the ones we lose. And so it goes on...

The idea of seasonal eating, of focusing our cooking on the best seasonal produce, should be the guiding principle in our approach to food in the complex maze that is the modern food market. By actively giving priority in our buying and cooking to seasonal produce, making it the focus of our attention, we can shift the balance towards an equilibrium. After ten years cooking in the Café Paradiso kitchen, I am certain that without the wonderfully fascinating, unpredictable and infuriating ebb and flow of the seasonal produce we work with I would have been bored to tears long ago. There is a deep pleasure and a never-ending challenge in working with the seasons that you can't get by phoning in orders for the flashest items available on the international market; and a sense of connection with the food which is difficult to evaluate but is often more depressingly obvious in its absence. When the magic works best, the cook is a medium, passing on the produce of the person who grows pumpkins, beans or artichokes to those lovely people who come every few weeks for... a birthday, a quiet night out, maybe... or just for the pumpkins, perhaps.

I hope that the recipes in this book help you to cook well but, equally, I hope that they encourage you to buy well. Give priority in your shopping and cooking to the best vegetables of the season; make conscious and deliberate choices about where you buy, who you buy from and the quality and origin of the food you buy. If you go home with good food that you have chosen carefully and are looking forward to cooking with it, you are more than halfway to eating well and you have hugely increased the pleasure potential of your food.

About the recipes

This collection of recipes is not intended to be a comprehensive collection. I haven't dredged up all the recipes I could think of for each vegetable but have instead tried, using a small number of recipes, to give a sense of the diverse uses each vegetable can have. There are many books, written by more knowledgeable people, that are far closer to being authoritative manuals of vegetable cooking, of which my two favourites are Alice Waters' *Chez Panisse Vegetables* and Digby Law's *A Vegetable Cookbook*.

The recipes are arranged in seasonal order, flowing through the year from the optimism of late spring and all that it promises, through the joy and bounty of summer and autumn, to the relief of early spring when the first greens tell you what you can hardly believe – that you survived another winter. Within that order, recipes focused on a specific vegetable are grouped together. The fact that some vegetables have very long seasons of high quality and bountiful production while others appear for only a short time makes a minor nightmare of arranging the order. In the flow of the book, I have placed a vegetable where it first becomes plentiful in the practical reality of our restaurant and home in Cork, where I buy primarily from West Cork and Irish producers but happily stretch the often short or rain-drenched seasons by buying organic produce imported from France, Italy and Spain. Thus spinach is placed in late spring, when it is a plentiful and mature leaf, after the other greens of late spring, but before the sunny produce of early summer. Broad beans are also in late spring, when I first begin with French ones, even though in a bad year their pods won't show a bulge in Ireland until mid-summer. Leeks which are with us for more than half the year are placed in late autumn, when they are plentiful and become very important as we lose the last of the late-summer and harvest vegetables.

However, almost to highlight how personal and utterly un-encyclopaedic this collection is, black kale finds itself slotted into early summer, although my research suggests it is naturally a vegetable of early winter in north Italy. While it certainly produces quite well after the first frosts, my supply from Hollyhill Farm has always run from early summer to mid-winter and my strongest feelings for it are when it first appears each year, when I am almost reduced to tears at the sight of its beautiful leaves.

One of the reasons for the loosely structured flow of the seasons is that I wanted it to reflect the reality of seasonal changes. I've never been comfortable with the neat compartmentalisation of the year into four even-sized seasons. I sometimes argue that there are probably seven, but when I tried to tie the recipes to these, they still didn't fit. It's not really possible, but often done, to put a menu together at the start of each of the four official seasons using ingredients that are all present at the start and end of the 'season'. In spring you would have no asparagus at the start and no sprouting broccoli at the end; in summer there would be no peppers, peaches or beans until halfway through or later. The reality is that vegetables are unaware of our breakdown of the year and show up in their own good time and in a raggle-taggle order. Some stay for months, others a few weeks. In Café Paradiso, I like to think that there has only ever been one menu. Rather than throwing it out at the end of August, for example, to be replaced by the 'Autumn' menu, that one menu responds to the ebb and flow of the vegetables through the year. They come and go one or two at a time, and the menu follows suit, changing a little here and there every now and again. The recipes in the book follow a similar flow.

Unlike the recipes in the *Café Paradiso Cookbook*, the ones gathered here were put together at home and most could never be categorised as restaurant food. Some are simple ways to prepare vegetables, and these are obviously open to personal interpretation. They can be simple dinners, side dishes or the starting-point for something more elaborate. A few are from the menus of Café Paradiso and are complex and conscious of their appearance, as restaurant food must be. However, these are no less flexible than the simpler recipes. They can be used as specific instructions or as vague guidelines to what goes well with what. The recipes are always about the primary vegetable and, if a recipe pairs a vegetable with a spice or a cheese, chances are those two will be good together in any context. Look closely at the 'spiced beetroot in coconut pancake' on pages 75-6 and you will see that it is in essence a recipe for beetroot curry, based on someone else's recipe and one which I first served (cold) with half a dozen other random dishes at a hastily arranged party. Only later did it become such a pretty and refined dish. Take what you want from the recipes. I hope they are as useful as reference points as much as fixed instruction documents.

It is also very important not to undermine your precious vegetables with poor support. You should be just as fussy about your oils, vinegars, cheeses, flours, grains and so on. Unless something else is specified in a recipe, 'olive oil' always means a good extra virgin one; 'balsamic vinegar' means a traditionally aged one from Modena, at least five years old but older is better; 'butter' means nothing less than real butter, and do try to use Irish butter – it has a richness of flavour I've never come across anywhere else.

Although this may seem a little uptight, many of the recipes give very specific instructions on chopping and slicing vegetables. This is not just for appearances; how the vegetable is cut affects how it cooks as well as the final texture and character of the dish. Look at the beetroot curry again. You can make the dish with huge lumps of beetroot, neat dice, or even thickly grated; all work, but I believe you get the best texture and balance of beetroot flavour with the spices by using the thin cut specified in the recipe. If you have a standard way of cutting a vegetable which you automatically use, try to lose it. You don't always have to follow my cutting methods exactly, but, when you approach a vegetable with a knife, first stop to think about the final dish, try to get a clear sense of it in your mind, and then decide how to cut the vegetable to suit the dish.

All quantities in the recipes are net values; that is, after all peeling and trimming – the amount, in other words, that you are putting in the pan.

Happy cooking.

Late Spring

rocket

asparagus

rhubarb

artichoke

broad beans

spinach

Rocket salad with avocado, spring onion, garlic croûtons and pecorino

A salad of rocket leaves is as frequent a part of feeding-time in our house as potatoes or bread. Most of the time it is simply a case of putting a bowl of leaves on the table close to a bottle of olive oil and a little bottle of balsamic vinegar with a clever home-made sprinkling mechanism. That way, the rocket is eaten before, during and after the meal, depending on your mood and the make-up of the main dish. Lightly dressed rocket is a great foil for rich food, adding that essential balance of freshness and pungency. Occasionally, we might dress the rocket up as a first course, and this version is only one of many possibilities. All the rocket needs is some olive oil, balsamic vinegar and one or two of a range of ingredients such as roasted baby beets, pinenuts, dried tomatoes, cherry tomatoes, broad beans, grilled asparagus, soft cheeses like fresh sheep's cheese or buffalo mozzarella, and so on.

A hard, salty cheese like pecorino is the perfect partner for rocket, but, if you can't get, or don't like, pecorino, use a cheese you do like.

FOR FOUR:

2 slices day-old bread
100mls olive oil
2 cloves garlic
3 spring onions
200–300g rocket
1 large avocado
2 tablespoons balsamic vinegar
salt and pepper, to taste
pecorino, or other hard cheese, for shaving

Brush the bread with a little of the olive oil, and then toast it lightly in a low oven (about 120°C/250°F). Rub the toast with the garlic before cutting it into small pieces.

Slice the spring onion very thinly on a long diagonal. Put the rocket in a bowl, add the spring onion and some of your croûtons.

Slice the avocado into long pieces and, if the flesh is firm enough, add it to the bowl. If the avocado seems too soft to survive being handled, leave it out of the mixed salad and simply tuck the slices into the individual plates of salad later. Sprinkle over the balsamic vinegar and the rest of the olive oil, add a little salt and pepper, and toss the salad gently a few times. Share out the salad and use a vegetable peeler to shave thin slivers of cheese over each serving.

Rigatoni with rocket, broad beans, cherry tomatoes, olives and fresh cheese

Rocket adds a little spicy kick and the tang of fresh greenery to a pasta dish, but only if you don't cook it too much. In fact, don't cook it at all, but stir it into the cooked pasta just before you serve. The first time I cooked rocket, in a potato cake with a clever hidden filling, I felt very pleased with myself in a modernist kind of way, pushing back the boundaries of cooking and all that jazz. That was fine until, one evening, a wise and kind experienced hand at the restaurant business in Cork ate it and said that the dish was nice but I could have saved myself some money by using grass or a few weeds for all the flavour or character of rocket that survived the cooking. Actually, he wasn't as cruel as that, but he was genuinely concerned at my waste of both money and fine produce. So, rocket is definitely one of those vegetables that gives a cook the challenge of conflicting interests: the contradiction between the cook's need to give the impression of doing something clever, and the knowledge that the vegetable is at its best with the minimum of interference – no more is required than a little teasing out of its best qualities and the careful selection of partner ingredients.

This pasta dish has the lightness, simplicity and bright pungency of spring, which is why I like to serve fresh cheese with it – made to be consumed young, fresh cheese also has those springtime characteristics of lightness and delicacy. I alternate between Knockalara sheep's cheese and Oisín goats' cheese crottins; you may have your own favourites, and ricotta, mascarpone or any mild soft cheese will be fine.

FOR FOUR:

450g rigatoni
4 spring onions
4 cloves garlic
100g cherry tomatoes
12 kalamata olives
120mls olive oil
4 tablespoons cooked broad beans
black pepper and salt, to season

100g rocket
100g fresh cheese, from goats', sheep's or cows' milk

Bring a large pot of water to a boil and cook the pasta until just tender. Drain it and return it to the pot. Meanwhile, chop the spring onions into long diagonal pieces. Slice the garlic. Halve the tomatoes; stone the olives and chop them lengthways into halves or quarters. Heat a generous amount of olive oil in a wide pan and cook the onion and garlic gently for a minute. Add the tomatoes, olives and broad beans and cook for one minute more until the tomatoes break down a little. Add just a splash of water to the pan to pick up all of the juices, then tip the contents into the pasta pot with another generous glug of olive oil, a generous seasoning of black pepper and a little salt. Heat the pasta through briefly, then stir in the rocket. Serve the pasta and crumble some cheese over each portion.

Avocado and rocket risotto with shavings of Oisín goats' cheese and a lemon chilli oil

Hard, mature goats' cheese is a rare enough thing, I suppose. It needs a careful hand, and a good goatkeeper, to make it as a civilised and sophisticated cheese rather than a pungent and smelly challenge to the palate. Rose and Rochus of Oisín Farm near the Cork/Limerick border, make a sublime gouda-style cheese that, in its youth, melts beautifully and has a mild taste with just a hint of goat. At eight or nine months, however, the cheese has hardened, even taking on some of the crystalline texture of mature Parmesan. All aspects of the flavour have deepened: the cheese has dried and become creamier, sweeter and richer on the tongue, yet the goaty element is still in balance. Shavings peeled from a freshly cut cheese add a perfect finishing touch to a risotto, pasta or a salad of strong character.

Rocket risotto is a fine combination, a little bit of peppery spirit in the king of comfort foods. But avocado? Some people look at me strangely the first time I suggest they put avocado in the risotto, and in fairness I wouldn't go chucking it into any old risotto. It is a particularly good companion to rocket, in salads as well as here. The avocado is added at the end so that it warms through but doesn't get heated to the point where it could become bitter. Take the trouble to source ripe but firm Haas avocados. They seem to ripen more evenly, and have a richer, full-fat texture. This is important when heating an avocado, as watery varieties become bitter at the mere sign of heat.

The lemon chilli oil used in this recipe, and the basic model chilli oil, is well worth having round the house, as a table condiment or to use in cooking. I don't like to encourage chilli addicts, or to enter macho chilli-eating contests, but sometimes you need to cook dishes for people with less kick than you would like and a little bowl of chilli oil on the table gives everyone great flexibility in the matter.

FOR FOUR:

FOR BASIC CHILLI OIL:
1 litre fruity olive oil
fresh or dried chillies (e.g. 20 bird's eye or 2 habaneros)

FOR THE LEMON CHILLI OIL:
200mls chilli oil (see above)
juice and rind of 1 lemon

To make a basic chilli oil, take a small amount, say 200mls, of fruity but not peppery olive oil. Chop or grind some fresh or dried chillies, maybe 20 bird's eye or two habaneros, and add these to the oil. Heat the oil gently for a couple of minutes, but don't quite boil it. Off the heat, add a litre of the same olive oil. Leave this to rest for a couple of hours – a day would be better – then test the oil. You may need to dilute it further, especially for table use, though a hot oil for cooking is fine, if your self-control is good. You can either sieve out the chillies, pour the oil off them into another container, or leave them to settle on the bottom – dried chillies will be fine left in, fresh ones may deteriorate.

Now, to make lemon chilli oil, take a small amount of the oil, say 200mls, as it is impossible to blend smaller amounts, add the lemon juice and rind, and use a hand blender to blend the two. The oil should thicken to a nice pouring consistency, though it might separate again later, in which case simply blend it again just before you use it.

FOR THE RISOTTO:

1200mls vegetable stock (see page 276)

60g butter

60mls olive oil

320g risotto rice, such as arborio or carnaroli

1 bunch spring onions, chopped

4 cloves garlic, chopped

120mls dry white wine

60g Parmesan, grated

1 large avocado

100g rocket

salt and pepper, to season

80g mature, hard goats' cheese

Bring the stock to the boil in a pot and keep it at a very low simmer. Meanwhile, melt one tablespoon of the butter with one spoon of the olive oil. Throw in the rice and stir it well to coat the grains with oil. Cook the rice gently for ten minutes, stirring often, then add the spring onion and garlic, and cook for one more minute. Pour in the wine, bring it to the boil quickly, then simmer until the wine is absorbed. Now add a ladle or cup of the stock, about 150mls, and continue to simmer, stirring often until it is all but absorbed. Add another cup of stock, and carry on absorbing, stirring and adding stock until the rice is almost cooked. Take care that the stock going into the rice pot is at a boil and, therefore, not interrupting the cooking of the rice. Test individual grains – the rice should be cooked through but firm, while the stock has become a little creamy and is almost completely absorbed. When the risotto reaches this stage, take it off the heat and stir in the rest of the butter and olive oil and the Parmesan. Quickly chop the flesh of the avocado into large dice, coarsely chop or tear the rocket and add these to the risotto. Season well with salt and pepper.

Spoon the risotto on to plates, and use a vegetable peeler to shave slivers of the goats' cheese over it. Drizzle a little of the lemon-chilli oil around the fringes. Leave the oil and the lump of cheese on the table for those who like more kick than comfort in their dinner.

Grilled asparagus with salt flakes and rosemary aioli

Grilled asparagus is the simplest and, in my opinion, the nicest way to cook this finest of spring delicacies – the vegetable that epitomises the point of seasonal eating. You can get it out of season these days, but only from the other hemisphere, whichever one you don't live in, and doesn't it taste sad? The flavour of asparagus is so delicate, so elusive and yet so in-your-face when it's right. Asparagus is perfectly of its time, and that's why we feast on it for the short time it is with us.

For every time you dress asparagus up in fine recipes during the season, you should eat it this way at least twice, simply grilled, with or without the aioli. Don't just go grilling the first bunch you find this year, though. To serve thin asparagus with aioli, it would be better to lightly steam or boil it for no more than one minute, just enough to change it from raw to cooked. Grilling works best for fine big, fat spears. The outside skin browns, crisps and caramelises a little while the inner flesh barely cooks, retaining its inherent moist sweetness. I think maybe cookbooks some-times over-encourage people to search out thin, elegant asparagus (come to think of it, asparagus isn't the only vegetable to suffer that fate) and I think there may be a little snobbish disdain for the bigger spears. I don't see it like that at all. The smaller, thinner spears are wonderful in salads and as crudités; and in risotto and pasta, hardly cooked at all but thrown in at the end for the last seconds of cooking. But to take on grilling or roasting, or in dishes with the flavours of strong cheese, you need a bigger asparagus, where there is enough body to give a contrast between the deli-cate, sweet flesh and the cooked green skin. The most important thing when buying asparagus is to check its condition and freshness. It is best if the heads are firm and fairly closed, but the other end is a better barometer. Those plastic or paper sheets around the shins of the asparagus, and the often-too-tight elastic bands, can hide old age and bad condition. Take a look below the knee-line and at the base of the stalks – they should be fresh and crisp, not dried up or beginning to show mould, even if the tops look fine.

FOR FOUR:

2 sprigs rosemary
300mls oil
5 cloves garlic
2 tablespoons olive oil
2 egg yolks
half teaspoon hot mustard
salt and pepper, to season
juice of half lemon

2 bunches asparagus
salt flakes

First make the rosemary oil. Pull the leaves of rosemary from their stems and put them in a small pan with 100mls of olive oil. Bring this slowly to a boil, remove the pan from the heat and leave to infuse for at least 30 minutes, much longer if possible. Strain the infused oil into the remaining 200mls of olive oil. Rosemary oil keeps very well and is very useful, so it is a good idea to make much larger quantities than this.

Snip the ends off the garlic cloves and put them on a small oven tray, drizzled with a little olive oil. Roast them in a low to medium oven for about 15 minutes until the garlic is soft. Squeeze the garlic from its skin into a food processor with the egg yolks and mustard. Blend these for a full minute before beginning to drizzle in the rosemary oil, then continue to add the oil slowly until the aioli

has taken on a thickish dip-like consistency. Check the flavour of the aioli, add salt and pepper, taste it again and add some or all of the lemon juice, to your liking.

Heat a grill to a high temperature. Snap the ends off the asparagus spears, and lay them close together on a tray. Drizzle some olive oil over the asparagus and put the tray under the grill. Cook the asparagus until it begins to colour a little in places, but remains firm – this should take only three or four minutes. Pile the grilled asparagus on to a serving dish and scatter over some flaked salt.

Serve with a generous bowl of the aioli to dunk the spears in.

Asparagus, caramelised onion and Knockalara sheep's cheese tart

Cooking with Knockalara sheep's cheese can sometimes make me nervous and unsure. Oh, it's a dream to use in salads, breaking off angular lumps from the wheel and tucking them into bitter salad leaves or wilted greens. It's a subtle, fresh cheese with a clean, slightly lemony zing that I fear will get lost in my big-flavoured cooking. Yet it often surprises me how that subtlety adds a touch of class to a dish I might have expected it to get lost in. And sometimes I pay attention to the subtlety of the cheese and keep my excesses in check. This tart is a simple affair, with little chance of the cheese getting lost. It is a natural-born partner to asparagus, in the way that foods of a season just seem so right for each other. That compatibility is at the heart of what I love about cooking seasonally. The foods of any one time of the year seem designed by nature to get along perfectly on the plate and in the pot. For example, if you do this tart with chopped watercress instead of asparagus, you will get the same fresh spikiness of spring. Do it with the strong, cabbage greens of a few weeks earlier in late winter/early spring and you might as well have used sour milk.

The tart doesn't really need embellishment, but I would often serve it with a sweetish sauce such as tomato pesto or a cherry tomato salsa, some new potatoes and a salad, perhaps even the watercress one on page 171.

The red onions will take about an hour to cook but they keep for a week or more and are very useful, so I would suggest you make a large batch the day before you make the tart.

You will need a pastry case 26cm in diameter.

FOR FOUR:

160g plain flour
large pinch salt
80g cold butter
40mls cold water

250g red onions
tablespoon olive oil
2 tablespoons brown sugar
2 tablespoons balsamic vinegar

1 bunch asparagus
150g Knockalara sheep's cheese
3 eggs
150mls cream
salt and pepper, to season

Sift the flour and salt, then cut in the butter. A food processor does this very efficiently, but remove the pastry to a bowl before stirring in the water with a few quick strokes. Shape the dough into a ball with your hands, flatten it gently and chill it for at least half an hour. Then roll the pastry to fit a 26cm pastry case and chill for a further half hour. Blind-bake the pastry case for about ten minutes at about 180°C/350°F.

Slice the red onions in half, then into thin slices. Cook them in a little olive oil, stirring often, until the onions are fully cooked and beginning to caramelise. Add the sugar and balsamic vinegar, and continue to cook until the onions are breaking down and the liquid is syrupy. Leave to cool.

Snap the ends off the asparagus and cook the spears in boiling water for two minutes. Break the cheese into small pieces. Beat the eggs and cream together and season with salt and pepper. Chop the asparagus spears into pieces about 1cm long and, setting aside the heads, mix them with the sheep's cheese. Spread a layer of caramelised onions in the pastry case and cover with the asparagus and sheep's cheese. Arrange the asparagus heads on top and pour over the custard. Bake in an oven at 180°C/350°F until the tart is just set, about 30 to 40 minutes. If you are using a fan oven, turn the fan off after the first ten minutes to allow the tart to cook without burning the top.

Fresh herb and feta omelette with warm asparagus, avocado and cherry tomato salsa

I've long had a secret desire to put omelettes on the restaurant menu, ever since I ate a perfect one in a café open to the street in Auckland one summer morning a year or ten ago. It was a concoction, filled with fashionable leaves and garnished with a salsa that included olive oil and a nice kick of chilli, and served almost lost at the bottom of a gigantic, wide and shallow dish. For all its flashy elements, it was also a perfectly executed omelette, soft and luscious. I remember it almost every time I beat a few eggs together for dinner. But that was a casual brunch menu – at Paradiso we don't do brunch, and somehow the omelette has lost its place on restaurant menus – mostly due to abuse, the usual tyrant, and long years of rubbery, watery frisbees made from factory eggs and plastic ham. One of these days… but probably not.

I don't claim to understand the scientific theory on the compatibility of asparagus and eggs, but it is one that works in many different ways – asparagus with scrambled eggs, soft-boiled eggs, hollandaise or aioli, and, of course, the omelette. Asked what I cook at home I sometimes fantasise about picking vegetables from my pristine plot, creating exquisite and intricate delicacies that are too difficult and spontaneous to reproduce in the restaurant. Often, I will go so far as to pass off these fantasies as truths, and later feel a mixture of guilt and mischievous glee. Sometimes, though, I will admit that dinner is most often pasta or eggs – simple, soul-reviving, Sunday-evening food. And in that territory, the omelette is king. A well-made omelette is a culinary double act. On the one hand, the most luxurious and decadent thing – your whole week's allowance of egg cholesterol with some butter or olive oil for good measure, maybe some cheese and a dollop of mashed or roast potatoes – yet, at the same time, the simplest, fastest, most fundamentally peasant kitchen-garden supper. Grab whatever number of eggs you can find, crack them into a pan, stir a bit and flip the thing on to a plate. Food.

The climactic scene in the movie *Big Night* is an omelette scene, and the first calm scene for some time. The two brothers, Primo and Segundo, cook and waiter, worn out from the extraordinary stresses of the day, meet in the kitchen and share some eggs. They call it an omelette, though in the Italian style it is just some beaten eggs fried in a pan – no lifting, flipping or filling. I think I had hoped to see a pristine demonstration of the art of the omelette, and was a little disappointed the first time I saw the film. But it's not about technique. As the simple, slow and careful movements are carried out to prepare and cook the eggs, the brothers, who had in the preceding madness fallen out, come back to each other, a sense of sanity and peace returns, and you realise that this is the true power of food: to bring people together. Earlier in the evening, the brothers had given intense pleasure to a wide range of characters, bringing the two together if only for one evening, with their flamboyant, labour-intensive and divinely flavoured restaurant food. But for their own coming together, that food would not have been enough. Sitting down to eight courses of rich food would have sparked more debate than reconciliation. No, for the brothers it had to be eggs, cooked in the family style, no questions asked. It is hard to imagine what other dish could have been used to facilitate the scene.

Speaking of technique, I re-read Elizabeth David on the matter of eggs recently, expecting to have confirmed what I thought I had learned from her. Instead, it turns out that I don't cook omelettes à la Ms David at all, and that she doesn't believe there is a proper way. She does, instead, allow for all manner of personal variations and encourages the ritualistic element of cooking, exactly the element that made the preparation of an omelette in *Big Night* such a redemptive experience. In essence, learn a comfortable way to do it, and do it often, so that it becomes a routine that brings you peace and pleasure.

This recipe is for two. If you have more to feed, share it or cook a second omelette – it will only take two minutes if everything is ready.

6 spears asparagus
8 cherry tomatoes, halved
1 clove garlic, chopped
half a fresh chilli, deseeded and diced
2 tablespoons olive oil

4–5 eggs
2 tablespoons water
salt and pepper, to season
handful of fresh herbs (of two or three types, such as chives, parsley, thyme, tarragon, marjoram)
50g feta
butter or olive oil to coat pan

half an avocado

Snap the ends off the asparagus, chop the spears into pieces about 3cm long, and grill or steam these for a minute or two until just tender. Put the cherry tomatoes in a small pan over a low heat with the garlic, chilli and olive oil. Cook gently for two minutes until the tomatoes just begin to collapse, then remove from the heat and add in the asparagus. Do all of this just before cooking the omelette, then, when the omelette is cooked, a mere two minutes later, dice the avocado flesh and stir it gently into the warm salsa.

Crack the eggs into a bowl and beat them briefly just to break them up, then add two tablespoons of water, some salt and pepper. Chop the herbs, crumble the feta and set them at the ready. Heat a heavy flat pan to a high temperature (your omelette pan – the one you never use for anything else and always wipe out immediately with never a scour, scrape nor detergent near it). Brush the pan with a coating of butter or olive oil, pour in the beaten egg, give them a quick stir, tilt the pan towards you, then away, each time lifting the edge of the omelette to let the raw egg run under the cooked. Do this once or twice more, then scatter the ready-prepared herbs and feta over the centre of the omelette. Flip one-third of the omelette over the middle, then the other. Remove the pan from the heat and divide the omelette on to two plates. Spoon some of the salsa over each.

Gratin of asparagus, roasted tomatoes and Gabriel cheese with chive and mustard cream

A main-course version of one of my favourite starters: asparagus gratin. We sell a lot of these in Café Paradiso, but when I cook it at home it is always just 'dinner', with some new potatoes, maybe a salad, and often, as here, another vegetable or two in the gratin. You need a lot of asparagus – eight big spears for each portion – but if you're eating seasonally, this is a fine way to feast on asparagus. This is another dish that is really best suited to bigger spears of asparagus, all the better to pick up the cream sauce.

FOR FOUR:

8–10 large tomatoes
salt and pepper, to season
drizzle of olive oil

80g fine breadcrumbs
80g Gabriel cheese, grated
1 sprig thyme
2 tablespoons butter, melted

60mls vegetable stock (see page 276)
60mls white wine
300mls cream
small bunch chives, chopped
1 teaspoon hot mustard

32 asparagus spears

Heat an oven to 190°C/375°F. Slice a thin sliver off the top and bottom of the tomatoes, then cut the tomatoes across into thick slices, three or four from each. You will need 36 slices in all for four portions. Place the slices on oven trays lined with baking parchment or greaseproof paper, season with salt and pepper, and drizzle lightly with olive oil. Roast the tomatoes until they are lightly browned and semi-dried. Depending on your oven, you may need to turn the slices once to cook them evenly on both sides.

Mix the breadcrumbs with all but one tablespoon of the cheese, the thyme and the butter. Season with salt and pepper.

Bring the stock and wine to the boil in a small pan, and reduce it to about half its volume. Add the cream and mustard, bring it back to the boil and simmer for two to three minutes or so to thicken the sauce to a pouring consistency.

At the same time, boil or steam the asparagus for two or three minutes until just tender.

Heat a grill. On each plate, place six slices of tomato, a neat line-up of three by two, and cover this with five asparagus spears. Place a single layer of tomato slices on top, and three more asparagus spears over the tomatoes. Spoon a little of the mustard cream over the vegetables, then finish with a generous sprinkling of the crumble. Cook the gratins under a hot grill for two or three minutes until the cream is bubbling and the top is crisp and browned. Put the remaining cream back on the stove, whisk in the rest of the Gabriel cheese and the chives, and pour this mixture around the finished gratins.

I would usually serve some simple new potatoes sitting in the cream around the gratin, or even a few small mounds of mash.

You could also finish this dish in an oven instead of on individual plates, as follows. Place a layer of tomato slices in an oven dish, cover this with a layer of asparagus, then pour over the thickened cream and finish with a generous sprinkling of the crumble. Bake for ten minutes until the cream is bubbling and the top is crisp and browned.

Rhubarb and glazed pecan crumble with a gingered rhubarb syrup

Rhubarb is the first fruit of the year – the only one to appear in spring – and it is greatly appreciated for its early showing. That said, it is not really a fruit at all, but the stalk of a leaf plant – a vegetable in fact. And it's certainly not sweet, but quite sour. Yet it is almost always cooked with sugar to make sweet dishes, which makes it an honorary fruit.

Rhubarb is a peculiarly old-fashioned food, which, I think, is best if treated in a fairly old-fashioned way. This recipe, a crumble, is a variation on a standard from another era, and the next most likely dishes to be made with rhubarb are equally simple and old-fashioned: stewed with custard, tarts and pies, fools and jams; the rhubarb and shortbread dish in *The Café Paradiso Cookbook* is simply a rejigged version of stewed rhubarb, biscuits and cream. I like to serve the gratins in individual portions by cooking them in steel rings. This is mainly for aesthetic reasons, but the rings also help to maintain the proportions between rhubarb and crumble, and I like to be able to serve a little extra syrup on the side. If you don't have rings or find all that too fussy, just layer the rhubarb and crumble into an oven dish and bake for longer.

Most rhubarb recipes begin by tossing chopped rhubarb with lots of sugar and cooking it gently. 'Gently' is important – rhubarb passes through the stage of being perfectly cooked and on to mushy in a timescale not much beyond the blink of an eye.

Of course, for every rhubarb lover there is another who can't stand the stuff, though I suspect that these unfortunate people may be carrying traumatic memories from childhood. In any case, it is on this love/hate aspect of rhubarb that I have based my philosophy on its place in restaurant menus. Simply, I believe that if you put a rhubarb dish on a menu (and you always should in spring) then it should have lots of rhubarb in it and should taste predominantly of rhubarb. The rhubarb haters won't go near any dish featuring the 'r' word on the menu, while rhubarb lovers will be inconsolably disappointed if they find that you led them on only to present them with a concoction with the merest scraping of rhubarb buried in the mix. No, they want rhubarb, you promised rhubarb, so it is best to satisfy their craving. And the truth of it is that, no matter what you do to trick out a rhubarb dish, nothing will please the true fan as much as a huge bowl of warm rhubarb and some homemade custard. Give in.

FOR THE SYRUP:

1 bunch rhubarb, 600g
net weight

400g caster sugar

FOR THE CRUMBLE:

100g flour

30g light muscovado
sugar

60g butter

half teaspoon ground
ginger

30g caster sugar

1 teaspoon maple syrup

50g pecans

2 preserved ginger nuts

Chop the rhubarb into pieces 2cm or 3cm long, and put them in a large pot with the caster sugar. Bring this to a boil and simmer, covered, over very low heat for five minutes until barely tender. Carefully lift the rhubarb out with a slotted spoon, then strain the liquid through a fine sieve to get a clear juice.

Put the flour, muscovado sugar, butter and ground ginger into a food processor and blend in brief spurts to get a fine crumb-like texture. Spread the crumble on a baking tray and bake it at 180°C/350°F for five or six minutes until lightly toasted.

Put the caster sugar and maple syrup in a small pan over very low heat until the sugar is melted. Stir in the pecans and immediately spread them on an oven tray lined with parchment. Put the tray in a low oven, 120°C/250°F for 20 minutes. Leave the pecans to become dry and crisp. Stir them into the crumble.

Pile the rhubarb into an oven dish, or into individual steel rings, and scatter a layer of the crumble over the top, pressing it on gently. Bake at 180°C/350°F until the rhubarb is hot; about ten minutes for individual crumbles, longer for one large one.
While the crumble is cooking, put the rhubarb juice in a pan. Slice the ginger nuts thinly and add them to the juice, then simmer for five minutes until the juice has the consistency of a thin pouring syrup. If it becomes too thick, simply stir in a little water and simmer again. Allow the syrup to cool to room temperature again before serving it. Serve the crumble with a stream of the syrup poured around it, and some citrus ice cream, or just a dollop of fresh cream or mascarpone.

Grilled artichoke with roasted pepper and basil aioli

I first ate artichokes this way in a sleepy small town north of San Francisco. We were lunching in a courtyard restaurant on the corner of the square, and I ordered grilled artichoke just to see how you did it. It was so blindingly obvious when the dish arrived, dressed with a tomato salsa kind of thing, and it was a very pleasant way to spend half an hour. Between the artichoke, the sauvignon blanc and the general cowpoke ambience, we so fell under the spell of the town that we booked into the old colonial hotel on the opposite corner of the square – you know, lots of ancient dark wood, fine white linen, bourbon, moose heads and rifles on the stair landings – and were kept awake all night, first by 'hoons' cruising the streets, and then the refuse truck, which started work at an ungodly hour, reversing around tricky corners, only shortly after the lads had revved off home to bed. In the morning the town looked less romantic through bleary sleepless eyes, and we moved on.

You could say that this is a sort of inside-out version of the classic method of eating an artichoke by picking the leaves from the outside in and scraping off the edible flesh from the base of each leaf with the front teeth, until the prized heart is reached. In keeping with the impatience of modern living, this reversed recipe allows you to get at the prize first and go on picking at the outer leaves only as long as you can be bothered. Oh my god, I'm going off this dish even as I type it! For those of you who don't like to dive straight in but want to play mind games with your food, and I'm completely with you on this, pick and nibble the leaves from the inside out but leave the heart until last when it is fully exposed and uncluttered.

FOR FOUR TO FIVE:

2 red peppers
4 cloves garlic
2 egg yolks
1 small bunch basil
300mls olive oil
4 large artichokes
juice of half lemon
salt and pepper, to season

Put the peppers on a tray under a hot grill, turning them as necessary until their skins are blackened all over. Pop them into a paper bag until they are cool enough to handle. Nick the ends off the garlic cloves and put them in a low to medium oven until they become soft.

Peel the peppers, discard the seeds and put the flesh into a food processor. Squeeze the garlic from their skins into the processor too. Add the egg yolks, tear the basil and toss it in. Blend everything for two minutes, then pour in the olive oil in a thin, slow stream, until the aioli has the consistency of a mayonnaise or dip.

Cut the artichokes into halves, then into quarters. Use a small knife or a spoon to remove all of the hairy choke, and drop the pieces into a bowl of water to which you have added the juice of a lemon. Bring a pot of water to a boil and cook the artichoke pieces in it until just tender. Check their consistency by sticking a sharp knife into the thickest part of the base.

Just before serving, heat the grill, brush the artichokes with olive oil, season with salt and pepper, and cook the artichokes until lightly browned.

Serve three or four quarters each with a little bowl of aioli to dunk in.

Lemon-braised artichokes with a white asparagus mousse and tomato – wild garlic concasse

Young, purple-leafed artichokes won't have a bottom big enough for stuffing but, if you're lucky, they won't have much in the way of a choke either. Indeed the smallest and youngest shouldn't have any at all, making them a cook's dream. While the larger ones are excellent for chopping or grilling, as in the previous recipe, the smaller ones are best suited to being fully prepared, as in this one.

I think it's fair to say that this dish is really two separate dishes that ended up together through circumstance more than design. I was serving the previous grilled artichoke dish in Café Paradiso, with the tomato concasse and an asparagus mousse, but one weekend I felt the artichokes were too skinny and too much trouble for the diner, so I replaced them with this version, whereby we did the work on the artichokes in the kitchen. Braised like this, whether with lemon, as here, or with garlic and herbs, the artichokes make a wonderful part of a meal as well as a starter, and are lovely with pasta or around a risotto.

Shortly before going to press with these recipes, a new grower showed up with a batch of what he called Imperial Star artichokes, an American variety. They are wonderful to work with, having more soft edible leaf than waste, very little hairy choke even when the vegetable is quite mature, and a divine flavour. I'm a little excited – no, a lot excited – at the prospect of working with these beauties for a few years. New growers! Such enthusiasm, determination, and such optimism. The older hands are never scared or worried, though, they just watch and wait for the lines of fretting and resignation to appear on those fresh faces.

I don't use a lot of white asparagus, being far too obsessed with the green varieties during asparagus season to pay it enough attention. It's funny how regional the devotion to it is, in Germany, north Italy and parts of Spain, and how absolute that devotion. White asparagus eaters don't think much of the green stuff, nor probably of the growers who must seem too lazy to go to the extra trouble to make it white by blanching – piling up earth to keep the stalks covered as they grow. Jörg Köster, this book's photographer, had a visit from his German parents during the spring shoot and they brought their own precious supply of incredibly fresh white asparagus wrapped in damp towels. They didn't get to try this mousse, so I can't say how it stands up in white asparagus dish territory. I can say that it makes a very elegant starter with the tomato–wild garlic concasse, and, if you don't use artichokes with it, some grilled green asparagus would make a lovely contrast.

I use small but deep ramekins of a capacity of 80mls to make tall, elegant mousses. If serving the mousses as a course in their own right, a slightly larger ramekin might be better.

FOR FOUR:

FOR THE MOUSSE:
400g white asparagus
2 cloves garlic
120g cream cheese
2 eggs
2 egg whites
salt and pepper, to season
oil, to coat the ramekins

To make the mousses, first peel the ends of the asparagus and cook the spears in boiling water for five or six minutes until tender. Drain the asparagus and leave it in a colander to cool; then purée it in a food processor with the garlic. Add the cream cheese and the eggs, and blend briefly to get a smooth purée. Finally add the egg whites and some salt and pepper, and blend again for a few seconds. Lightly oil the ramekins and put a piece of baking parchment paper in the bottom of each. Fill the ramekins right to the top with the mixture and place them in an oven dish. Pour boiling water into the dish to come halfway up the sides of the ramekins

and place the dish in an oven at 180°C/350°F. If you are using a fan oven, turn the fan off. Cook the mousses for 50 to 60 minutes, until they are just set. Test by pressing the top of a few mousses – they should be quite firm. Leave the mousses in the ramekins for at least ten minutes. Run a small knife round the outside of each mousse, then tap the base of each ramekin to turn the mousses out on to plates.

If you cook the mousses ahead of time, they can be reheated after being loosened in their ramekins by putting the ramekins back in the oven, in hot water.

FOR THE CONCASSE:
2 tomatoes
80mls olive oil
salt and pepper, to season
6 wild garlic shoots

Cut a small cross into the base of each tomato, then drop them into boiling water for a few seconds. Remove the tomatoes to a bowl of cold water, and peel the skin off when the tomatoes are cool enough to handle. Halve the tomatoes and cut out the stalks and seeds. Dice the flesh and put it in a

small pan with the olive oil. Bring it to the boil and simmer for one minute. Season with salt and pepper and leave the sauce to cool to room temperature before serving. Just before you serve, chop the wild garlic shoots, saving the flowers, and stir them into the tomato.

FOR THE BRAISED ARTICHOKES:
8–10 artichokes
juice of half lemon
150mls olive oil
150mls vegetable stock (see page 276)

1 lemon
large pinch salt
black pepper, to season

Pull the hard outer leaves from each artichoke until you are left with edible, yellowish leaves of at least 2cm at the wide base. Cut across the leaves at this point and rub the cut part with lemon juice. Trim the widest part of the base and peel from there down to the stalk and about 2cm along the stalk. Use a small knife or a vegetable peeler, depending on how thick the skin is. If the artichokes are very fresh and young, there will be quite a bit of edible flesh in the stalk. Slice the prepared artichoke in half lengthways and use a knife or a teaspoon to remove any hairy choke. Put the artichoke into a bowl of water into which you have squeezed the juice of a lemon.

Repeat with the rest of the artichokes. Bring a pot of water to the boil and place the artichoke halves in it for five minutes to partly cook them. Transfer the artichokes to a wide, shallow pan and add the olive oil and stock.

Chop the lemon in half lengthways, then into quarters, and slice the quarters quite thinly. Place the lemon slices on some kitchen paper, put some more paper on top and press the slices to dry them a little. Add the slices to the pan with a large pinch of salt. Bring it to the boil and simmer, covered, for 20 to 30 minutes, checking occasionally and shaking the pan to keep the artichokes from sticking. At the end of cooking, grind in plenty of black pepper. Serve warm.

Roasted globe artichoke with sheep's cheese and pinenuts, wilted greens and tomato pesto

For this, you will need large, wide, pale-green artichokes. You should be able to get artichoke bottoms with diameters of 6cm to 8cm, but in your search for large artichokes don't forget that the leaves should still be tightly closed – you want large ones, not old and overgrown. It is a lot of work preparing the artichokes, though you can get up quite a speed a few weeks into the season at a rate of 20 a day! Mind you, when a supplier came up with a late crop last autumn, I had to turn it down, fearing mutiny from my hard-working but fragile-spirited crew, who were certain they'd seen the last of these monsters for a few months. The real beauty of this dish is that the eaters of the artichokes will be overwhelmed with admiration for the person who has presented them with a ready-to-eat version of a vegetable they are usually obliged to work on at the table, picking one leaf out after another.

The filling is a variation on a combination I use in many dishes: sheep's cheese and pinenuts. They just seem so made for each other. I have used other fillings successfully but, as in all artichoke dishes, the important thing is to keep the additional flavours low-key, light and fresh, to allow the artichoke's strong but subtle character to shine through.

FOR FOUR:

FOR THE TOMATO PESTO:
100g sundried tomatoes
2 cloves garlic
300mls olive oil
salt and pepper, to season

Soak the sundried tomatoes for 20 minutes in enough warm water to cover them. Purée them in a food processor with the garlic, then pour in the olive oil, with the motor running, until you get a thick but pourable consistency. Season with salt and pepper.

4 large globe artichokes
juice of 2 lemons
25g pinenuts
200g sheep's cheese
a few leaves fresh basil
olive oil, as required
4 handfuls black kale, chard or spinach

Working with one artichoke, cut the artichoke stem about a centimetre from the base. Snap off the outer green leaves as close to the base as possible until the leaves revealed are a pale yellow-green shade right up to the widest part of the artichoke. Now cut the top from the artichoke at this widest part, and peel the tough outer green skin from the base. Finally, use a spoon to scoop out the hairy choke from the centre. This leaves you with a completely edible artichoke bottom. Drop each finished artichoke into cold water to which you have added the juice of one lemon – this will help to prevent discolouring. Bring a pot of water to the boil, add the juice of the other lemon and drop in the artichokes. Boil them until just tender; about ten minutes should do it but check by piercing one with a sharp knife – it should be firm but easily cut. Plunge the artichokes into cold water again to cool them and stop the cooking.

While the artichokes are cooking, lightly toast the pinenuts, crumble the cheese and mix it with the pinenuts, some chopped basil and a little salt and pepper.

Brush the artichokes with olive oil, season them, and roast them in a hot oven for about ten minutes, until they start to brown a little at the edges. Now, pile some of the cheese filling into each artichoke, leaving the filling loosely packed. Drizzle a little oil over the top and put them back in the oven for a few minutes to heat through. Just before you take the artichokes out of the oven, heat some more olive oil in a wide saucepan. Tear the greens into pieces, drop them in and stir over a high heat until they wilt and soften – an occasional splash of water will help. Season with salt and pepper, then place a small pile of greens on each of four plates. Put one artichoke on each pile and run a stream of pesto around the edge.

Broad bean salad with grilled haloumi, wild garlic, lemon-thyme oil and crispbreads

Broad beans crop up here because this is the time I associate them with, the time I first buy fresh organic broad beans. They come from Italy or the south of France, and I admit I take them as soon as I can get them, and even at that I've been hanging out for them for a few weeks. Local Irish organic broad beans don't kick in until mid-June, or mid-July in a bad year. This approach allows me to get a very long season with new young crops arriving every couple of weeks as the season moves up through Europe. We're all good Europeans now, and I've decided to apply that concept to seasonal food. The first broad beans are tiny and edible raw: through the season the beans grow larger and thicker-skinned, and they need longer cooking and sometimes peeling too. It's worth mentioning that frozen broad beans are generally very good quality, though I do believe you will appreciate the vegetable more if you prepare it from its pod rather than simply slitting a plastic bag.

Broad beans, or fava beans as they are known in other parts of the world, seem to divide that part of the population that pays them any attention: you either love and crave them or you hate them. Now, I am a fully paid-up member of the broad bean fan club and self-elected chairperson of the committee to encourage more broad bean eating, but I'm fascinated as much by the foods people hate as those that are loved. And while I can certainly understand people gagging at the thought of seaweeds, stinking mushrooms from dank forests, pickles… I can even understand phobias from childhood experiences – boarding-school parsnips or the texture of over-ripe bananas – but broad beans? Maybe it's just exaggeration and what people mean when they say those horrible things is merely that they don't really care too much for broad beans. I love everything about them, starting with the almost ludicrously luxurious soft white fur lining the inside of the pod, which makes shelling broad beans a more amusing job than you might expect.

This salad recipe is currently my favourite way to eat broad beans, but they are such a useful vegetable to have around; we put them in risotto and pasta, in stews, soups and ravioli; mash and salsas; and anything else we're cooking while broad beans are in the house.

This is a vibrant salad, full of the fresh sparkle and zing of lemon, lemon thyme and wild garlic. During spring, I use a lot of wild garlic – the variety with a grass-like leaf and a pretty white flower, like a white bluebell. If I forget to pick it at home, there is an emergency crop on the walk to work, growing on a grassy bank and even out of the supporting wall.

Haloumi is a fantastic food to work with – a cheese that can be fried without melting. The many brands available vary a little in quality (and in the rennet used) but most seem to be made with a combination of cows', goats' and sheep's milk, which is a few steps away from its origins in Cyprus as a sheep's milk cheese.

For years, I resisted the temptation to buy a lined griddle pan, having seen too many cookbooks full of pictures of fashionably striped food, and having eaten far too much restaurant food that cared more about its stripes than its taste. However, it became obvious that Johan, in Paradiso, would apply himself so much more enthusiastically to preparing this salad if I would fork out the measly €20 for a griddle pan to cook the haloumi on. I was right – he turned out perfect salads for the season; and, as always, he was right too – doesn't the haloumi look divine with its go-faster stripes, elevating peasant food to the heights of culinary fashion? Even the broad beans seem quite chuffed to be in such dandy company.

The flexible weight of broad beans in the recipe is dependent on the yield you get from the whole pods, and how much podding you are willing to do. I think shelling broad beans, and peas too, especially if done outdoors on a stoop in the sunshine, is guaranteed to make you feel in touch with nature in the way that sharpening a pencil with a knife makes grown men feel, well, manly. I don't enjoy peeling the beans though, and never would when they are young and small; nor do I like to tell other people to do it, as it can make the vegetable seem a chore too far, and I love broad beans too much to be putting people off them. However, the late-season monsters can be a bit thick-skinned, so do peel them if that offends you. However, I would always encourage you to eat the skin rather than give up broad beans.

FOR FOUR:

4 slices day-old bread
200mls olive oil
salt and pepper, to season
juice and rind of 1 lemon
2 sprigs fresh lemon thyme
300g broad beans, net weight
small bunch wild garlic
240g haloumi
some salad leaves

First make the crispbreads. Cut any crust off the bread, brush it all over with a little of the olive oil and season with salt and pepper. Bake the bread in a moderate oven, 180°C/350°F, until nicely browned and crisp all the way through. Break the slices into rough pieces about half the size of the haloumi slices.

Put the rest of the olive oil, lemon and thyme in a jug and use a hand blender to blend them to a slightly thick emulsion. If it separates after a while, blend it again just before you use it, and speak firmly but kindly to it.

Cook the shelled broad beans in boiling water until just tender. Drain them and cool them to warm, not cold, in cold water, then put them into a bowl. Chop the wild garlic and add it to the beans.

At the same time heat a griddle pan or a heavy frying pan to quite hot. Slice the haloumi block into six pieces and cut each of these in half diagonally. Brush the slices lightly with olive oil and place them on the hot pan. Cook over a high heat until lightly browned, then turn the slices to cook the other sides. Drop the haloumi into the bowl, put in an equal quantity of crispbread pieces and pour in enough of the oil to coat everything.

Serve the salad as it is, in the bowl, as part of a meal. To serve it as a starter, first put a little pile of salad leaves, such as rocket or mizuna, in the centre of each plate and spoon the salad over and around the leaves, taking care that everyone gets their fair share of haloumi.

Broad bean, feta and basil mash

I made this after a trek to London, the highlight of which was a broad bean mash I had in the River Café in London. I think theirs was made with a hard Italian cheese, pecorino maybe, and the basil was a later addition. I put the basil in to try to maintain a green colour without peeling the broad beans. It didn't really work, but when I relented on the peeling, I left the basil in because I'd come to love the taste of sunshine it brought to the mash. So, unfortunately, this is one broad bean dish where I would have to say that peeling is almost essential. There: I back-pedalled, I said 'almost'.

The mash is very useful as a rich accompaniment to many dishes, though you should think of it as a relish more than a vegetable dish. I love a dollop of it on a simple omelette or pancake; it's great on toast or bruschetta or with grilled polenta and salad. It doesn't keep well, but it rarely gets the chance anyway.

You will need about a kilo of broad bean pods to get 400g of beans.

FOR FOUR:

400g shelled broad beans
150g feta cheese
50g basil leaves
50mls olive oil

Pop the broad beans from their pods and cook them in boiling water until just tender. Cool the beans in cold water, then peel them by squeezing them individually between your fingers. Place the beans in a food processor with the feta, a generous handful of basil and a generous splash of olive oil. Blend the mixture in short bursts to get a rough mash. Season with salt and black pepper, though salt may be unnecessary with the feta. Use the mash at room temperature.

Broad beans with olive oil, marjoram and garlic

A simple way to serve broad beans as a side dish, combining them with flavours they love. It can be served hot or at room temperature. Marjoram doesn't get a lot of exposure these days, being overshadowed by its better-known but very similar cousin, oregano. The simple combination can also be used as the base for a more elaborate dish – with the addition of other vegetables after the cooking, such as tomatoes and asparagus or artichokes – or a warm salad, by scattering the beans over some salad leaves.

FOR FOUR:

300g broad beans
2 spring onions
6 cloves garlic
2 tablespoons olive oil
a few sprigs marjoram
salt and pepper, to season

Pop the broad beans from their pods and place them in a pan with just enough water to almost cover them. Slice the spring onions, chop the garlic roughly and add both to the pan with the olive oil. Bring this to a boil and simmer, covered, until the beans are tender, which should take about five to ten minutes, depending on their age and size. The water should evaporate; if it doesn't, simply turn up the heat and boil it off quickly. Add in the marjoram and seasoning and serve.

Ravioli of pinenuts, currants and Knockalara sheep's cheese in a lemon-thyme cream, with spinach and sundried tomato

I've just realised how much I use these flavours together. Knockalara sheep's cheese… pinenuts… lemon… thyme… spinach… tomato. Not always all at the same time, though, as they appear here. Well, I've given a few moments' thought to fiddling about with the recipe to disguise my predictable nature, to give off more of an air of maverick spontaneity and a diverse range of ideas. But then some other recipe would be swanning around your kitchen while my favourite version would be sulking at home in Paradiso, a reject, almost-wanted. So, then, here is another in an ongoing series of recipes featuring sheep's cheese, pinenuts, spinach, lemon, thyme and tomato. Oh, and currants. I love currants, the runts of the dried-fruit world. I'll admit there's an awful lot of gnarled tasteless droppings sold as currants, but get a supply of the best organic currants you can find and you have little pinpricks of concentrated sweet fruit. They add a lovely edge to these ravioli where their bigger cousins would be flabby intruders. I don't soak the currants for this recipe, but I do sometimes soak them to add to salads, and it always bewilders me when a diner asks for the salad without the currants – I mean, how offensive or scary can a currant be? Do give them a chance.

FOR FOUR:

4 halves sundried tomatoes

2 tablespoons pinenuts

200g sheep's cheese

1 tablespoon finest organic currants

2 sheets fresh pasta, approx 16cm x 60cm

150mls light stock (see page 276)

150mls white wine

rind and juice of 1 lemon

400mls cream

1 sprig lemon thyme

salt and pepper, to season

100g fresh spinach

Put the sundried tomatoes in a bowl for 20 minutes with just enough warm water to cover them, then drain and slice them into long thin strips.

Lightly toast the pinenuts, then chop them coarsely. Don't grind them, you don't want powder here, you want pieces of pinenut, half-nuts and suchlike. Crumble the cheese and gently mix in the pinenuts and currants.

Lay the pasta on a work surface and cut out two sets of circles, one slightly larger than the other, 12 of each size. From the size of pasta sheet specified, one circle of 8cm and one of 7cm would be perfect, but do whatever best suits the pasta size and your cutting equipment. One of those sets of pastry cutters with Russian doll-like ever-decreasing metal rings inside each other is ideal. Take a small-ish amount of the filling, small but as much as you think the parcel will hold… perhaps a rounded teaspoonful… roll it into a ball and place it in the centre of one of the smaller circles of pasta. Brush the visible part of the pasta circle with water and place one of the larger pieces on top. Now press the edges together firmly while, at the same time, taking care not to leave any air pockets inside the parcel. Repeat this with the rest of the parcels – you need three each for a starter, more for a main course.

Bring the stock, wine and lemon to a boil in a pan, and simmer until the volume is reduced by half. Add the cream and thyme, and simmer for a few minutes until the sauce thickens to a nice pasta-coating consistency – try some on the back of a wooden spoon to get an idea. Season carefully with salt and pepper. Keep the sauce warm, or make it before you start to cook the ravioli and reheat it gently.

Bring a large pot of water to a boil and drop in the ravioli. If you think the parcels might be overcrowded, do two batches. As with all pasta, the only way to decide that it's cooked is to test it. Nick a tiny bit off one of the ravioli and taste it. Remove the ravioli with a slotted spoon and put them in a bowl with a little olive oil to prevent them sticking to each other. If you do two batches, tip the first one back into the pot just as the second batch is cooked and remove the lot in half a minute.

Cook the spinach in the same water while you transfer the ravioli to warm plates. Drain the spinach and chop it into slices similar to the tomatoes. Strew a few of these and a few of the tomato slices over the ravioli, then pour a generous amount of the lemon-thyme sauce over each portion.

Almond pastry galette of wilted spinach, Knockalara sheep's cheese and crushed potato with tomato-cardamom relish

The foundation, in every sense, of this elegant dish is the way the layers of pastry and ground almonds are put together to give a very crisp, puffed-up finish. There are three pastries, each of three layers, so the final effect is of lightness and a crisp, airy texture. The layers are cooked separately and assembled on the plate, which helps to keep this crisp texture all the way to the table. The filling is a very simple and very traditional mixture of spinach and sheep's cheese. This approach came about after a long abstinence from filo pastry. I had become uncomfortable with it, having read a piece by a Turkish cook, I think, in which he insisted that filo pastry's natural affinity was with honey and nuts, and that the characteristic multiple layering would only work when there were very few, and very dry, ingredients between the layers, i.e. honey and nuts. He finished by invoking the gods, some gods or other, to keep filo pastry away from 'creative' chefs, and he didn't use those words in a complimentary way. It made me look at what I was doing with the pastry, and where I had learned to use it. On the positive side, we came up with a very good baklava recipe of about ten layers of honey, nuts and rosewater, which has been on the menu ever since.

There is one more layer underneath the pastry, which is not strictly necessary – one of crushed potato flavoured with coriander seeds. This is loosely based on my father's speciality, his one signature dish, known simply as 'Dad's fried potatoes' to distinguish them from my mother's more polite and more correct version of potato slices carefully fried to crisp on both sides. His would only be served after a long Sunday afternoon's rambling and strenuous cowboy and Indian carry-on. Where my recipe uses halfway floury rooster potatoes, he used the leftover ultra-floury ones from Sunday lunch; where I use olive oil, he used the white lard scooped off the top of a bowl in the fridge. You can see why he only served it after strenuous exercise, and even then he would pronounce that our wolfing down of the fried potatoes was driven by a 'false appetite', brought on by too much oxygen. The technique is all his, though. Frying pan on high heat, he melted a substantial piece of lard, which he would add to during the cooking with a few more spoonsful. Then he flung in the potatoes, half-crushed in his hands, and continued to turn, beat and chop them until he had a very rough mash that was flecked all through with crisp, fried shards. Even then he would carry on cooking it a little more; I think just to drive us crazy. Since I first sheepishly tried to recreate it with less life-threatening ingredients, I have found it to be a very useful part of many dishes, and it is very popular with tired staff late at night after the kitchen equivalent of cowboys and Indians.

6 tomatoes

2 scallions or 5cm piece of leek

1 clove garlic

12 cardamom pods

half teaspoon grated ginger

drizzle olive oil

1 tablespoon white wine vinegar

1 tablespoon sugar

salt and pinch of cayenne pepper

4 filo pastry sheets, 40 x 30cm

50g unsalted butter, melted

100g ground almonds

400g spinach

400g fresh sheep's cheese, Knockalara or similar

salt and pepper, to season

1kg rooster potatoes or similar, cooked and peeled

2 scallions

salt and ground black pepper, to season

De-seed the tomatoes and chop the flesh into small dice; finely chop the scallions (or leek) and garlic. Remove the black seeds from the cardamom pods by your favourite method – mine is to crush the pods with a rolling pin or the side of a cleaver, pick them open and pop the seeds out – and add them to the tomatoes, with just a scrape or two of freshly grated ginger. Heat a drizzle of olive oil in a small pan and cook the tomatoes for just two minutes, then add the vinegar, two dessert-spoons of water, the sugar and a little salt and cayenne. Cook again for just two minutes more, then leave the relish to cool to room temperature.

For the almond pastries, preheat the oven to 150°C/300°F. Place one filo pastry sheet on to the work surface, with one long edge facing you. Brush with melted butter, sprinkle with some of the ground almonds and then lay another sheet of pastry on top. Brush again with butter and then fold over the nearest third. Brush again with butter and fold down the top third. Brush again with butter. Repeat with the other two sheets of pastry and then cut each of these lengths of folded pastry into six even-sized rectangles, 12 in all. Bake the pastries on lightly buttered baking sheets or on baking parchment for eight to ten minutes until crisp and very lightly coloured. Do this in batches if necessary, using the safest middle shelf of the oven, and, if you have the option, turn the oven fan off to avoid burning the top of the pastries.

Cook the spinach briefly by dropping it into boiling water for a minute, then cool it in cold water and squeeze it as dry as possible. Chop the spinach and mix it gently with the sheep's cheese, and season with salt and pepper.

Carefully spread the sheep's cheese and spinach over eight of the almond pastries. Place four of these on to a baking sheet and then place another four on top of those. Heat gently in the oven for eight to ten minutes, then put the remaining pastries on top of each galette and warm them through for another few minutes.

While the pastries are cooking, chop the potatoes coarsely, or break them up in your hands. Chop the remaining pair of scallions. Heat some olive oil in a wide, heavy frying pan, a little more than for shallow frying, then toss in the potato chunks. Keeping the temperature high, brown the potatoes, all the while turning them and breaking them down into smaller chunks with the side of a slice, until you have an effect somewhere between very well-fried potato and chunky mash. It's not pretty but it tastes divine. Mix the scal-lions in for the last few minutes of cooking, and season very generously with salt and coarsely ground black pepper.

Spoon a neat-ish rectangle of potato on to each plate and place a galette on top, pressing down firmly on top of the galette – this helps to make the dish a harmonious unit rather than a silly restaurant construction, which it veers very close to, I'd be the first to admit. Spoon some of the relish around each galette, and serve with some simple green beans or sugar snaps.

Spring vegetable and herb soup with a fresh goats' cheese ravioli

This is as likely to be called 'summer vegetable soup' in Paradiso. In fact I seem to remember that, last year, it was on the dinner menu from April to September, a variation on the old 'soup du jour', which is exactly what it came to be nicknamed in the kitchen, and is the essence of the recipe: it's a soup made from the best of the day's vegetables. The character of the soup changed through the months as asparagus and radishes were replaced by mangetout and courgettes, and in turn by sweetcorn and black kale; and the dominant herbs became basil and oregano. In late September, we put the 'soup du jour' into retirement. So, take the ingredients list only as a guide. Use the best you have or can get. The important thing is to take a minute to decide in which order to add them to the soup and how cooked you want each vegetable to be.

The stock is a very important element. Because of the short cooking time of the soup, about five minutes after the stock boils, the vegetables in the soup impart only a little flavour to the broth. Instead they retain their own flavour and freshness, and the stock has to be good enough on its own with the help of the herbs. The stock needs to be fresh and vibrant, made the same day and well flavoured with herbs.

The ravioli floating in the soup is a very simple one – it's in there to add a little richness and a touch of class to the clean flavours of the soup. You could cook the ravioli from scratch in the soup, but I find it hard to get the timing spot on for the ravioli and the vegetables. More importantly, if you have a split-ravioli accident, it's better to have it in a separate pot, meaning you only have to make another ravioli, not a new soup.

FOR FOUR:

FOR THE SOUP:
1200mls vegetable stock, freshly made (see page 276)
100g spinach
1 tablespoon olive oil
8 spears asparagus
8 baby carrots
2 tablespoons broad beans
2 tablespoons fresh peas
2 cloves garlic, chopped
4 radishes
4 spring onions
small bunch herb leaves (two or three from fennel, dill, thyme, parsley, chives, wild garlic…), coarsely chopped or torn

Bring the stock to a boil in a large pot and drop in the spinach for one minute; then take it out and chop it coarsely.

Heat a little olive oil in a wide pan. Slice the asparagus into 3cm-long diagonal pieces and the baby carrots in half lengthways, and cook them with the broad beans, peas and garlic for two or three minutes. Slice the radish thinly and the spring onion in 1cm pieces, and add them to the pan to cook for one minute more. Add the boiling stock, the spinach and the herbs. Bring the soup back to a boil and serve immediately. Slide a cooked ravioli (see below) into each portion.

FOR THE RAVIOLI:
1 sheet fresh pasta, approx 16cm x 32cm
80g fresh goats' cheese

Cut out eight squares of pasta, four at 8cm square and four a little smaller. Take a 20g piece of cheese, roll it into a ball, flatten it a little and place it on one of the smaller pasta squares. Brush the edge of the pasta with water, place a larger square of pasta on top and press the edges to seal them, taking care not to leave any air pockets inside the ravioli. Bring a large pot of water to a boil and cook the ravioli for five minutes until almost fully cooked, then drop them into cold water.

Summer

gooseberries	strawberries
cherries	raspberries
apricots	peas and beans
kale	watermelon
chard	peaches
courgettes	melon
squash	tomatoes
beetroot	peppers

Gooseberry fool with gingered sponge fingers

The first and most important thing to say here is that you don't have to top and tail the gooseberries. That delicate and tedious operation must be the biggest reason for the relative unpopularity of berries in general, though I'm sure their sour taste has more relevance in the case of gooseberries. It's difficult to give specific quantities; so much depends on how strong you like your fool, so the basic instruction must be to make a syrup of the gooseberries and sugar, a light mousse of the cream, and to fold as much gooseberry into the cream as you see fit, to your own taste.

Fool is, surprisingly, one of the most popular lunch desserts in Café Paradiso, whether it be made from sour berries, rhubarb or sweet fruit like apricots.

FOR FOUR:

1kg gooseberries
1kg sugar
500mls cream

2 eggs, separated
50g caster sugar
50g plain flour
20g cornflour
half teaspoon ground ginger
icing sugar, to serve

Put the gooseberries in a pan with the sugar and a tablespoon of water. Bring it very slowly to a boil and simmer very gently, stirring occasionally, until the fruit is very soft. Blend the fruit in a food processor, pass the purée through a sieve and leave it to cool.

Whisk the cream to soft peaks and fold in the gooseberry purée to your taste. Save a little of the purée to swirl on to the top of individual portions. You can serve the fool now or chill it again for up to a few hours before serving.

To make the sponge fingers, whisk the egg whites until stiff, then add half the caster sugar and whisk again for a minute. In another bowl, whisk the egg yolks and the rest of the caster sugar until pale and fluffy. Sift the flours and ginger together and fold into the egg yolks. Then fold in the egg whites. Use a piping bag to pipe lengths of the batter, 10cm by 2cm, on to baking trays lined with parchment. Bake at 180°C/350°F for 25 to 30 minutes, until pale golden. Leave to cool on the trays. Dredge the fingers with icing sugar before serving.

Cherries in kirsch with chocolate-olive oil mousse

Cherries have such a short season they are hardly on the menu before they disappear again. But that's okay because cherries are the first of the luscious summer fruits and their passing is only a sign that the rest are on their way: the strawberries, raspberries, peaches and currants. It could be said of most summer fruits that the nicest thing to do with them is to eat them on the way home from the shop, or on the way back up the garden path if you are so lucky as to have your own, and cherries are definitely in this category. Buy more than you intend to serve or you won't have enough for dinner. In Paradiso we make little tartlets packed with cherries, and cheesecakes too, but sometimes we serve them very simply, maybe doused in an alcoholic syrup, as here.

This recipe is equally an excuse to give you the chocolate mousse with olive oil. If it didn't show up here with the cherries, it would have later with raspberries, or even later with poached pears in the winter. It is an extraordinary mousse with a slightly chewy texture, almost-but-not-quite-nougat, which holds a lot of air bubbles, yet melts divinely in the mouth. I came across this recipe by Gabriela Llamas, a Spaniard, in the New Zealand magazine *Cuisine*, but I lost the magazine and the first year we made the mousse by guessing. It was all right, but nothing earth-shattering, and we persisted more for the novelty value than anything else. Then the magazine popped up from whatever misfiling system it had become lost in, we tried out the proper recipe and were blown away. Now, I envy anyone trying it for the first time. Use a good-quality chocolate with at least 70 per cent cocoa solids, and a fruity, nutty olive oil.

FOR FOUR:

150g dark chocolate
140mls olive oil
4 eggs, separated
125g caster sugar
1 tablespoon Cointreau or other orange liqueur
pinch salt

200g sugar
200mls water
50mls kirsch
400g fresh cherries

In a bowl over a pan of simmering water, melt the chocolate and slowly stir in the olive oil. Beat the egg yolks with half the sugar until pale and fluffy. Stir in the chocolate oil mix and the Cointreau. Whisk the egg whites with a pinch of salt until stiff, then continue whisking while adding the remaining sugar gradually in small batches. Fold the egg white mix into the chocolate and put the mousse into a fridge to chill for at least four hours. It has a strong structure, and should easily keep overnight.

Place the sugar, water and kirsch in a small pan and simmer for five minutes. Leave this syrup to cool to room temperature. It should be slightly thickened, just enough to coat the back of a spoon.

Leave the cherries whole and their stalks attached. When ready to serve, dunk the cherries in the syrup, put them on serving plates and pour a little more syrup over. Serve with a generous scoop of the mousse.

Vanilla-poached apricots with lemon and almond polenta cake and yoghurt

We rarely get Irish apricots, though I'm sure there are some optimists growing them here. However, imported apricots do show up for a brief time in June, and though it's easy to miss them, even to dismiss them as poor cousins of the peach and nectarine, they have their own charms, not least of which is the delightful way they give up their stones – anyone who has ever wrestled with a stubborn but ripe peach, trying to use a combination of gentleness, quickness and force while the flesh turned to mush and the juices ran off your elbows, will appreciate apricots. Vanilla goes very well with their rich sweetness, though very light touches of cinnamon or sweet ginger are good too.

The very lemony cake is a perfect foil for the sweet, poached apricots. Use a 24 x 34cm tin for the lemon cake, the shallow one often known as a Swiss roll tray. The quantity of cake mixture might appear to be a bit mean, but it will cook to a thickness of about 2cm, which is thin enough for the lemon syrup to penetrate almost to the bottom.

Because I think of this as an eastern Mediterranean dish, I would serve it with thick yoghurt rather than cream.

FOR FOUR:

200g butter
200g caster sugar
rind and juice of 3 lemons
3 eggs
100g plain flour
100g fine maize meal
50g ground almonds
1 teaspoon baking powder

100g light muscovado sugar

1 vanilla pod
150g sugar
8 apricots

Heat an oven to 180°C/350°F, and line your tin.

Melt the butter and caster sugar, and stir in the rind of one lemon. Whisk the eggs briefly, then whisk the butter/sugar mix into the eggs. Sift the flour, maize, almonds and baking powder together, then fold this into the batter. Pour this into the tin and bake it in the oven for 30 minutes. When the cake is done, prick it all over with a fork. Warm the muscovado sugar with the lemon juice and the rind of two lemons, then pour this all over the cake. Leave to cool to room temperature before eating.

Split the vanilla pod lengthways and scrape the inner seeds into a pan with the 150g of sugar, the vanilla pod and 250mls of water. Bring this slowly to a boil, while you halve the apricots and remove their stones. When the syrup boils, turn it down to a very low simmer and drop in the apricot halves. Cover the pan and simmer very gently for five minutes, maybe a few more, checking occasionally. Take the pan off the heat shortly before the apricots are fully cooked, remove the lid and leave the apricots to cool in their syrup. Serve the apricots warm or at room temperature over a slice of lemon cake, with a dollop of thick yoghurt.

Black kale with plum tomatoes, olive oil, garlic and chillies

My first and only source of black kale was, and still is, from Hollyhill Farm in West Cork, which grows vegetables for Café Paradiso. They have always grown it both outdoors and in tunnels, and have often managed to keep up a skeleton supply through ten or eleven months of the year. I love the vegetable too much to complain, though I did moan a bit last year when they only managed six months. I believe it is more naturally a winter vegetable but, over the years, I have come to welcome it most in early summer. Basically, I take it when I can get it, and I would advise anybody who comes across it to do the same.

This vegetable might be better, or even more properly, known as 'cavolo nero' or 'Tuscan cabbage'. 'Black kale' has been the functional name we use in Café Paradiso when identifying it to each other, the customers and even the growers. After a few initial phone conversations in the early days where it was identified as 'you know, that cavolo nero stuff, the black kale-type thing, the big stalky cabbage down the back of the tunnel', we fell into the habit of saying only 'black kale'. If a name is a form of identity, then it is well named. The plant grows as a stalk of two or three feet and puts out long leaves of the most extraordinarily beautiful green, so green it is almost black in a deep-blue-purple kind of way. If you could buy cloth of this shade, I would fill my wardrobe with it and wear nothing else. The leaves can be picked and the plant will go on producing more. The leaves can be pulled from their stems very easily; indeed it is a very satisfying chore. For all its beauty and generosity of production, it is the flavour of black kale that makes it by far my favourite green leaf vegetable. At once strong, earthy and sweet, the kale also seems to become rich and juicy when cooked, especially cooked in olive oil. It is still frustratingly rare commercially. Despite the elitist pleasure of having someone grow it exclusively for us in Paradiso, I would love it to be grown and cooked more widely.

This simple recipe contains what is just about my favourite food flavour combination. It is a slight variation on the basic model of green leaves wilted in olive oil. Strong, potentially bitter greens, cooked just right and long enough so they come up sweet and luscious with the help of the fruity richness of a good olive oil and some ripe tomatoes, topped off by a solid hit of chilli. It is almost extraordinary that it is the flavour of the kale itself that shines through this. If you think I exaggerate, try biting off a piece of raw kale, or cabbage, to see what the raw material is. Bitter, isn't it? Check this against the divine balance of sweet, rich, green and hot that this recipe produces in five minutes and you have the magic of simple cooking. As you chew almost-melting black kale, its inherent sweetly rich but strong and earthy flavour pushes through the upfront flavours of chilli, garlic and olive oil, and when they have faded the sweet kale is the last to linger. Eat kale this way with anything – your finest rich dinner, your simplest supper, or a poached egg and toast.

FOR FOUR:

200g black kale
4 plum tomatoes
2–4 cloves garlic
1–2 fresh red chillies
olive oil
a little stock and salt

Pull the leaves of kale off the stalks and tear them coarsely. Slice the tomatoes into thin wedges. Slice the garlic, but don't chop it finely. Check the heat of the chillies by nicking off a little bit and tasting it, decide how much chilli to use and whether to leave the seeds in or out, then slice them in half lengthways and chop the lengths into thin slices crossways.

Heat a couple of tablespoons of olive oil to quite hot in a pan and drop in the kale. Use tongs to toss the kale in the oil and keep it from burning. Add a splash of water or stock after a minute to add a touch of steam to the cooking. I would add a little salt now too.

The kale will wilt and take on a glossy sheen very quickly, and as soon as it does add the tomatoes, garlic and chillies. Keep tossing and stirring over a high heat, occasionally adding splashes of stock or water when the pan seems too dry, though the juice from the tomatoes will help here. Four or five minutes' cooking should do it. Pick out a little piece of kale to test. It will be softly chewy, sweet and oily when it's done… and perfectly warmly spiced if you got your guess right on the chillies. Check for seasoning and add a little salt, if needed.

Fresh pappardelle in sage butter with black kale, broad beans, artichokes and green peppercorns

Nine times out of ten, I would cook black kale as in the previous recipe, wilted in olive oil with or without the tomatoes and spices. Then it is a perfect side dish or can be stirred into pasta, risotto, pancakes and so on, and I could write a dozen recipes based on that prototype. Here is one recipe cut from a different cloth, where the kale is flavoured with sage butter.

Pappardelle is a very wide strand of pasta, 2–3cm, though it is often cut to less than half the length of, say, tagliatelle to compensate for the width. I use it for this recipe because I like the way the wide acreage of the pasta holds a rich coating of the sage butter. It's not an easily available cut of pasta, and even my local pasta supplier no longer makes it. Her new machine is too clever and pleased with its efficiency to take pappardelle on board. Chances are that the pasta roller in the back of your cupboard doesn't have a wide enough blade either. Never mind. When I want to use pappardelle, I either make my own pasta or buy a length of fresh pasta sheet from a good shop, and cut it myself with a knife. To do this using fresh local or homemade pasta, first cut pieces of pasta about 18 to 20cm long. Roll each length up loosely and slice them into strips about 1 to 1.5cm wide – bearing in mind that the strands will almost double in width when boiled. A slightly jagged and uneven cut of the pasta is a characteristic that will impress your friends, whether or not you've admitted that you didn't actually make the pasta. If you do make your own, cut the final strands by hand, without too much fuss, to give the pasta a lovely handmade quality. It's surely a golden rule that, if you go to a whole lot of trouble preparing dinner, the food shouldn't look like you bought it from a chilled food shelf on the way home from the office.

It is a rare day when I use butter or cream with pasta in the summer. Usually it's olive oil every time in our house, from the first of the glorious Irish summer downpours to the last. But when I first put this combination together a few years ago it was a big hit, so I've left well alone. The black kale and the pasta become rich and luscious with absorbed sage butter, and the cracked green peppercorns add a lovely warm kick. I love the combination in green peppercorns of heat and fragrance, and the light, hollow freeze-dried ones are my favourite.

Looking at the recipe now, however, it is obvious that it is a very adaptable one. The basic combination of pasta and sage butter will happily take on other greens throughout the year, and leeks and mushrooms love sage too.

Make the sage butter anything up to a few hours, or even days, before you need it, and make plenty. It keeps well for weeks in a sealed container in the fridge, and if you get to like it you will find yourself dousing lots of stuff with it – potatoes, pasta, eggs, steamed vegetables…

450g butter
1 bunch sage leaves
2 fresh artichokes
a little lemon juice
100g shelled broad beans
160g black kale
1 tablespoon freeze-dried
green peppercorns
a little water or stock
pinch salt
400g fresh pappardelle
Parmesan, to serve,
grated or shaved

Clarify the butter to remove the milk solids: do this by melting the butter and putting it in a tall, narrow jug; in an hour or so, the milk will gradually settle to the bottom and you can take off the clear oil by a combination of careful pouring and dipping with a small ladle. Don't be greedy though; leave it when you don't feel confident of getting any more clear butter without a taint of milk. Put the clarified butter back in a clean pan with the sage leaves and bring it to a boil. Leave this to cool and for the butter to absorb the sage flavour.

Trim the inedible leaves from the artichokes, scoop out and discard the chokes and cook the artichokes in boiling water with a little lemon juice, until tender. Chop or slice the cooked artichokes.

Cook the broad beans in boiling water until just tender, cool them and set them aside. The cooking could take from three to ten minutes, depending on the age and size of the beans.

Pull the leaves of kale off the stalks and tear them coarsely into pieces. Gently crush the peppercorns – you want cracked and halved ones, not powder.

In a pan large enough to hold the finished dish comfortably, heat two tablespoons of the sage butter and drop in the black kale. Use tongs to toss the kale in the oil and keep it from burning. Add a splash of water or stock after a minute, to add a touch of steam to the cooking, and a pinch of salt. The kale will wilt and take on a glossy sheen. Keep tossing and stirring over a high heat until the kale is tender, about five or six minutes, occasionally adding tiny amounts of stock or water when you feel the pan is becoming too dry. Add the artichoke slices for the last two minutes of cooking.

Meanwhile, bring a large pot of water to a boil and drop in the pasta. Use tongs to stir and separate the strands of pasta while the water comes back to the boil. If the pasta is going to stick, this early stage is the most likely time, and if pappardelle sticks you get a very big lump of dough. Test the pasta after a few minutes and drain it into a colander when it is just tender. Shake the colander a few times, but not too much – it's not necessary, or even desirable, to dry out the pasta completely – then tip the pasta into the kale pan. Add the broad beans and peppercorns, four tablespoons of the sage butter and a little salt. Toss a few time with the tongs, then serve immediately into warm bowls. Offer some Parmesan, either freshly grated or as a lump to be shaved over the pasta.

Rigatoni with chard, red onion and cannellini beans in a roasted pepper and garlic oil

Chard seems to suffer from a poor public image, and is often perceived as being a crude country cousin to the more refined spinach. It is true that most dishes featuring chard can be done with spinach, and the effect will be a softer, sweeter and more melting dish, whereas chard takes longer to soften and, even when stewed to sweetness, retains a little of that green astringency that lovers of strong fresh greens crave. This pasta dish has some strong flavours, and I think chard lives comfortably with them, where spinach might wilt, in every sense. So, chard has a place in the pantheon of greens. It does need to be used very fresh, especially the stalks, which can become stringy with age. This makes it difficult to sell commercially, while making it a fantastic garden vegetable. It is also very beautiful, especially if you grow a mix of white-, yellow- and ruby-stemmed varieties, and of course it has that very useful knack of going on producing more leaves as you pick the larger outer leaves, a cooking gardener's dream vegetable. Such vegetables always remind me of the only thing my father ever grew after he had left the farm he was brought up on. In our back garden, he planted what he called 'cut and come' cabbage; maybe it was a spring cabbage, the miracle of which was that the plant went on producing lovely soft cabbage leaves for a long time. He revelled in this lazy, almost cheating, version of farming; he must have had enough of the back-breaking real thing as a child, as he left the farm and headed for town as soon as he could.

FOR FOUR:

6 cloves garlic

2 large red peppers

300mls olive oil

100mls water

a little salt

generous pinch ground chilli or cayenne pepper

2 small red onions

6–8 medium-sized chard leaves

1 tablespoon olive oil

4 tablespoons cooked cannellini beans

450g rigatoni

salt and pepper, to season

Cut the ends off the garlic cloves and roast the cloves in a low to medium oven until the garlic is soft and lightly coloured. At the same time blacken the skin of the peppers, either over a flame or under a hot grill. Pop the peppers into a paper bag and leave them to steam and cool for 20 minutes or so. Peel the skin from the peppers, and scrape out and discard the seeds. Squeeze the garlic from its skin, and put it in a small pan with the pepper flesh, the olive oil and water. Add a little salt and a generous pinch of ground chilli or cayenne pepper. Bring to a boil and simmer for two minutes. Pour the contents of the pan into a jug and use a hand blender for a minute, or even two, until you have a thick, well-emulsified sauce.

Chop the onions in half, then into thin slices. Pull the leaves of chard off their stalks and chop them roughly. Slice the stalks across into pieces about 1cm thick. In a pan large enough to hold the finished dish, heat some olive oil and toss in the onions and the chard stalks. Cook at a medium heat for two minutes before adding the leaves. Keep the heat fairly high and stir the leaves until they wilt. Add the cannellini beans and continue to cook for a further minute or two until the leaves are tender.

Meanwhile, bring a large pot of water to a boil and cook the pasta to your liking, drain it and add it to the chard pan. Stir to mix the dish well, and season with salt and pepper. Turn off the heat and add four to six tablespoons of the pepper-garlic oil, stir once or twice to coat the pasta and serve immediately.

Braised chard parcels of potato and lentil with spiced red pepper and tomato jam

Chard, being a little tougher than spinach, is a very good parcel wrapping. It is easier to handle than spinach, which – being more delicate – can easily tear and break your heart. Medium-sized chard leaves with thin stalks are ideal for this dish. However, many people would consider it a shame to be picking chard before it matured to a decent size, and that, in any case, big leaves are more tender to eat. If you're from that camp, first pull the large leaves from their stalks and you will be able to make two parcels from each leaf. The stalks can be cooked separately, fried or braised, and served alongside their leaves.

I have specified rooster potatoes here because they are floury and starchy enough to make the chunky texture that works best, but not so floury that they become mashed potato against your will. The filling is a gently flavoured thing, soft in texture, easy eating as braised food always is, although I have added a green chilli to the potato mix, a mild one with seeds removed. Do check the heat of the chilli beforehand: you really don't want a big wallop of chilli in this filling – the heat is in the tomato-pepper jam.

We make this tomato-pepper jam, or a variation of it, when we get a glut of tomatoes that are too ripe to be seen in public. Don't make it from anything less ripe. In fact, if you're in any doubt, tinned tomatoes are probably better. The jam is an addictive combination of hot and sweet, one of my favourite tastes, and it keeps very well for weeks in a fridge, though you will have to make a much bigger batch than this if you want it to last for long.

FOR FOUR:

FOR THE JAM:
4 red peppers
500g ripe tomatoes
2–4 fresh red chillies
1 tablespoon cumin seeds, ground
1 tablespoon fresh ginger, grated
250g caster sugar
100mls balsamic or red wine vinegar

Blacken the skins of the peppers under a grill or over a flame, then put the peppers in a covered bowl or in a paper bag to cool. Peel off the skins and scrape out the seeds. Chop the pepper flesh finely. Dice half of the tomatoes. Blend the rest in a food processor with half of the peppers, the chillies, cumin and ginger. Put this puree in a pan with the sugar and vinegar, and bring it to a boil. Add the chopped tomato and pepper, and simmer for 30 to 40 minutes, stirring often. Scrape the sides of the pan with a spatula occasionally too. Pour or spoon the jam into jars and leave it to cool.

FOR THE PARCELS:

400g rooster potatoes, or similar, peeled

80g puy lentils

1 mild green chilli

4 spring onions

2 cloves garlic

1 sprig thyme

2 tablespoons olive oil

salt and black pepper, to season

1 teaspoon coriander seeds, ground

12–16 medium chard leaves

olive oil, to coat the parcels

Peel the potatoes and steam them. Coarsely chop the cooked potato into a rough mash. Meanwhile, boil the lentils in plenty of water for 12 to 15 minutes until tender but not soft. Drain the lentils and set them aside.

Slice the chilli lengthways and scrape out the seeds, then chop the chilli halves crossways in thin slices. Chop the spring onions and garlic finely. Pull the thyme leaves from the sprig. Heat two tablespoons of olive oil in a pan and cook the onion, chilli, garlic, thyme and coriander for one minute. Add the lentils and cook for one minute more. Stir the contents of the pan into the potato and season it well with salt and black pepper.

If you are using whole chard leaves with thin stalks, crush the stalks gently with a rolling pin or the flat of a knife. This will help the stalks to cook as fast as the leaves. Bring a pot of water to a boil and drop in the chard leaves. Cook for just one minute, then pull out the leaves and drop them into cold water to stop the cooking. Lay a leaf on a work surface and put a tablespoon of the potato mix at the end nearest you. Roll the leaf up

once, tuck in the sides and roll the leaf to the end, keeping the parcel fairly tight. Press the parcels on the work surface to square off the edges. Repeat with the rest of the leaves, then place the parcel in an oven dish. Brush on a very generous coating of olive oil and pour over enough water or stock to just cover the base of the dish. Cover the dish with foil in which you have cut a few slits. Cook the parcels in the oven at 180°C/350°F for 30 minutes. Check once, after 20 minutes, to see that the dish isn't completely dry.

Leave the parcels to cool for a while before serving them warm or at room temperature, with a bowl of the tomato-chilli jam to dunk into.

Pan-fried courgettes with cherry tomatoes, basil and garlic, on a new-potato tortilla

A lovely way to cook, and to present, 'baby' courgettes. I hesitate to use the phrase 'baby courgettes', because I don't really consider those little ones to be babies at all, but proper-sized courgettes. I tend to go along with the definition of a courgette I first read in Digby Law's *Vegetable Book*. The courgettes should be picked and eaten when no bigger than your little finger, while the flesh is still sweet and fairly concentrated, and before they have developed bitter seeds and taken on too much water to taste of anything.

The annual glut of courgettes is one of the banes of my life – a lot I've got to worry about, eh? – and one of the few things about summer that makes my heart sink. Because the plant is so productive, too many people grow too many courgette plants as a cash crop, selling the swollen marrow by the kilogram, thereby transferring from the kitchen to the garden that old cynical catering ambition to find ways to sell water. Mostly, I avoid courgettes completely except for the crops grown locally for Café Paradiso by people who will agree to pick small ones for me. We stuff the flowers, with or without little courgettes attached, and we cook courgettes either whole or halved, in recipes like this one where the vegetables are cooked briefly with their favourite summer partners of olive oil, garlic, tomatoes and basil. The courgettes themselves are never more than a day or two old and never much bigger than, well, let's say my biggest finger. Even so, the crop is still huge. At first, I used the carrot of higher prices to persuade growers to pick the courgettes early. Now, they prefer them that way, and they are beginning to think that the plant still produces close to the same amount of vegetable by weight as it would if left to grow monster marrows. They still like the higher prices, though.

This dish is one of those that came about from trying to make a special dinner from very fresh seasonal vegetables, and realising that no amount of twisting, wrapping, stuffing, layering or anything else would do the vegetables as much justice as cooking them briefly with ingredients they love to be with. Here, the courgettes, cooked in a simple way that might often relegate them to a side-dish role, are served on an individual new potato and egg tortilla, which might properly be the focus of the dish. In a sense, the dish is inverted, or at least the focus is shifted to bring the courgettes into the limelight. The tortilla differs from traditional tortilla in that it contains boiled waxy new potato slices set in the egg rather than chipped and fried floury potatoes, and it tastes lighter and more summery for it. Don't try to please Spanish guests with it though; they may doubt your grasp on the basics of life.

Of course you can cook one big tortilla to fill a frying pan and cut wedges from it, and it will taste good, but I think these individual ones suit new potatoes and the composed, elegant look you are aiming for in the finished dish.

If you do cook this, or indeed any courgette dish, with big, fat truncheon-like marrows, slice them in half lengthways and scrape out the seeds before slicing the flesh. But, first, let your vegetable supplier know you're a bit grumpy about having to work with such monsters. Oh, and agree to pay more for proper, smaller, courgettes.

FOR FOUR:

400g small waxy new potatoes

6 eggs

4 spring onions, sliced thinly

salt and pepper, to season

600g courgettes

1 small red onion

6 cloves garlic

200g cherry tomatoes

olive oil, to brush pan and rings

2 tablespoons olive oil

large pinch salt and pepper

splash of stock or water

1 handful basil leaves

Cut the potatoes into half moons of half to 1cm thick and cook them in boiling water until just tender. Beat the eggs well and stir in the potato, spring onion, and plenty of salt and pepper.

Slice the courgettes in half lengthways, or leave very small ones whole. Quarter the red onions and slice them thinly. Slice the garlic cloves quite thin. Halve the cherry tomatoes. Place four steel rings of 8–10cm diameter, 2cm high, in a wide frying pan. Put the pan over a low, wide flame and brush the pan and the sides of the rings with olive oil. After a few minutes, fill each ring with the egg and potato mixture. Leave the tortillas to cook for at least five minutes before flipping them over quickly. Tap down the sides of the rings to prevent too much egg leakage – the egg will set very quickly anyway, so there shouldn't be much spillage, even if your flipping is not up to speed. Let the tortillas continue cooking over a low heat. Turn them once or twice more to check the cooking side, and press the tops gently to test their firmness. If the tortillas are cooked before the courgettes, turn the heat off and leave them in the pan, or keep them in a low oven.

While the tortillas are cooking, heat two tablespoons of olive oil to a fairly high heat in a wide pan and toss in the courgettes. Cook for two minutes, stirring and tossing, then add the red onion and garlic, and continue cooking for one minute more, reducing the heat to avoid burning the garlic. Add a splash of stock or water to help prevent this. Now add the cherry tomatoes and a large pinch of salt and pepper. With the heat on medium, cook for one minute more until the tomatoes just begin to soften. Tear the basil leaves and stir them in, adding a splash each of olive oil and stock or water. These will combine with the tomatoes to form a lovely juice.

Place the tortillas – cut in half if you like – on plates, and pile a generous mound of courgettes over each, pouring every last drop of juice from the pan over the vegetables.

Poached courgette flowers with herbed ricotta stuffing in a tomato and basil broth

The recipe I reach for when the first courgette flowers arrive is the one in *The Café Paradiso Cookbook* for lightly battered and deep-fried flowers. Stuffed with sheep's cheese and pinenuts, and served with tapenade, it is fun in the way of deep-fried foods, yet light and sublime too. This poached version, inspired by Alice Waters' *Chez Panisse Vegetables* book, is a more delicate affair, perhaps more in keeping with the idea of cooked flowers, but it still has some richness and strong flavours, especially in the broth, which has a lot of olive oil and basil. But whichever way your own tastes lean, don't let the summer go by without frying a few courgette flowers, even if cooked in a simple batter without a filling, as I encountered a few years ago in Italy – served in a big communal plate, as though they were a dish of bountiful green beans or suchlike. Sometimes it's a shock to see what you consider an exotic delicacy being cooked and devoured as an everyday dish; then you realise that this is the essence of seasonal eating – always feasting on the current bounty and letting it go when its time ends, moving on to the next crop.

The filling in this recipe uses ricotta cheese as a base, with Parmesan and herbs as added flavour. It's not a cheese I'm particularly fond of, but it has a dry texture that is very useful in cooking. I have tried to make this dish using some of my favourite soft, fresh cheeses, like Knockalara sheep's cheese or Oisín goats' cheese, but the ricotta cooks faster, so the courgette flowers don't get overcooked waiting for the filling to cook.

The broth quantities will give you a small cup of highly flavoured rich broth to pour over the flowers, but you will need more stock to poach the flowers than for the final broth. If you are worried about overcrowding in the poaching pot, cook the flowers a few at a time and reheat them by placing the first lot back in the stock for a minute.

FOR FOUR:

200g ricotta cheese

1 tablespoon melted butter

1 egg

50g Parmesan, grated

2 tablespoons flour

1 tablespoon chopped chives

1 sprig thyme

salt and pepper, to season

8 courgette flowers, with tiny courgettes attached if possible

4 tomatoes

3 cloves garlic

800mls vegetable stock (see page 276)

4 tablespoons olive oil

2 tablespoons diced courgette

1 small handful basil leaves

Beat together the ricotta, melted butter, egg and Parmesan until smooth, then stir in the flour and herbs, and season lightly with salt and pepper. Open the flowers carefully and fill them about two-thirds full with the stuffing. Gently twist and squeeze the flowers to close them just above the filling.

To peel the tomatoes, cut a tiny cross into the base of each and drop them into boiling water for a minute, then transfer them to cold water. The skins will come off easily. Dice the tomato flesh and chop the garlic.

Bring the stock to a boil and poach the flowers in it until the filling is set, about seven or eight minutes. Check by pressing or squeezing the flowers – they should become quite firm. Lift out the flowers and put two each in shallow bowls. While the flowers are cooking, heat the olive oil in another pan and cook the tomatoes and garlic (and diced courgette, if using it) for five minutes, then pour in 300mls of the stock and boil for one minute. Tear the basil leaves and toss them in, season with salt and pepper, then ladle the broth over the flowers.

Summer squash salad with cashews, coconut, yoghurt, lime, ginger and coriander

Like potatoes, squashes and pumpkins come in types all along a scale of starchiness, or flouriness, from dry, perfectly mashable, to moist and firm. Those at the dry end of the scale ripen mainly in the autumn and tend to have deep orange flesh, intense and sweet flavours. The moist and firm squashes ripen earlier and have more delicate flavours, sometimes vaguely nutty. While my true passion for pumpkins is almost exclusively devoted to the autumn ones, especially when roasted and spiced, I do admire the sprightly lightness of summer squashes too. There are dozens of varieties, most of them very pretty, though I think the most commercially available is the spaceship-shaped scallop squash or pattypan; though it's easy to forget that courgettes are squash too. Butternut squash, which is, strictly speaking, a winter squash, stores brilliantly and seems to be available all year round these days. It has a lovely balance on the starch scale, being rich and dry enough to roast, yet moist enough not to fall apart too easily when boiled. A combination of different squashes is lovely for this salad and if you can find a butternut or similar orange-fleshed one it will add a lovely splash of colour. The salad has some lively, tangy and spicy flavours, but the subtle taste of the squashes won't be lost if they are cut into large enough chunks. Use a mild chilli with the seeds removed – chilli should not be the dominant flavour here.

FOR FOUR:

2 tablespoons whole cashews

1kg squash

2 spring onions

1 tablespoon sushi ginger

1 mild fresh red chilli

rind and juice of 1 lime

1 bunch fresh coriander leaves

large pinch salt

100mls coconut milk

200mls plain yoghurt

Toast the cashews in a low oven for half an hour or so, until lightly coloured right through. Peel the squash, unless the skin is very thin and edible, and cut it into two-bite sized chunks. Steam or boil the chunks until just tender, then drop them into cold water for a few minutes to cool them. Chop the spring onions into thin diagonal slices, and the ginger into thin slivers. Scrape the seeds from the chilli and slice the flesh thinly. Put the squash in a bowl with the cashews, onion, ginger, chilli, lime rind and juice, most of the whole coriander leaves and a large pinch of salt, and toss them gently. Stir the coconut milk and a pinch of salt into the yoghurt. When you are ready to serve the salad, either on individual plates or in a large bowl, pour the yoghurt dressing over the squash without tossing, and scatter the last of the coriander leaves over the top.

Roast beetroot with balsamic vinegar, caraway and wilted greens

Although I try to use beetroots for as much of the year as I can get them – in any variety or size, and changing the dishes for the large stored roots of winter – my true love is the first crop of tiny, rock-hard beets freshly pulled from the warm ground in summer. And, as with most vegetables whose annual arrival is anxiously awaited, the first thing I do with it is cook it my favourite way. In beetroot's case, that's roasted in olive oil until the beets begin to caramelise on the outside, then finished with a dash of balsamic vinegar for a few minutes more roasting. I serve these beets to anyone who will have them, to complement all kinds of food but especially rich dishes like risotto, crêpes, baked goats' cheese or feta dishes, and so on.

However, the first time I put caraway seeds with roasted beets was to serve with some Moroccan-spiced spring rolls – I don't know if caraway is particularly Moroccan, and I doubt that beetroot is, but the combination had an exotic flavour that was exactly what I was looking for. I don't think caraway gets much attention in modern cooking, but maybe it never did. The only way I remember caraway being used in the food of my childhood was in the caraway bread made by a local bakery at Christmas – a slightly sweetened and enriched yeast bread eaten in thick slabs with butter. It was my grandfather's official and often-declared favourite food: he would look forward to it for weeks, and devour it for the few days it was available. Now it puzzles me that neither he nor anyone else questioned its short seasonal appearance, or begged the bakery, which was two doors from his home, to make it more often. Anyway, if caraway isn't your favourite spice, the more popular cumin is a lovely replacement.

If the beets come with young leaves attached, use these as part or all of the greens in the recipe. If you are not using the beets immediately, chop off the greens and store them separately, as the greens will draw moisture from the root, causing the roots to dry out and soften sooner. But I bet you knew that already.

FOR FOUR:

20 small beetroots
olive oil
salt
1 tablespoon balsamic vinegar
1 teaspoon caraway seeds
1 red onion, thinly sliced
4 large handfuls greens, such as beet, chard or spinach
salt and pepper, to season

Trim the greens from the beets, leaving just a centimetre at the top of the roots, and leave any tail on for now. Cook the beets in boiling water for 30 minutes or so, then lift the beets out to a bowl of cold water. Rub the skins of the beets while in the cold water or, better still, under running water. The skins and the tail will slip off easily.

Put the beets in an oven dish, splash on a tablespoon of olive oil and some salt, and toss the beets to coat them. Cook the beets in a fairly hot oven, about 190°C/375°F, until beginning to crinkle and caramelise, about 15 minutes. Shake the dish now and again to ensure even cooking. Now sprinkle on the balsamic vinegar and the caraway seeds and return the dish to the oven for a further five minutes.

Heat two tablespoons of olive oil in a large pan and toss in the greens and onion slices. Stir the greens with tongs until they shrink and take on a glossy look, adding a splash of water if they seem too dry or inclined to burn. Season well with salt and pepper.

Lift the greens on to a serving dish and place the beets on and around them

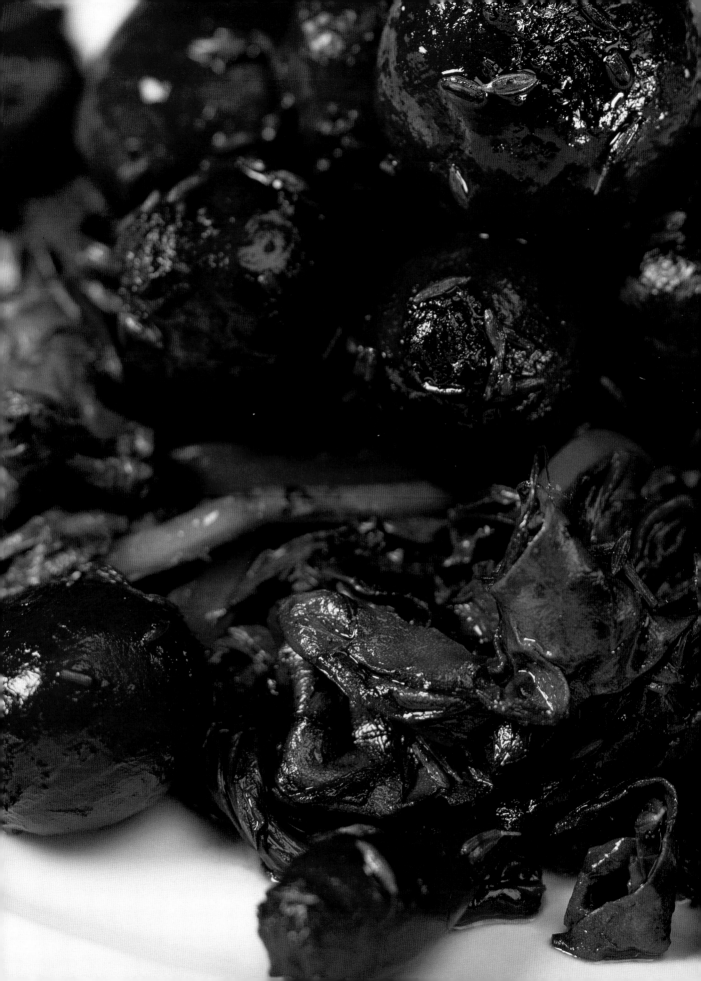

Beetroot with spices in a coconut-rice flour pancake with a scallion and pistachio cream

This dish is based on a beetroot curry I ate as part of a wonderful feast we had one evening in Rasa, the extraordinary vegetarian Indian restaurant in London. We also had a garlic curry but I haven't thought of anything to do with that yet! Here I have put a version of the curry into a coconut and rice flour pancake, which I use for many dishes. The pancakes are not as flexible as crêpes, which is why I cook them just before serving, when they are most pliable. They do keep for a few days and reheat well, but might not fold so easily. The curry has such a beautiful colour that I only partly cover it with the pancake. You could serve some rice and maybe one or two other curries with the pancake, or make it part of a series of individual courses. I think it's too good-looking to be dumping other curries on the plate.

The recipe includes a quantity of fresh coconut. Do try to use fresh if you can get it but, if not, desiccated will do. To get the flesh from a coconut, break the nut with a hammer and pull the hard shell off the white flesh. Grate the flesh with a wide grater.

The scallion cream was an idea I took from the book *Charlie Trotter's Vegetables*, an incredible and stunningly beautiful volume, full of the most outlandish things to do with, or to, vegetables. Any of you who know Trotter's books, or his food if you're lucky, will be familiar with the constant sense of 'How does he do that?' or even 'What kind of a mind even started down that path… with potatoes and peas?' Well, there I was one evening, flicking through the book looking for inspiration, when my eye fell on one of the many beautiful green oils, sauces and emulsions in the photographs. I checked the recipe and then had my first Charlie Trotter 'I could do that!' moment: it was ecstatic, I can tell you. I added the pistachios and cardamom to give it an eastern twist and a little cream to enrich the sauce.

500g beetroots

50g shelled pistachios
6 cardamom pods
2 bunches scallions
2 tablespoons olive oil

3 fresh green chillies
1 tablespoon oil or
clarified butter (see page
60)
1 tablespoon grated ginger
1 teaspoon yellow
mustard seeds
1 teaspoon fennel seeds
100g fresh coconut,
thickly grated
salt, to season

200mls thick plain
yoghurt

50g plain flour
50g rice flour
1 teaspoon cumin seeds,
ground
quarter teaspoon ground
turmeric
pinch cayenne pepper
large pinch salt
1 egg
200mls coconut milk

150mls cream

Boil the beetroots until tender and peel them under cold running water, then chop them into thick matchsticks.

While the beetroot is cooking, toast the pistachios in an oven for a few minutes. Crack the cardamom pods and remove the seeds, discarding the pods. Slice the white ends off the scallions and chop them finely. Drop the green ends into a pan of boiling water for a few seconds, then plunge them into cold water. Chop them coarsely and put them in a food processor with the pistachios, cardamom seeds and two tablespoons of olive oil, and blend, adding a little cold water in a slow stream until you get a thick but smooth purée. Pass this through a sieve, fine enough to take out any coarse pieces of scallion but not the ground nuts, into a small pan.

Halve the chillies lengthways, and chop them into slices. Heat a tablespoon of oil or clarified butter in a shallow pan and cook the scallion whites, chillies, ginger, mustard and fennel seeds over medium heat, stirring, for five minutes, then add the beetroot and coconut, and cook for five minutes more. Season with salt. Just before you serve, stir in the yoghurt.

Put the flours, cumin, turmeric, cayenne pepper and a large pinch of salt in a bowl. Whisk the eggs and coconut milk together, then whisk them into the flours to get a pouring batter. Heat a crêpe pan, brush it lightly with butter or vegetable oil and pour in enough batter to cover the base generously, a little thicker than a dessert crêpe. Flip the pancake over after a minute or so to cook the other side. Keep the pancakes warm in a low oven while you cook the rest.

Add the cream to the scallion-pistachio purée and reheat it gently while you serve the pancakes.

Put one pancake on each plate, spoon some of the spiced beetroot over one half and fold the other half. Pour some scallion cream over each pancake.

Warm salad of beetroot with fennel, broad beans and a star anise – citrus cream

Beetroot doesn't go with everything, but it has a wonderful affinity with certain flavours that seem to tease out hidden qualities. Think of beetroot with mint or dill, with balsamic vinegar or the salty tang of feta; beetroot with orange is classic. Beetroot is generally perceived as being a cold-climate, north-European vegetable with a thing for soured cream, cabbage and vinegar. Yet, when it comes to spices, it has a definite taste for the exotic, fragrant spices that conjure images of the sultry, mysterious eastern Mediterranean and Asia: cumin, cardamom and caraway certainly, but especially the aniseed- or liquorice-scented spices like fennel and star anise. You've got to admire a vegetable that likes to travel. For a salad, small freshly picked beets are best.

It's important to get very fresh fennel for salads; look for nice fat bulbs, very white with no blemishes, and some bright green feathery leaves at the top. Old fennel can be too stringy to eat raw or lightly cooked, while still being suitable for long braising.

Use any salad leaves you've got to hand, but do try to include some of the smaller, more pungent leaves like rocket, mizuna, mustard leaves or cress.

FOR FOUR:

2 star anise
1 orange
1 lemon
100mls plain yoghurt
100mls cream

12–16 small beetroots
120g shelled broad beans
1 bulb fennel
4 handfuls salad leaves

To make the dressing, put the star anise in a small pan with the finely grated rind of both the orange and lemon, and the juice of half of each. Double the volume of liquid by adding water, bring it to a boil and simmer gently until the liquid is reduced by half again, then leave this to cool. Remove the star anise and stir the liquid, including the citrus rinds, into the yoghurt, then use the cream to dilute this to a pouring consistency.

Boil the beetroots for 30 minutes or so until tender, and peel them under cold running water. Halve the beetroots, toss them in a little olive oil and salt, and roast them in an oven until they are warmed through but not yet caramelising.

Cook the broad beans for five to ten minutes, depending on their size and age, then cool them to warm, not cold, by putting them in cold water for a short time.

Discard any stringy outer leaves of the fennel, slice the bulbs in half lengthways, then crossways, into very thin slices. Toss these slices in a little olive oil and add a squeeze of lemon juice.

Toss the salad leaves with a light coating of the dressing and place them on plates. Put some beetroot, fennel and broad beans on each portion and drizzle over some more of the dressing.

Strawberries with balsamic vinegar and Thai basil

As sweet as strawberries are, a spoonful of sugar does wonderful things for them… but vinegar? A regular smartarse order in Café Paradiso is 'the balsamic strawberries without the balsamic'. That's strawberries, sugar and cream, then, sir, just like mummy used to make? Actually, my own mother was one of the first to try to get away with the 'hold the balsamic' line, but I wouldn't budge. Afterwards, she said it was 'quite nice, unusual, but not as nice as strawberries without balsamic vinegar'! It is a bit of a cheffy concoction but, no, I didn't invent it – it goes back at least as far as nouvelle cuisine, and may well have an authentic Italian pedigree, for all I know. You do need a very good balsamic vinegar, however, one with a rich, intense and rounded flavour, with natural concentrated sweetness as well as the acidity of vinegar. It should be traditionally aged for at least six years, though ten years and older is better for sweet dishes. Cheap balsamic is no better than general red wine vinegar and will only make your strawberries sour.

The basil element of the dish is not my idea either. John Foley, the book designer, called me one morning to say, among other more urgent things, that he had made a fantastic discovery the previous night while rummaging in his fridge for dinner… strawberries and basil. I briefly fantasised about what other combinations he had pondered and rejected before settling on that, but said nothing and carefully filed the information on a scrap of paper from my back pocket. Then when our organic strawberries came on stream, I tried this version, which combines John's with the balsamic strawberries I had been toying with; mostly, I admit, for the fun value of pairing such 'savoury' flavourings with everybody's favourite summer fruit. I was pleased that it worked, but I was surprised at just how well. Yum, that's delicious. I tried a number of different basils because I had the luxury of having visited the gardens of Ballymaloe Cookery School a few days earlier and had been sent home with 10 of their 20-something varieties. This 'Thai basil' was my favourite with strawberries; it has a quite pronounced aniseed flavour and hints of mint over a fairly mellow layer of classic basil taste. Most basils will work, though some that I tried were overpowering – avoid the fashionable dark purple ones, which are very strong and a little bitter. Having enjoyed the variety of basils at Ballymaloe, I'm going to grow a few of my own in a pot, though not 20! I suggest you do the same.

FOR FOUR:

2 punnets strawberries
1 tablespoon balsamic vinegar
4 tablespoons sugar
10 small leaves Thai basil

Slice any large strawberries in half and leave the rest whole. Toss the strawberries in a bowl with the balsamic vinegar and sugar, and leave them for 10–20 minutes. This will draw out the sweet juices of the strawberries to form a thin syrup with the balsamic and sugar, but any longer and the strawberries may start to become a little mushy. Just before you serve, tear the basil leaves and stir them gently into the strawberries.

Strawberry baked Alaska with summer berry compote

I didn't realise how daunting this recipe could be until I started to write it down. It looks like a lot of work, doesn't it? Well, if you come into the kitchen at 5pm to find you have sponge circles already cut out, a batch of ice cream in the freezer, then it's a simple matter of whipping up a meringue and assembling the Alaskas. You could knock up 30 or 40 before dinner. I suggest you take that approach to it. Make the sponge whenever you've got time and freeze the cut circles. Same with the ice cream, which is a very simple ice cream recipe, based on whipped cream and yoghurt rather than egg custard, yet it makes the best strawberry ice cream. Now, I'd say there's no more than a comfortable half hour's work to finish the Alaskas, even the first time you make them.

If you're still daunted by the whole rigmarole, and if you never make the Alaskas, please make the ice cream for its own sake, for your sake. It's divine: strawberries and cream, frozen. Although I use an ice cream churner, the ice cream will be almost as good if you simply put the mix straight in the freezer.

Baked Alaska may have started life as a novelty or an experiment, but the pleasure people take from eating one is no novelty. I've never seen an Alaska pushed to one side, half-finished, to cries of 'Well, that was a laugh, but I'm bored now', as can happen with gimmick food.

FOR FOUR:

FOR THE SPONGE:
3 eggs
90g caster sugar
90g plain flour
half teaspoon baking powder

Heat an oven to 190°C/375°F. Whisk the eggs and sugar until they are thick and pale. Sieve in the flour and baking powder, and fold in gently. Bake the sponge in a parchment-lined sandwich tin, approximately 20cm x 25cm, for 20 to 25 minutes. Leave the sponge to cool, then cut out six rings of about 8cm diameter.

FOR THE ICE CREAM:
250g strawberries
100g clear honey
juice of half a lemon
100mls cream
100mls plain yoghurt

Blend the strawberries, honey and lemon juice in a food processor. Whisk the cream to soft peaks and gently whisk in the yoghurt. Fold in the fruit and churn this in an ice cream machine until thick and almost frozen, then transfer to a freezer to freeze fully. (This ice cream method will also work quite well without an ice cream machine.)

FOR THE MERINGUE:
4 egg whites
240g caster sugar

Whisk the egg whites until they are stiff, then gradually whisk in the sugar in batches.

TO FINISH:
100g strawberries
100g mixed berries and/or currants
100g sugar

Roughly chop the strawberries and divide them between the six sponge rings. Top each with a large scoop of the strawberry ice cream. Cover this completely with a generous amount of meringue. Freeze the prepared Alaskas again for at least half an hour. Bring the mixed berries and sugar to a boil, simmer for one minute to melt the sugar, then blend to a smooth purée. To serve, bake the Alaskas in a hot oven, at least 200°C/400°F, for just three or four minutes until the meringue is lightly browned. Serve immediately, surrounded by a drizzle of the berry sauce.

Dark chocolate tart with raspberry sorbet and fresh raspberries

Raspberries and chocolate go together so well that we serve this chocolate tart with the raspberries prepared two ways: raw and as sorbet.

Raspberries could be seen as the more refined cousins of strawberries, somehow more precious, physically delicate with a slightly elusive flavour. Look at them there in the shops, the strawberries with their green stalks on, tumbled together in large punnets, full of the joys of summer – maybe a little bruised, but never mind; and the raspberries, resting delicately on slightly absorbent paper, trying desperately to stay in good shape until you take them home. Imagine farming raspberries… really, think about it for a minute or two. Those of you who do grow raspberries, take a bow, while the others ponder your crazy life.

Given their exquisite flavour, their fragile but perfect form and their high cost, you might think it a waste to go making sorbet of raspberries. So did I – I mean, couldn't you make the sorbet from frozen raspberries and save the fresh ones to serve raw with the chocolate tart? And indeed you can, because frozen raspberries are sometimes very good. But the sorbet is noticeably better made with fresh raspberries, so I have to bite my tongue on the cost, and so should you.

FOR FOUR:

200g sugar
450g raspberries
2 tablespoons lemon juice
2 tablespoons raspberry liqueur
2 egg whites

50g cold unsalted butter
100g plain flour
30g caster sugar
1 egg yolk

250g dark chocolate
150g white chocolate
100g unsalted butter
3 eggs
4 egg yolks
100g caster sugar
200g raspberries, to serve

Make a sugar syrup by putting the sugar and 200mls water in a pan, bringing it to a boil and simmering for one minute. Leave the syrup to cool.

Purée the raspberries with the lemon juice and raspberry liqueur in a food processor, then pass this through a sieve. Beat the egg whites lightly with a fork and add them to the purée with the sugar syrup. Freeze, using an ice cream machine.

Cut the butter into small dice and rub these into the flour using your fingers, or a food processor in short bursts, until you get a fine breadcrumb texture. In a bowl, stir in the sugar. Beat the egg yolk with a fork and add a tablespoon of cold water to it; then stir this into the flour, using a few quick movements with your fingers to bring the dough together. Knead it very briefly to form a smooth ball, flatten it gently and place it in the fridge for at least an hour, though, in my experience, overnight is best with this dough. Roll the pastry to fit a 24cm round tin and refrigerate it again, this time for 30 minutes. Finally blind-bake the pastry at 180°C/350°F for 10 to 15 minutes, until lightly coloured and firm.

Chop 100g of the dark chocolate finely – using a knife or food processor – and scatter it over the base of the prepared pastry case. Melt the remaining dark chocolate with the white chocolate and the butter in a bowl over simmering water. Whisk the eggs, egg yolks and sugar until pale and fluffy, then fold in the chocolate mixture. Pour this into the pastry case and bake at 220°C/425°F for 15 to 18 minutes only. Leave the tart to cool before serving. If possible, refrigerate it for a couple of hours.

Serve slices of the tart with a scoop of raspberry sorbet and a little pile of fresh raspberries.

Roasted green beans and shallots with couscous and marinated feta

The key to avoiding this pilaf becoming a stodgy and dull dish is to see it as a vegetable dish more than a couscous one – a big pile of sweet, roasted beans and shallots wrapped in a flavoursome blend of herbs, citrus and chilli, all bound together by the starchy, puffed-up granules of couscous. Marinated feta adds a richness that I can't resist putting in, though you may well find that the pilaf is perfect without the cheese. Cooking beans this way, by oven roasting, is best suited to the rougher element in the bean family. Delicate fine beans will end up all charred skin with no inner sweetness. You need runner beans, flat beans, the long, wide and substantial ones. Shallots are a bit of a chore, but worth it sometimes for their lovely caramelised sweetness. Small red onions or baby leeks, sliced, would be the next best thing.

Marinating feta gives it an extra dimension. In a few hours, the marinade doesn't penetrate far into the cheese; it's more like putting a coat of warm, fragrant spice over the cheese's body of salty creaminess. I use a simple marinade of garlic, chilli and rosemary in olive oil. Use a generous amount of olive oil in the marinade; it won't go to waste, as the oil also takes on the flavours of the marinade; and even some of the feta's saltiness. Drizzle some of it over the finished pilaf, and keep the rest to drizzle over tomorrow's dinner or to make a salad dressing.

You can use this pilaf as a simple main course, and it also makes a lovely warm salad, either as a starter or as part of an outdoor picnic or barbecue. Or you can take it as a basic model and add other vegetables, both roasted and steamed.

FOR FOUR:

200g feta cheese
4 cloves garlic
2–4 hot chillies, halved
a few sprigs thyme or rosemary
olive oil

20 small shallots
300g couscous
1 teaspoon turmeric
rind of 1 orange, finely grated
rind of 1 lime, finely grated
salt and pepper, to season
500g green beans
4 cloves garlic, sliced
2 fresh red chillies
1 tablespoon cumin seeds
1 tablespoon fennel seeds
splash of stock or water
4 tablespoons cooked chickpeas
small handful mint leaves, torn roughly
small handful fresh coriander, chopped
1 lime

Marinate the feta at least an hour before you want to serve the couscous. Chop the feta into rough cubes of about 15mm. Put the pieces in a bowl with the whole garlic cloves, chillies and the rosemary or thyme sprigs. Pour in enough olive oil to cover the cheese. Peel the shallots, toss them in a little olive oil in an oven dish and roast them at about 160°C/325°F until they have softened a little and are beginning to colour.

While the shallots are cooking, soak the couscous. Stir the turmeric, orange and lime rind into the dry couscous, season with salt and pepper and pour in 300mls of hot, not boiling, water. Stir the couscous once and leave it to soak until the vegetables are cooked.

Slice the green beans diagonally into pieces of about 5cm, add these and the garlic to the shallots. Toss well to coat everything in oil, turn the heat up to 190°C/375°F and put the dish back in the oven. Cook for five minutes, then slice the chillies into rings and add them, along with the cumin and fennel seeds.

Add a splash of stock or water to keep the beans from burning, and cook for a few minutes more until the beans are browning a little and just tender. Stir in the chickpeas, mint and coriander. Sift the couscous with a fork or your fingers and stir it into the vegetables. If you want to serve the dish hot, rather than warm, return the entire dish to the oven for a few minutes. Otherwise serve it as it is now – I think this kind of food is good at just above room temperature, probably better. Spoon the vegetables on to plates, scatter some cubes of feta around each and drizzle some of the oil from the feta marinade around and over the vegetables. Finish by squeezing some lime juice over the vegetables.

Green bean salad with olives, capers, cherry tomatoes and a lemon-garlic dressing

The very finest green beans, thinner than pencils and crisp-fresh, are best served lightly cooked as a salad. To boost the sense of summer sweetness, I sometimes like to use some raw sugar snaps and mangetout mixed into the cooked beans. You can also use a wide range of cooked beans, different varieties and colours, such as the common green one, yellow and purple beans, flat beans and young pink-streaked borlotto. Late-season broad beans are always welcome too in my kitchen, though you may have your own thoughts on that. The only essential stipulation is, as so often, to use only young and fresh beans. It will give you no pleasure, and do your reputation no good, to be making this with beans that are only fit for stewing, disguising in hot stir-fries or composting.

FOR FOUR:

rind and juice of 1 lemon

200mls olive oil

3 cloves garlic, crushed

300g green beans

150g sugar snaps and/or mangetout

200g cherry tomatoes, halved

1 tablespoon small capers

16 kalamata olives, stoned and halved

salt and pepper, to season

handful fresh oregano leaves

Make a dressing with the lemon, olive oil and garlic. Whisked or shaken together is fine, but I would use a hand blender to get a slightly thickened emulsion – it coats the beans better that way.

Cut the tops and tails off the green beans. Pull the strings off the sugar snaps and mangetout. If the mangetout are very big, cut them in half on a long diagonal. Cook the green beans in boiling water for just two minutes, then put them into cold water for half a minute. This will stop the beans cooking any more, yet leave them a little warm. Put the beans in a bowl with the sugar snaps and mangetout, the cherry tomatoes, capers and oregano leaves. Add the olives to

the salad. Pour in enough dressing to generously coat the salad, add a little salt and some coarsely ground pepper, and toss the salad to mix everything well. If you are serving this on individual plates, some of the smaller beans, capers and olives may gather at the bottom of the bowl. To avoid fighting at the table, divide them equally over the salads.

Risotto of fresh peas, mangetout and sugar snaps with mascarpone, mint and chives

I feel a little silly writing down specific quantities of each of these vegetables to put in this risotto. It might be better to think of the recipe as a basic summer model with a couple of handfuls of sparklingly fresh peas and raw edible pods added at the end. Any one or all of these three sweet vegetables will be equally lovely, as would some young broad beans. I put the mangetout and sugar snaps into the risotto raw because I don't think cooking does anything for them and I love that crunchy, summery texture they give to any dish. If you are buying peas, rather than picking your own, do make sure they are very fresh and sweet. The truth is that frozen peas are better and far cheaper than all but the best and freshest of fresh ones. If buying the latter, the pods should be smooth, shiny and crisply firm, but the only way to be sure about the sweetness is to pop a pea in your mouth.

The mascarpone gives the risotto an extra-creamy finish, and it goes very well with the peas here, as peas always love a little blob of cream. I gather from the customers in Café Paradiso, who are not shy about feedback, that mascarpone in risotto is not to everyone's taste. If you are that way inclined, leave out the mascarpone and double the amount of Parmesan added at the end of cooking.

FOR FOUR:

1200mls vegetable stock (see page 276)

60g butter

60mls olive oil

320g risotto rice such as arborio or carnaroli

1 bunch spring onions, chopped

4 cloves garlic, chopped

120mls dry white wine

30g Parmesan, grated

6–8 mint leaves, chopped

1 bunch chives, chopped

120g shelled peas

80g mangetout

80g sugar snaps

salt and pepper, to season

40g mascarpone

Bring the stock to a boil in a pot and keep it at a very low simmer. Meanwhile, melt one tablespoon of the butter with one spoon of the olive oil. Throw in the rice and stir it well to coat the grains with oil. Cook the rice gently for ten minutes, stirring often, then add the spring onion and garlic, and cook for one more minute. Pour in the wine, bring it to a boil quickly, then simmer until the wine is absorbed. Now add a ladle or cup of the stock, about 150mls, and continue to simmer, stirring often until that is all but absorbed. Add another cup of stock, and carry on absorbing, stirring and adding stock until the rice is almost cooked. Take care that the stock going into the rice pot is at a boil and, therefore, not interrupting the cooking of the rice. Test individual grains – the rice should be cooked through but firm, while the stock has become a little creamy and is almost completely absorbed. When the risotto reaches this stage, take it off the heat and stir in the rest of the butter and olive oil, the herbs and the Parmesan.

While the risotto is cooking, cook the peas in boiling water for a few minutes until just tender. Pull any strings from the mangetout and sugar snaps, and slice them in half diagonally. Stir the vegetables into the risotto just after the Parmesan. Season well with salt and pepper.

Before you serve, use a teaspoon to drop lumps of the mascarpone on to the risotto and fold them in gently with a few strokes of a spoon or spatula. It's lovely if the mascarpone doesn't completely melt but remains, at least in part, as warm, half-melted blobs of creamy richness.

Green beans with tomatoes, garlic, orange and oregano

At home we use green beans a lot as the 'greens' part of dinners based on eggs, potatoes or rice, or fried food like fritters and spring rolls and so on. This, the basic model of the recipe, has a lovely hint of orange in the tomato sauce. Depending on the dominant flavours of the rest of the meal, the orange and oregano can be replaced with ginger, cumin, chilli, basil and so on. While the recipe works best with flat beans and runner beans, it is good with all but the very thinnest of fine beans.

FOR FOUR:

500g green beans
5 ripe tomatoes
3 tablespoons olive oil
5 cloves garlic, thinly sliced
1 tablespoon fresh oregano leaves
rind of 1 orange

Top and tail the beans, and slice them if you are using large beans. Boil the beans for two minutes. Halve and thickly slice the tomatoes. Heat three tablespoons of olive oil in a pan and cook the beans for two minutes over medium heat, then put in the tomatoes and garlic, and cook until the tomatoes have softened. Stir in the oregano and orange rind, and cook for one minute more. Serve hot or warm.

Watermelon and feta salad with lime, pumpkinseed oil, toasted pumpkin seeds and green peppercorns

I first came across this weird and wonderful salad in Peter Gordon's *Sugar Club Cookbook*, but didn't pay it any more attention than a passing glance, a bemused shrug and the observation that 'that Gordon fella's got a fierce imagination', until Bridget came home from her annual pilgrimage to New Zealand raving about the amazing salad her sister was making regularly… from the Peter Gordon book. I added the toasted pumpkinseed oil simply because I had just been given a small bottle of it, and the green peppercorns because I love their fragrant heat. It is, I think, the savoury elements of the pepper and the salty feta that give the salad character and save it from the whimsy of the old cliché that is melon as first course. Shortly after I had begun to use it on the Café Paradiso menu, I was accosted by Sevinc, a Turkish woman working in Paradiso. She had just eaten the salad for lunch and was close to tears. Now what had I done? Thankfully, for she is a fiery woman, it turned out that the salad was apparently a perfect encapsulation of a flavour combination very familiar to her from home. Peter Gordon suggested the salad had a history in Israel; it seems it has roots, much older ones, all along the eastern Mediterranean, and probably originally came out of the Lebanon.

The quantities here will give you enough for four starters. However, if the salad is for a party or an unspecific number of people, it might be appropriate to start with one whole watermelon and gauge the other quantities from that. If you can't find toasted pumpkinseed oil, use sesame oil.

FOR FOUR STARTERS:

2 tablespoons pumpkin seeds

1 tablespoon freeze-dried green peppercorns

1kg watermelon

200g feta

2 limes

4 tablespoons olive oil

pumpkinseed oil

Toast the pumpkin seeds in an oven until lightly coloured. Crack the peppercorns gently between your fingers or with the flat of a knife. Chop the watermelon into two-bite sized chunks and peel them. (By the way, that's a phrase I use quite a bit, 'two-bite', and I presume, maybe wrongly, that it is easily understood. Basically, it means a piece of food that should reasonably take two bites to be eaten, so twice the size of 'bite-sized'.)

Chop the feta into small cubes and put it in a bowl with the watermelon and the pumpkin seeds. Grate the rind of one lime finely and squeeze the juice from it. Add both, and the olive oil, to the bowl, and toss gently. At this point, if you are serving individual portions, pile a mound of the salad on to each plate, scatter some peppercorns over each and drizzle a little pumpkinseed oil over and around the salad. Finally, squeeze a little more lime juice over each salad. If the salad is to be served from the bowl, toss the peppercorns through it and drizzle the pumpkinseed oil and lime juice over the top.

Oven-roasted peaches with lavender and honey ice cream and pistachio biscotti

The truism that the best thing to do with perfectly ripe fruit is to eat it from the tree must surely apply to the peach more than any other. The combination of the rich, sweet flavour and the uncontrollable juices streaming down your chin and elbows can cause you to wolf down the peach in a sensuous frenzy that leaves you a little shocked afterwards as you suck the last of the flavour from the stone, looking for somewhere polite to put it. Unfortunately, it is also true that, as the peach has become more commonplace, the perfectly ripe peach is becoming more elusive. How often do you buy peaches at the supermarket and find them disappointing in a ho-hum ordinary kind of way; or, worse still, you eat one without noticing, mindlessly reading a newspaper. A peach as ordinary, humdrum mild disappointment is a travesty. It could be seen as a symbol of the marketing of food as dull, safe, acceptable but cheap and ever-present, which should shock us into anger and disgust. Mostly we carry on reading the paper and gradually forget what a peach tastes like. In Paradiso we have a wonderful supply of organic peaches from France, which I wait for, in prayer, each summer before using this recipe, or indeed any peach recipe. I recently demonstrated this dish to a group of enthusiastic food lovers, a large number of whom said they had never tasted such wonderful peaches; and they didn't mean the way they were cooked. As much as I like people to appreciate my cooking, I get a bigger kick when they fall in love with the ingredients.

Peaches are a gift from the gods or one of the greatest pleasures of nature, depending on which way your beliefs lean. Do take the trouble to search out good ones, pay whatever is asked and, above all, reject common, cheap imitations.
Check peaches by smell first and then texture, rather than colour. Ripe, good-quality peaches will give off a rich fragrance and will be heavy and firm but not hard. Though they should have no green skin, a lot of red skin doesn't mean the peach is either ripe or tasty, as they are often bred and modified to turn red easily and quickly.

In fact, what strikes people about this dish, often more than the peaches, is the lavender ice cream, an idea that Bridget brought back from a trip home to New Zealand. Lavender flowers bloom just in time for the peach season, making this a perfect match. The number of lavender flowers given here makes a sublimely flavoured ice cream; don't be tempted to go for a bigger flavour as I was the second time I tried it, or you'll end up throwing out an ice cream that tastes like soap. Also, not all lavenders are good in food; the one we use is known as English lavender, or sometimes French lavender. The one I use has an inch-long head of tight purple pods.

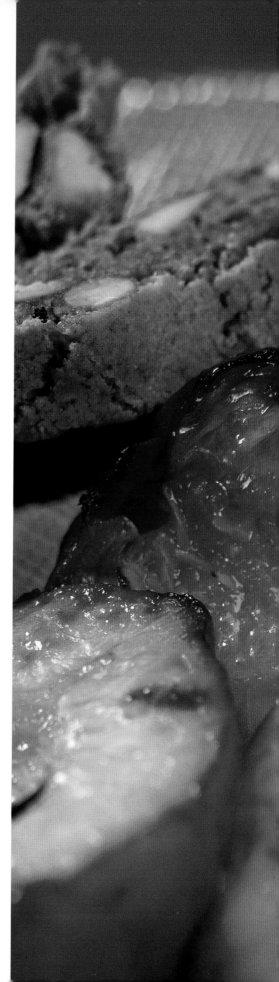

FOR FOUR:

FOR THE ICE CREAM:
350mls milk
6 heads lavender flowers
5 egg yolks
100g sugar
1 tablespoon honey
300mls cream

Bring the milk to a boil and drop in the lavender flower heads. Simmer very gently for two minutes, then remove from the heat and leave for 30 minutes.

Whisk together the egg yolks, sugar and honey until pale and creamy. Strain the milk into the egg mix, then heat this custard gently, stirring all the time, until it has thickened slightly. Cool the custard completely, then stir in the cream. Freeze the ice cream custard using an ice cream machine.

FOR THE BISCOTTI:
200g plain flour
200g caster sugar
2 teaspoons baking powder
2 eggs, lightly beaten
rind of 1 lemon
40g sultanas
40g dried apricots, sliced
40g dates
80g shelled pistachios
40g hazelnuts

Mix flour, sugar and baking powder together in a food mixer. Add half of the egg and mix well. Add the remaining egg and beat well to get a soft, slightly sticky dough. Now add the lemon rind, dried fruit and nuts, and mix everything well.

Weigh the dough and divide into it into four. Roll each quarter into a long tubular shape of about 3–4cm diameter. Place these tubes well apart on parchment-lined oven trays, and bake at 180°C/350°F for 30–40 minutes until pale golden. Remove from the oven and cool for 15 minutes. Turn the oven down to 140°C/275°F. Slice the cooled biscotti dough across at an angle into slices of about 10mm thick. Lay the slices on the baking sheets and bake them again for ten minutes, then turn the slices over and bake for ten more minutes. The biscotti will still be slightly soft, but will become crisp very quickly as they cool. They will keep for weeks in a sealed jar or tin.

TO SERVE:
6–8 peaches
4 tablespoons clarified butter (see page 60)
1 tablespoon honey

Halve the peaches, remove the stones, and place the fruit in an oven dish. Melt the clarified butter and stir in the honey. Spoon the honey-flavoured butter over the peaches and roast them under a grill, on a barbecue or in a hot oven. Serve the peaches warm with ice cream and biscotti.

Charentais melon sorbet with honey and rosewater baklava

Having been brought up with the notion that melon was some icily cold, tasteless thing you got as a starter for Sunday lunch in country hotels, even in the dead of winter, I am wary of melons in general – a wariness that has become subconscious and that I have to struggle with every summer. Those hotel starters were almost always made from the variety called 'honeydew', though they could have been called anything for all the flavour they carried. Nowadays, there are two varieties of melon that I work with, though I know I should try harder to expand that repertoire… but the memories begin to surface and I turn away. Watermelons I have come to love, as much for their thirst-quenching qualities and their dramatic size and colour as anything else. Watermelon may be the flashiest of melons, and the most satisfying to scoff from the fridge on a scorching afternoon, but the charentais, or cantaloupe, is far and away the king when it comes to flavour. Rich, sweet and fragrant, it has a dense, orange flesh and a beautiful scent – a good, perfectly ripe cantaloupe will call to you with its fragrant perfume as you pass it in the market.

You definitely need a well-flavoured melon to make into sorbet, as there is some dilution of flavour in the process. Here we serve the melon sorbet with baklava, but it is great on its own or with a salad of fresh melons.

The baklava recipe is essentially the classic version of pastry and nuts baked in as many layers as you can make, then drenched with a very sweet honey and rosewater syrup, which not only gives the baklava most of its flavour but helps it to keep fresh and crisp for a long time. I know this because one evening a woman told a waitress in Paradiso that the baklava was dry and tasteless; luckily I checked before taking a stand in defence of my baklava; we had been selling all evening a baklava made without syrup. It was worse than dry and tasteless, she was being polite. No one was seriously injured in the fallout in the kitchen.

FOR FOUR:

FOR THE SORBET:

200g sugar

200mls water

1 medium charentais melon

2 tablespoons lemon juice

2 egg whites

Make a sugar syrup by putting the sugar and 200mls water in a pan, bringing it to a boil and simmering for one minute. Leave the syrup to cool.

Peel the melon and blend the flesh with the lemon juice in a food processor, then pass this purée through a sieve. Beat the egg whites briefly with a fork to froth them a little, then stir this into the melon purée with 350mls of the sugar syrup. Freeze, using an ice cream machine.

FOR THE BAKLAVA:

400g whole almonds

50g light muscovado sugar

half teaspoon ground cinnamon

half teaspoon ground ginger

1 packet filo pastry

225g unsalted butter, melted

100g caster sugar

125g honey

1 and a half tablespoons rosewater

You need a 24 x 30cm oven dish, which will give 16 portions: 32 triangular pieces. Lightly toast the almonds, then chop them finely and mix them with the muscovado sugar, cinnamon and ginger.

Cut the filo pastry to fit the dish, saving any cut-off pieces to make up layers in the middle of the procedure. Brush the dish with butter, lay a sheet of pastry in it, brush that with butter, cover it with another sheet and brush that also with butter. Scatter on a layer of the almonds, then put two more layers of pastry as before. Continue in this way until the almonds and pastry are all used up. Make sure the almonds are scattered evenly to the edges so that the dish is building up evenly. Brush the top pastry sheet with butter and chill the dish for 30 minutes. Heat the oven to 190°C/375°F, with the fan turned off if you have one.

Using a sharp knife, cut the baklava into 16 rectangles, four by four, then cut each one in half diagonally to get 32 triangles. Make sure you cut right to the base of the dish. Bake the baklava for ten minutes, then turn the oven down to 160°C/325°F for an hour. The baklava should be lightly browned on top and crisp all the way through.

Heat the caster sugar, honey and rosewater together in a small pan until bubbling, leave it for one minute, then pour it over the hot baklava. Leave the baklava in the dish to cool completely before removing the pieces. It will keep for a week or more in a sealed container.

Buffalo mozzarella with organic tomato salad and a warm olive-basil dressing

The tomato has become such a staple of modern food that it would be hard to get through a day without meeting one. The world, or at least the parts of it we live in, takes the tomato completely for granted. Tomatoes are available every day of the year in every cornershop and supermarket, fresh and tinned, puréed and juiced. In the ketchups, sauces, chutneys, frozen foods and so on of our pantries, the tomato is a fundamental ingredient. In Paradiso, as everywhere, tomatoes are used in many ways in so many dishes, all through the year. Even in winter, we use dried tomatoes, roasted tomatoes, frozen tomato sauces and tinned tomatoes. During the times of year when we can get good fresh tomatoes, they still mostly tend to play either supporting or partial roles in dishes, or act as the base for sauces, stews and relishes. But in late summer, when tomatoes are at their prime, I serve them raw with olive oil, salt and pepper. This is the time to remind ourselves what a tomato tastes like. Because despite the tons of tomatoes we all get through during the year, we rarely stop to pay them much attention. So, when the time and the tomatoes are right, I like to present a plate of perfectly ripe, organic tomatoes, three or more varieties grown for their flavour rather than for their keeping qualities or crop yield, and ripened in their own good time in summer sunshine. In the right atmosphere, in the right frame of mind, everybody will notice the flavour and love it; most will be surprised. I enjoy those moments, seeing the look on a face, whether it is a first appreciation of a food or an unexpected flashback.

However if you write 'tomato salad' on a restaurant menu containing all sorts of other exotic attractions, then the reality is you're going to end up with a few boxes of over-ripe tomatoes at the end of the week and then it's tomato soup again all next week. So I usually serve the tomato salad with one or more eye-catching foods, something irresistible or of perceived high value. From a list including pesto-topped crostini, roasted sweetcorn, a herbed mousse, sheep's or goats' cheeses, shaved Parmesan, olives and anything including the word basil, my favourite is the classic combination of tomatoes with fresh buffalo mozzarella. Sometimes we dress the salad very simply with olive oil and salt; on other days we will concoct a slightly more complex dressing like the one in this recipe. But whatever we serve with them, we never lose sight of the fact that it is the tomatoes themselves that we want the diners to notice. This is the time to treat tomatoes as the extraordinary fruits that they are, the crown jewels of the most glorious time of the year.

If you don't have the simple luxury of your own tomatoes, take care to buy sun-ripened organic ones and try different varieties if you have the opportunity. Tomatoes taste better at room temperature, so avoid putting them in the fridge if you are going to eat them soon.

FOR FOUR:

2 x 200g pieces buffalo mozzarella

600–800g tomatoes

salt and black pepper, to season

10 kalamata olives, stoned and chopped into fine dice

150mls oil, 1 bunch basil

Tear the mozzarella pieces in half and put one half on each plate. Using a variety of tomatoes from tiny sweet cherry tomatoes through to the giant, dense fleshy ones. Slice or chop the tomatoes. Arrange the slices around the mozzarella and sprinkle some salt, coarsely ground black pepper and the finely chopped olives over both the tomatoes and the cheese. Blend the olive oil and basil and drizzle a generous stream of basil oil over everything and serve. To make a fabulous and substantial lunch of this starter, add some crusty bread or warm crostini, and take it out into the garden.

Tomato rasam

All summer long, and into the autumn, we make a roasted tomato soup in Café Paradiso, an almost shockingly intense concentration of tomatoes with garlic and summer herbs. The very simple recipe for that soup is in *The Café Paradiso Cookbook*, so this time around I thought I might give you a recipe for another, very different, tomato soup. I first came across rasam in the books of Das Sreedharan, two slightly different recipes in two books, which intrigued me, so I went looking for other versions of the dish. I found plenty, all different, some radically so, including one that claimed it to be the precursor of mulligatawny, that most English of Indian dishes. In the end I went back to Das's versions, because they were closest to what I had originally liked about the dish, that it was a thin invigorating broth rather than a soup, and I liked his description of it as a healing drink, a pick-me-up, a refreshing and cleansing tonic for any time of day. In Paradiso, we use our own ginger broth in the same way. The customers get it as part of a noodle dish but in the kitchen we drink it from cups to kick-start the evening. So the aim here was to make an Indian-spiced version. The main difference between my version and Das's is that I use only the broth from the lentils, not the lentils themselves, which gives a lighter finish, and I roast the tomatoes first to intensify their sweetness.

There is a chilli element in the spicing of the rasam, but it's not too upfront. Instead the broth is a soothing blend of the fruity sourness of tamarind, the sweetness of roasted tomatoes and the earthiness of the lentils. The dominant flavours are provided by the fragrant spices, which are barely cooked in oil and swirled into the broth at the last minute. If you were to make large batches of this to keep for days, I would recommend that you only fry sufficient spices as you intend to stir into each serving, as the lively freshness of recently introduced spices will fade to a more absorbed effect if left overnight. That's not a bad thing, merely different.

The broth is a first course, a light lunch or a cure, depending on your needs. It hasn't quite displaced the ginger broth in the Paradiso kitchen, but mostly because it is a little more complicated to make.

This recipe makes two litres, enough for eight to ten starters, but it's worth making at least that much, especially if you become fond enough of it to take a cupful as a refreshing drink.

FOR EIGHT TO TEN
STARTERS:

100g red lentils

1200mls vegetable stock
(see page 276)

1kg tomatoes, quartered

olive oil, to coat

salt, to season

8 cloves garlic

3cm x 4cm piece of
ginger, chopped

2 fresh green chillies,
chopped

2 teaspoons turmeric

small bunch fresh
coriander

150g tamarind pulp

3 tablespoons olive oil

1 teaspoon green
peppercorns, crushed

2 teaspoon mustard seeds

2 teaspoon fennel seeds

1 teaspoon cumin seeds

Wash the lentils and put them in a pot with the stock. Bring it to a boil and simmer over very low heat, covered, for 20 minutes. Take it off the heat and leave to cool.

Put the tomatoes in an oven dish with just enough olive oil to coat them, and some salt. Roast the tomatoes in a moderate oven for 15 minutes, until soft and juicy but only lightly coloured. Add the garlic and ginger for the last five minutes of the roasting. Take the tomatoes from the oven, stir in the chillies, the turmeric and the fresh coriander, then pour the tomatoes into a food processor and blend them to a fine purée.

Break up the tamarind and put it in a jug with 800mls of warm water to soak for ten minutes, then strain the liquid through a fine sieve, pushing the pulp with the back of a spoon to squeeze all the liquid through the sieve. Pass the lentils through the same sieve, without pushing, to save the broth and discard any of the lentil mush that doesn't pass through. Don't force it but don't fret about any solids that sneak through. Put the lentil broth, the tamarind juice and the tomato purée into a pot, bring it to a boil and simmer for 15 minutes.

In a frying pan, heat three tablespoons of olive oil and add the green peppercorns and the mustard, fennel and cumin seeds. Fry the spices for a few minutes until the mustard seeds begin to pop. Ladle the soup into bowls and swirl some of the spiced oil through each portion.

Tomato, saffron ricotta and olive tart

My love of tomato tarts would be more or less evenly split between those that are set by a custard, like the one below, and those that are little more than roasted tomatoes placed in pastry with some herbs. A tart without custard is a wonderful way to show off good tomatoes, but I think they work best as individual tarts, or as small ones at least – and, for some reason, I had it in mind to include a large tart recipe here. This tart, though of the custard variety, is crammed with tomatoes, so in some ways it's a compromise between the two styles. It's a very simple tart, as tomato dishes should be when tomatoes are at their best. Because the tomatoes retain a lot of their juiciness, the tart doesn't really need a sauce or relish, but I would sometimes serve it with a classic basil pesto.

The tart case is a basic shortcrust pastry. The pastry can be rolled and stored in the freezer any time in the days before you use it.

FOR FOUR:

160g plain flour
1 teaspoon salt
80g cold unsalted butter
40mls cold water

10 tomatoes, halved
salt and pepper, to season
drizzle olive oil
6 strands saffron
250g ricotta
4 eggs
100mls cream
50g Parmesan, finely grated
2 tablespoons tomato pesto (see page 32)
10g kalamata olives, stoned and sliced

Put the flour and salt into a food processor. Chop the butter into pieces, add it to the flour and process in short bursts until you get a fine crumb texture. Tip the mix into a bowl, pour in the water and bring the dough together with a few quick stirs with a spoon, then tip the dough out on to a lightly floured surface and knead it a few times to form a smooth ball. Press the ball gently to flatten it a little, wrap it tightly and refrigerate it for half an hour or more. Roll the pastry to fit a 26cm tart tin, preferably one with a loose base and with a 3–4cm-high side. Prick the pastry all over with a fork and refrigerate it again for at least half an hour, or until you need it. Before you use the pastry, blind-bake it in a medium oven until the pastry is just firm.

Place the tomatoes, cut side up, on an oven tray. Season with salt and pepper and drizzle over some olive oil. Roast the tomatoes in the oven at a medium temperature until softened and coloured a little. Soak the saffron threads in a tablespoon of hot water for a few minutes. Put the ricotta, eggs and cream, and the saffron and its water, into a food processor, and blend briefly to get a smooth custard. Season with salt and pepper. Stir in the grated Parmesan.

Spread a thin layer of the tomato pesto on to the base of the prepared pastry case, then pour in the custard. Scatter the sliced olives over it, then place the tomatoes, cut side up, into the custard. Press them in gently. Bake the tart at 180°C/350°F for 30 to 40 minutes, until the custard is set and lightly browned. Leave the tart for ten minutes before slicing it.

Balsamic-roasted tomatoes

I use tomatoes cooked this way as an accompaniment to risotto, tarts, potato cakes, aubergine and egg dishes – rich foods that need the acid of the tomatoes and vinegar. This way of cooking tomatoes works very well with cherry tomatoes, or indeed any tomatoes sweet and ripe enough to stand up to the balsamic vinegar.

FOR FOUR:

1kg tomatoes, halved
salt and pepper, to season
drizzle olive oil
handful basil leaves or
sprig of thyme
2 tablespoons balsamic
vinegar

Place the tomatoes in an oven dish. Sprinkle with salt and pepper and drizzle over some olive oil. Roast at 190°C/375°F for ten minutes until the tomatoes soften and begin to caramelise. Tear the basil leaves or pull the leaves from the thyme sprig, and scatter them over the tomatoes, then drizzle the balsamic vinegar over that and return the tray to the oven for two or three minutes. Serve warm.

Summer stew of sweet peppers, new potatoes and sugar snaps with basil, garlic and olives, and goats' cheese ciabatta

A variation on the peperonata recipe from *The Café Paradiso Cookbook*. Here, the meltingly delicious olive oil-based pepper stew is given some added substance with some new potatoes, fresh waxy potatoes that don't break up or leak into the stew in the way you might want potatoes to do in a winter stew. And then, at the end of the slow cooking, I throw in a handful or two of crunchy sugar snaps, the vegetable that seems to best capture the essence of a fine, sunny summer. The stew is complete in itself, a lovely summer lunch, and needs only some crusty bread or, if you want something more elaborate, goats' cheese ciabatta. The recipe for the ciabatta doesn't have proper quantities – simply cover the bread with cheese. I like to scrape a thin layer of olive tapenade, preferably a green olive one, on to the bread under the cheese. Any pesto works very well too.

The flavour of the stew is a fairly upfront matter, in the sense that there aren't many background elements. There is a lot of garlic, but it remains in big pieces and cooks to a mellow sweetness. The peppers and garlic trade flavours with the olive oil, giving as well as taking, and that blending of flavours becomes the body of the stew. In such a blending the oil is more than a mere carrier, and its own flavour is very important. My favourite style of oil for this stew is a deep green one, very fruity but not really peppery or spicy. If you have some basil oil in the house, add a tablespoon or two of it with the tomatoes.

FOR FOUR:

FOR THE STEW:

2 small red onions

100mls olive oil

6–8 red and/or yellow peppers

1 fresh mild red chilli

10 cloves garlic, halved or sliced thickly

4 ripe tomatoes

12 black olives, stoned and halved

320g new potatoes

200g sugar snaps

1 bunch basil leaves

salt and black pepper, to season

Chop the red onions in half, then into thin slices. Heat the olive oil in a wide pan and start the onions cooking in it. Chop the peppers into quarters lengthways; scrape out the seeds and white membrane, and discard. Chop the pepper quarters into diagonal slices about 15mm thick. Slice the chilli in half lengthways and chop the halves into thin slices. Add the peppers, chilli and garlic to the onions in the pan, tossing well to coat everything in olive oil. Chop the tomatoes in half, slice them thickly and add them to the pan with the olives. When everything heats through again, cover the pan, turn the heat to the lowest setting and simmer the stew for 20 minutes.

Meanwhile, chop the new potatoes in half if they are golfball-sized or smaller, or cut them into thickish slices, say 15–20mm, if they are bigger. Steam or boil the potatoes until just tender, then add them to the pepper stew for the last few minutes of cooking. The stew is done when the peppers are soft and very sweet. Just before serving, string the sugar snaps, and stir them into the stew with plenty of roughly torn basil leaves. Season well with salt and black pepper.

FOR THE CIABATTA:

1 ciabatta loaf

some pesto or olive tapenade

goats' cheese

To make goats' cheese ciabatta, slice a ciabatta loaf in half lengthways and spread the cut surfaces with a thin layer of basil or tomato pesto, or a green olive tapenade, and cover that with thin slices of strong goats' cheese. Bake in a hot oven, 200°C/400°F, until the bread is crisp and the cheese lightly coloured.

Pan-fried couscous cake of red onion, feta cheese and pinenuts with green olive tapenade and spiced roast peppers with spinach

The first time I made this was for dinner and I used leftover couscous from lunch. After a few slightly disappointing results, I came to the conclusion that this isn't really a leftover-couscous dish, though I must state that it doesn't actually fail if you use leftovers. I have tried soaking the couscous in less water than it would normally take to make perfect, fluffy couscous – 300g of couscous would usually require 280–300mls of liquid. It now seems that less liquid in the initial soaking leaves scope for the couscous to mop up any spare moisture later without becoming soggy itself.

I'd like to say that I use picholine olives, my favourite green olives, to make the tapenade. We did use them in Paradiso for a few turns at it, but there's no easy way to get the flesh off the stones. Well, if there is, we didn't hit on it. Then we had the bright idea of buying stuffed green olives, the ones with garlic, almonds or peppers inside them. The olive flavour is fairly well preserved by this method, and you will find some use for the stuffings. I have never found a good-quality stoned and unstuffed olive, and there is no point in making the tapenade with tasteless olives.

Even though it is hidden under the cake, the peppers with spinach and spices is definitely the most strongly flavoured element in the dish. It is the fresh and vibrant part of the meal and, to my mind, the real focus. The cake is relatively lightly flavoured to allow the vegetables to shine from below.

You will need a metal ring of 9–10cm diameter and 3cm high for each of these cakes.

FOR THE TAPENADE:

300g green olives

2 cloves garlic

1 bunch basil

2 tablespoons capers

3 tablespoons olive oil

Stone the olives or pop out the stuffing. Put the olives in a food processor with the garlic, basil, capers and three tablespoons of olive oil, and blend to a smooth thick purée. To use the tapenade as a sauce, dilute with more olive oil.

FOR THE COUSCOUS
CAKE:

240g couscous

200mls warm water or stock

2 red onions

4 cloves garlic

1 tablespoon olive oil

200g feta

40g pinenuts, lightly toasted

small bunch fresh coriander, chopped

salt and pepper, to season

2 eggs

Soak the couscous in 200mls of warm water or stock. Finely chop one red onion and the garlic. Cook them for two minutes in olive oil in a small pan, then stir them into the couscous. Break the feta into a rough crumble and add it to the couscous with the pinenuts and fresh coriander. Season with salt and pepper. Add the beaten eggs just before you fry the cakes.

FOR THE PEPPERS:

4 red peppers

1 teaspoon cumin seeds

1 teaspoon coriander seeds, crushed

1 red chilli, chopped

400g spinach

Halve the second red onion and chop it into slices, not too thin. Quarter the peppers lengthways, scrape out the seeds and white membrane and discard, and chop the peppers into slices about 1cm thick. Toss these with the onion slices and some olive oil in an oven dish and roast them at 190°C/375°F for 15 minutes or so. Turn the vegetables occasionally. They are done when both the onion and peppers have softened and caramelised a little around the edges, and are beginning to look a little charred.

Meanwhile, on the stove, heat a large wide frying pan to a low-medium heat. Place four metal rings in the pan and brush their inside surfaces and the pan itself with olive oil. Pack each ring with some of the cake mix, pressing gently on the top of each. Fry the cakes gently for a few minutes before flipping them over. Keep the heat low and flip the cakes a few more times until they are cooked through and the outsides are slightly crisped.

A few minutes before the cakes are ready, heat some olive oil in a pan and put in the cumin, coriander and chilli. Almost immediately, add the spinach and stir it with tongs over high heat until it wilts and takes on a glossy, darker shade of green. Add in the roasted peppers and any juices from them, turn the heat down and wait just long enough to heat the peppers through.

Serve each couscous cake on a generous pile of the peppers and spinach, and put a teaspoon of tapenade on each cake.

Fresh pasta in a sweet pepper cream with mangetout, aubergine, spring onions and basil

There seems to be an unwritten rulebook for pasta – more a code than a set of rules – of unknown length or breadth, which can still strike terror into nervous cooks. How long to cook it, how fast to boil the water, salt or no salt, oil in the water or not, how severely to drain it of water, to cool in water or not? Is too high a proportion of sauce and vegetables to pasta a sin, something to be indulged in the dark on your own? Should I throw it against the wall to test its done-ness? (If you do this, stop immediately, clean the walls and use your teeth to test the pasta in future.) I have my own opinion on all of these matters, but the world is crawling with pasta authority spies, so I'll hold my tongue. One rule I seem to almost always adhere to is to use cream sauces on wide and long noodles, and olive oil or tomato sauces on thin noodles and tubes like penne and rigatoni, though sub-clause xi307 says that cream is also good on tubes. This recipe has a very rich sauce, sweet with the intensity of roasted peppers, and is definitely best on a wide noodle like fettuccine or pappardelle. However, it is also one of my favourite things to eat on penne, with extra greens and lots of Parmesan or goats' cheese, late at night after a hard evening's cooking. This is not recommended for those whose sleep is easily disrupted.

FOR FOUR:

2 red peppers
1 tablespoon olive oil
2 cloves garlic, chopped
100mls white wine
100mls vegetable stock or water
300mls cream

1 aubergine
200g mangetout
6 spring onions

400g fresh pasta noodles

handful basil leaves

Blacken the skins of the peppers under a hot grill or over a flame, then pop them into a paper bag and leave to cool. When cool, peel the peppers, discard the seeds and white membrane and coarsely chop the peppers. Heat a little olive oil in a pan and briefly cook the peppers and garlic. Pour in the wine and the stock, bring it to a boil and simmer over a low heat until the liquid has almost evaporated again. Blend the contents of the pan in a food processor and return it to the pan. Add in the cream. While the pasta is cooking, bring the sauce to a boil and simmer for a minute.

Slice the aubergine into rounds of about 1cm thick. Brush the slices lightly on both sides with olive oil and roast them in a hot oven until crisp and well browned. You may need to turn the slices once to get an even cooking. Pull the strings from the mangetout and cut them in half diagonally if they are too big to eat whole. Chop the spring onions into thin, 3 or 4cm long, diagonal slices.

Bring a large pot of water to a boil and cook the pasta until just tender. Drain it in a colander. While the pasta is draining, put the pepper cream and the vegetables into the pasta pot over heat. Tip the pasta back in and stir to mix everything well. Tear the basil leaves and stir them in. Serve immediately with some Parmesan or soft goats' cheese.

Outdoor Cooking

Outdoor cooking

There is a fundamental difference between outdoor eating and outdoor cooking. Our family eats outside a lot, though more because Bridget is a New Zealander than because Ireland has a climate conducive to it. By eating outside I mean that we bring our meals outside to eat in the sunshine (and the rain). Increasingly, we also cook outside. One recent cold evening in early spring, after a hard shift in the restaurant kitchen, I came home to find Bridget and Uncle Ron huddled over the barbecue, a homemade contraption involving the legs of an old sewing table, some red bricks from the garden wall and a thick slab of slate. Every window and door of the house was open to the harsh elements, and Bridget was sipping chilled pinot grigio and frying haloumi. At midnight. Not quite two weeks back from a trip home to New Zealand, she was clearly not yet re-acclimatised. The airspace immediately around the barbecue was the only place not to freeze to death, so I reluctantly joined them.

Generally, I like stoves and grills and ovens and all the paraphernalia of a well-designed kitchen. I like to cook calmly, in the evening when the day's work is done, with a glass of red wine… and a cosy room to eat in. The macho routines of the average barbecue never called to me, the burned flesh and the weak beer and… oh, my god… the apron worn over shorts! But I am a growing convert to outdoor cooking, if not its fashion sense. The first time I gave it any serious thought was a few years ago when I was asked to do a demonstration of vegetarian barbecuing at a barbecue festival in Bantry in West Cork. Sounded like hell to me at first, but the location was beautiful and gradually the challenge grew on me. With a lot of help from Bridget and our South-African cook, Johan, I set about coming up with a feast of vegetable dishes that would cook well on a very basic barbecue. The dishes we cooked that day form the basis of the following section. What surprised me, and what sparked my ongoing and growing interest in outdoor cooking, was that some of the food tasted better than it did when cooked on a domestic indoor stove. Partly because of the very high cooking temperatures and the short cooking times, some of the food cooked in a way I didn't expect. The baby carrots, briefly marinated and grilled, were a revelation. Artichokes and asparagus revealed hidden characteristics. Fennel did not resemble the fennel I like to cook indoors, usually braised slowly in wine and olive oil.

The day was a fabulous success, not only as a food experiment and demonstration, but as a surreal day out in the Irish countryside. Just as we were about to start cooking the main dishes of the afternoon, with a display of the simpler grilled vegetables already laid out to attract attention, a huge black cloud carrying a heavy storm charged into the town square from the bay and drenched everybody before we could look up to point at it and warn each other. We stood around laughing at the predictable unpredictability of it, while some fast-thinking observers scoffed the cooked food, and some of the uncooked stuff as well, in their ravenous panic. Then, out of the downpour, four strong men appeared with long poles. On their shoulders, like a papal procession, they carried the 12-foot long, scorching-hot barbecue across the square and into the fire station, where the demonstration carried on heroically. Only in Ireland… only in the summer…

Although all of these recipes can be very successfully prepared and presented indoors, when writing them down I have focused on recipes for cooking on a simple barbecue of bars over hot coals. A separate solid plate is a very useful addition but,

if you don't have one, it is easy to replicate by placing a thin oven tray on the bars. Some of the recipes do require some preparation of vegetables and sauces, which will have to be done in an indoor kitchen, unless you have a state-of-the-art multi-function outdoor cooking unit, in which case you know more about how to cook on it than I can tell you. Where such pre-preparation is necessary, it is of a kind that can be done well in advance if that suits you best, or just before the final cooking, if you prefer.

With a little practice and experimentation, a lot of recipes can be adapted to outdoor cooking, but an important aspect of food for outdoor eating is that it is durable and flexible. You don't want the kind of food that collapses in an indignant puddle because it wasn't consumed immediately it left the heat of the cooker. The food must be flexible enough to be cooked for five minutes or ten, at 250°C/300°F or 200°C/400°F; dishes need to be good if kept warm at the edges of the barbecue until wanted, and still good to eat much later and cooler when someone gets a fresh appetite, notices they missed a treat or arrives late.

I think there are two different types of outdoor meal, which require different planning and a different approach to the food. First, there is the most common: you come home from work, there is still some heat in the sun and the prospect of a nice, long evening ahead. You decide to eat outside, crank up the barbecue and cook a simple meal, with all the characteristics of a typical balanced meal: one main item, say some simple grilled haloumi or some aubergine sandwiches; some potatoes thrown in the embers and some grilled vegetables, with that jar of chutney your mother left last week; make a nice fresh salad, uncork a bottle of crisp white wine and away you go. In effect, 'dinner', cooked and eaten outside.

The other way that we eat outside is a more elaborate affair where, typically, people gather to spend a few hours eating and drinking. This scenario is nothing like inviting people to dinner, and the food therefore takes on a different role. I would even go so far as to say that it's not important that you choose dishes that complement each other, because people won't eat them in that way. Some will eat a little of everything over the course of the day, others will feast on the three starchy food dishes in one go and eat no more, still others will have nothing but some salad and corn chips. The best approach is to provide as much variety of dishes as you can, keep it flowing as long as it is wanted, and don't worry if someone has mayonnaise instead of satay with the tofu kebabs. I think an ideal menu would have three or four cooked dishes, two or three grilled vegetables, two or three salads, and an awful lot of corn chips and crisps for children and nervous adults.

The quantities I have given in the following recipes are for ten small portions as part of a range of dishes in a party situation, unless otherwise stated. For example, one kebab skewer or two aubergine fritters per portion. These quantities will be enough for four to six people in a more formal setting where you cook only one main dish. They are also easy to multiply if you're throwing a very big party.

Looking through the recipes now, I notice that quite a few are laced with spices or accompanied by spiced relishes and chutneys. It isn't deliberate, just the way they came out, and yet it doesn't surprise me. Spiced food seems to suit outdoor eating, and vice versa, and it suits the drinks that go with a day in the garden: sparkling wines, white wines, ice-cold beer and, Bridget's speciality, real margaritas of tequila, Cointreau and fresh lime juice. Yum.

Barbecued vegetables with a lemon, thyme and garlic marinade

A lovely way to start a long evening's cooking and eating in the open is to grill some vegetables, as many as are near to hand, and to present them as a simple antipasto before the richer kebabs, fritters, stuffed vegetables and so on. In a simpler meal where there is, say, just one type of kebab with potatoes and salad, then one or more of these grilled vegetables will add variety and freshness. It is essential that the vegetables are vibrantly fresh and in peak condition, so use only as many types as you can find in such condition. The cooking instructions are the same for all the vegetables: simply brush them lightly with olive oil and grill them on the barbecue, turning as necessary, until lightly browned and just tender. However, the vegetables will need different preparation, as detailed below. I would suggest you cook one or two types of vegetable at a time, as they may have different cooking times. Transfer the cooked vegetables to a serving plate and drizzle them with some of the marinade, and move on to the next batch. I wouldn't fuss too much about trying to keep the vegetables warm; perfectly cooked vegetables at body temperature are more what you're after. Some vegetables cook better if they are very briefly cooked in water before grilling, and these can be put into the marinade while warm to absorb the flavours. It's not that they won't cook fully by grilling alone, but they will be more succulent for having taken on some moisture.

FOR THE MARINADE:

the following proportions are good – multiply or divide them to the quantity you need, and simply whisk or stir the ingredients together.

250mls olive oil

rind and juice of 1 lemon

1 tablespoon fresh thyme leaves

4 cloves garlic, finely chopped

salt and black pepper

Any combination of the following vegetables will be good to barbecue:

globe artichokes – slice the artichokes in halves or quarters lengthways and take out the choke with a teaspoon; boil the artichokes for two minutes

fennel – halve or quarter the bulbs, depending on size, and boil for two minutes

baby carrots – simply wash them, don't peel

fat asparagus – snap the ends off nice fat spears

new potatoes – halve or leave whole if small, and boil for five minutes

spring onions or *thin young leeks* – simply trim the top and any tough leaves

courgettes – use small ones, whole or halved lengthways

sweetcorn – boil for five minutes and slice each ear into two or three pieces

pumpkin or *butternut squash* – chop into large chunks and boil for two minutes

runner or *flat beans* – top and tail, and slice in half if very long

portobello or *flat mushrooms* – leave whole, cook open side first

Grilled haloumi with lime and mint

Grilled with a squeeze of lime or lemon is the simplest and most common way to serve haloumi, and is usually the basis of more complex recipes using the cheese too. Haloumi loves the tang of lemon or lime and it is a certainty that even after you have dressed it with lime people will squeeze more precious drops directly on to the cooked cheese. Haloumi is sold in small blocks of about 250g, and is often already mildly flavoured with mint, though you are more likely to know this from the ingredients list on the packaging than the flavour of the cheese, so I have taken to occasionally scattering some fresh mint over it. The cheese has a slightly tough texture when raw, and it can become chewy if it sits around after cooking. Not to an unpleasant extent, indeed some people like it to take on this texture, but you should try to cook it just before serving. On a barbecue, cook small batches at a time.

2 x 250g packs haloumi
olive oil
1 small handful mint leaves
pepper, coarsely ground
3 limes

Cut the haloumi into slices of about 10mm thick – you should get ten slices from a 250g block. Brush the slices on both sides with olive oil and cook them for a few minutes in a frying pan, on a griddle pan or on a barbecue, turning once, until the slices are lightly coloured on both sides. Put the cooked haloumi on a serving dish; chop the mint and scatter it over the haloumi. Sprinkle a little coarsely ground pepper over also. Grate the rind of one lime and sprinkle it over the haloumi, and squeeze the juice of the same lime all over the dish too. Slice the other limes into wedges and serve them with the haloumi for those who like an extra tangy dimension.

Roasted pepper rolls of black kale and pinenuts

These pepper rolls make great barbecue food but they actually began life as an elegant dinner dish, served with a cream sauce of lemon and basil or thyme. Hot cream sauces aren't really practical outdoors, so I would serve the rolls with classic basil pesto or a lemony aioli.

If you don't have black kale, use spinach or chard.

FOR TEN ROLLS:

5 large red peppers
250g black kale
80g pinenuts
60g Parmesan, finely grated
salt and pepper, to season

Blacken the skins of the peppers under a hot grill or over a flame. Pop them in a paper bag or into a sealed bowl for 20 minutes or so to cool, then peel off the skin and scrape out the seeds without breaking the peppers. Carefully, slice the peppers in half lengthways.

Bring a large pot of water to a boil, drop in the black kale and cook it for five or six minutes, then transfer it to cold water to cool. Drain it well, squeezing out all the liquid with your hands, then chop it quite finely. Toast the pinenuts for a few minutes in an oven until lightly coloured, then chop them coarsely with a knife. Don't blend or grind them– you want broken and halved nuts, not powder. Stir the pinenuts into the kale with the Parmesan, a little salt and some black pepper.

Place a dessertspoon of the kale and pinenuts along one length of roasted pepper and roll up the pepper tightly, making sure the parcel is well packed. Repeat until all the filling or the peppers are used up. To cook the rolls, brush them lightly with olive oil and cook them on a barbecue, under a grill, in an oven or on a griddle pan, turning as required, until the rolls are browned in places and heated through.

Corn-crusted aubergine fritters with tamarillo chutney

There are so many things to do with aubergines and a barbecue, but this isn't an aubergine book, so there are more left out than included. In a state of indecision, I asked Bridget what her favourite one was, and she surprised me by suggesting this: her mother's standard no-frills fritters, which are usually coated with fine bread-crumbs and topped with a dollop of tamarillo chutney. A woman of simple taste is our Bridget. Unable to leave well alone, and with apologies to Gretchen, I have cooked the aubergines in a coating of corn instead of crumbs. I started by using coarse maize, which I had used previously on various fritters, but after a little exper-imentation I have decided I like medium-ground corn best. It gives a crisp but not quite crunchy texture. If you can't get medium-ground maize, use coarse, or the original fine breadcrumbs.

Tamarillos are one very good reason to go and live in New Zealand. Shaped like plum tomatoes, they are very often used like tomatoes to make relishes, chutneys and savoury sauces, or served grilled on toast. The flavour, however, is more fruit-like, rich and sweet, though quite acid, which means it can be used in sweet dishes too. Tamarillos make fantastic sweet crumble, which puts them one up on the old tomato. Unfortunately they don't travel well – I've brought in only tiny quantities – as they seem to ripen very quickly after picking. In the absence of tamarillos, use a tomato chutney and promise yourself a trip to New Zealand.

FOR 20 FRITTERS:

FOR THE FRITTERS:
2 eggs
200mls milk
salt
200g medium-ground maize
4 bird's eye chillies, ground
1 teaspoon dried oregano
200g plain flour
2 medium to large aubergines

Beat the eggs and milk together with a pinch of salt and put them in a shallow dish. Sift together the maize, chilli, oregano and a large pinch of salt and put this in another dish. Put the plain flour in a third dish. Cut a slice of both ends of each aubergine and slice the rest of the aubergines into round slices about 1.5cm thick. Toss some of the slices in the flour to coat them evenly. Shaking off any excess flour, dunk the aubergine slices in the beaten egg, and then into the corn. Toss the slices well to coat each fully in corn, then remove them to plate or tray, and repeat the process for all of the slices. Cook the fritters on a barbecue or a griddle pan, or in a frying pan, turning them at least once to cook both sides to a nice golden finish. Brush the hot cooking surface with olive oil before you put the aubergines on it, and again when you turn them.

FOR THE CHUTNEY:
1kg tamarillos
300g apples
200g onions
300mls cider vinegar
half tablespoon salt
1 teaspoon mustard powder
half teaspoon mixed spice
500g brown sugar

Peel the tamarillos and the apples, and chop them coarsely. Chop the onion into thin short slices. Put the vegetables in a stainless steel pan with the rest of the ingredients, bring to a boil and simmer for two hours, stirring, and scraping the sides occasionally. To store the chutney for a few months, fill some glass jars with almost-boiling water for a few minutes, then tip out the water and fill the jars almost to the top with the hot chutney. Screw on the lids and leave the jars to cool before storing in a dark cupboard or in the fridge. Left to cool and stored in containers in the fridge, the chutney will still keep for a couple of weeks.

Ginger-glazed kebabs of sweet potato, tofu and shallots with coconut satay

I probably use tofu more at home than in Café Paradiso these days. Every time you try to create a restaurant dish with tofu, you have to confront the public perception of it and its association with the worthy but dull end of vegetarian catering. Now I don't mind a challenge in work, but sometimes I like to let things go too. Let's say I'm in a rest period in my professional relationship with tofu. At home, tofu is without baggage; it is simply a very useful food to have around. We fry thick slices to eat with spiced greens and rice, toss cubes into stir-fries, float strips in noodle broths; and, best of all, it cooks great on a barbecue. Mostly we grill thick slices, but that's hardly a recipe, so I've opted for this kebab, which combines the salty marinated tofu with the sweet flavours of shallots and sweet potato, and everybody's secret favourite sauce, peanut satay.

FOR TEN KEBABS:

FOR THE KEBABS:

3 x 200g packs tofu

200mls soy sauce

1 teaspoon tomato purée

3 tablespoons fresh ginger, grated

600g sweet potatoes

30 shallots

200mls olive oil

1 tablespoon honey

rind and juice of 1 lime

1 teaspoon toasted sesame oil

Cut the tofu into cubes about 3cm thick, and put them into a shallow dish. Whisk together the soy sauce, tomato purée, 100mls water and half of the grated ginger. Pour this over the tofu to marinate for an hour at least, preferably three to four. Peel the sweet potatoes and cut them into chunks approximately the same size as the tofu. Peel the shallots. Bring a pot of water to a boil and cook the sweet potatoes for about five minutes until almost done. Remove the potato chunks to a shallow dish and cook the shallots in the water for just two minutes, before adding them to the sweet potatoes. Warm the olive oil gently in a small pan and whisk in the honey, lime, remaining ginger and the sesame oil, until the honey is melted, then pour this marinade over the sweet potatoes and shallots. Leave for half an hour.

Put a shallot on a skewer, followed by a chunk of sweet potato, then a piece of tofu, another shallot, tofu, sweet potato and, finally, a shallot. Repeat to get ten kebabs.

Brush some of the honey marinade on to the kebabs, and cook them on a barbecue or a griddle pan, or under a hot grill. Turn the kebabs to cook them evenly and brush a little more marinade over them if they seem dry.

FOR THE SATAY:

juice of 1 lemon

100g fresh or tinned pineapple

half tablespoon grated ginger

2 cloves garlic

2 bird's eye chillies

1 tablespoon soy sauce

150g peanut butter

400mls coconut milk

Blend the lemon, pineapple, ginger, garlic, chillies and soy sauce in a food processor. Pour the puree into a pan, bring it to a boil and simmer for two minutes. Add the peanut butter and whisk slowly while it comes back to a boil. Cook for a few seconds only before pouring in the coconut milk, then bring it back to a boil and simmer for one minute more. If you want the sauce to be thicker, simmer for longer, stirring frequently.

Aubergine and mozzarella sandwiches with fresh green chilli pesto

A slightly more involved dish than the aubergine fritters. This time, the aubergine is cooked twice, or cooked and reheated, more like. I don't think the aubergine will cook all the way through if you make the sandwiches with raw aubergine slices, but, even if they did, the mozzarella would melt all over the grill in the time it required.

The sandwiches are well flavoured enough to be served alone, and any pesto will give them a lift. Mind you, this fresh chilli pesto can easily give them more of a kick than a gentle lift. It's best to check how hot the chillies are before you make the pesto, then decide whether you want to leave the seeds in or not. If the chilli flesh has any reasonable heat, I would leave the seeds out, and you may even want to increase the proportion of herbs if the chillies are hot – the pesto is meant to be fun, not a rugby club post-match sport. Chilli in pesto, or any oil-based sauce, is fun in a deceptive kind of way. At first the oil masks the heat, as do the almonds in this recipe, and then the same heat-carrying oil coats the mouth and lingers for a while. So keep it under control.

FOR TEN SANDWICHES:

FOR THE SANDWICHES:

4 tomatoes

2 large aubergines

some olive oil

2 x 250g blocks fresh buffalo mozzarella

salt and pepper, to season

Slice the tomatoes into three or four slices each and roast them in a hot oven or cook them on a griddle plate, turning once. Cut a slice off both ends of each aubergine and slice the rest of them into round slices about 1.5cm thick. You will need 20 slices. Brush the aubergine slices lightly with olive oil and cook them on the barbecue, on a griddle pan or in a hot oven until just done and lightly browned on both sides. Cut each mozzarella block into five slices. Place a grilled tomato slice on an aubergine slice, season well with salt and pepper, then top that with a slice of mozzarella and another aubergine slice. Press down gently but firmly on the sandwich, and repeat to make ten sandwiches. Cook the sandwiches on the barbecue or in the hot oven for just a minute or two on each side. Serve with a dollop of chilli pesto on top (see below), or on the side for the faint of heart.

FOR THE PESTO:

200g fresh green chillies, chopped coarsely

2 cloves garlic

50g basil

50g coriander

50g ground almonds

250mls olive oil

Put the chillies in a food processor with the garlic, basil and coriander, and blend to a coarse paste. Add the almonds and olive oil, and blend again to get a thick pouring consistency.

Grilled squash with spiced coating

This also works well with sweet potato. A less chilli-hot variation is to use cumin only, or grated ginger with the rind of a lime.

2 tablespoons butter

2 tablespoons olive oil

1 teaspoon salt

4 bird's eye chillies

1 tablespoon cumin seeds

half tablespoon coriander seeds

1 butternut squash, hokaido pumpkin or similar

Put the butter, olive oil and salt in a large bowl. Grind the spices and add them to the oil. Chop the squash into chunks. Butternuts should be peeled but most others have thin edible skins. Bring a large pot of water to a boil and cook the chunks for just one minute, then remove them with a slotted spoon and put them in the bowl with the oil and spices. The heat from the squash will soften the butter. Toss gently to coat the chunks of squash evenly in the spices and oils. Grill on a barbecue or in an oven, turning occasionally.

Barbecued sweetcorn with basil and peppercorn butter

You simply can't have a barbecue without sweetcorn, if for no other reason than to feed the kids.

1 handful basil leaves

1 tablespoon olive oil

2 teaspoons coarsely ground black peppercorns

100g butter, softened

1 ear sweetcorn per person

Put the basil leaves in a food processor with the olive oil, and chop very finely. Add the peppercorns and butter, and blend briefly until the basil and pepper are evenly mixed through the butter.

Cook the sweetcorn ears in boiling water for five minutes, then brush them with olive oil and cook on the barbecue, turning often, until lightly coloured and tender. Put the corn on serving plates and use a brush or knife to smother each ear with the basil and peppercorn butter and a little salt.

Kebabs of haloumi, plum tomatoes and bay leaves with olive and caper tapenade

This time the haloumi is marinated in olive oil flavoured with haloumi's favourite partner, lemon, and some garlic, bay and chilli. The bay leaves flavour the marinade and are then put on the skewers, as much for their appearance as for the lovely smell they give off while cooking. Someone will always try to eat them, of course, but I haven't seen them swallowed yet.

The first time I cooked these, I used cherry tomatoes. They were a little too small, a little too juicy. The plum tomatoes are fleshier and so grill better. The medium-sized Gardeners Delight, or a similar tomato, are good too.

FOR TEN KEBABS:

FOR THE KEBABS:
250mls olive oil
4 dried chillies, halved
5 cloves garlic, roughly chopped
3 x 250g packs haloumi
20 fresh bay leaves
10 small plum tomatoes, halved

Put the olive oil in a jug. Add the chillies and garlic. Cut each block of haloumi in half lengthways and cut each half into five pieces. Put a layer of bay leaves into a shallow dish and cover them with the haloumi. Pour over the marinade. Leave for a few hours (up to 12 hours if possible).

Put one piece of haloumi on to a kebab skewer, followed by a bay leaf, a tomato half, more haloumi, another tomato half, a bay leaf and finally another haloumi piece. Repeat to make ten kebabs. Cook the kebabs on a barbecue, under a grill or on a griddle pan, turning to cook all sides equally, and occasionally brushing on some of the marinade if the haloumi seems dry.

Parmesan and chilli polenta

Polenta is intrinsically bland, but carries flavour well, and this just happens to be my favourite polenta flavouring at the moment: chilli and Parmesan. Not so good with spiced food, obviously, but great with greens or haloumi, or as a snack in its own right, with a cool dip or raita. To serve with spicy dishes, flavour the polenta with fresh coriander and/or lime instead of the cheese and chilli.

1200mls vegetable stock (see page 276)
250g coarse maize
1 teaspoon salt
half teaspoon chopped dried bird's eye chillies
60g Parmesan, grated
1 tablespoon parsley or fresh coriander, finely chopped

Bring the stock to a boil in a large pot, then whisk in the maize, salt and chillies, whisking over high heat until the stock comes back to the boil, then quickly turn the heat to a very low setting and replace the whisk with a wooden spoon. Cook the polenta for 15 to 20 minutes, stirring frequently, until the grains are soft. Stir in the Parmesan and herbs, and tip the polenta out on to an oiled tray. Spread the polenta evenly and quickly using a spatula, or your hands dampened with cold water. In about 20 minutes, the polenta will be ready to cut, but leave it longer if you can. In fact, the polenta can be made up to a day in advance. Cut it into triangles and grill them, lightly brushed with olive oil, on a barbecue or griddle pan.

Grilled sandwiches of artichoke paste, spinach and Coolea cheese

This works equally well with commercial wraps, flour tortilla and soft flatbread like focaccia. The important thing, if using focaccia, is that the top and bottom of the loaf is soft and pale – if the bread is already well done, slice off a thin sliver. I use tinned artichokes to make the paste, mostly for the convenience of it, and partly because it would seem a waste of time, energy and precious artichokes to purée fresh ones. However, if you have a glut of fresh artichokes and you are up to speed with your paring knife, go ahead. The quality of prepared artichokes can vary wildly, and some cheap ones will taste of nothing but the brine they are stored in. The Real Olive Company in Cork's English Market, and in markets all round Ireland, sells very good artichokes dressed in olive oil. If that's not a good reason to visit Ireland, I know a lovely pub that serves the best Beamish stout, far superior to tourist Guinness, and it's close enough to the Cork market to fit into the same itinerary. Coolea is a Gouda-style cheese from mid-Cork, which melts beautifully; would you believe you can buy it in the same market as the artichokes, which is only a short walk from the Beamish brewery? If you're staying home and you can't find Coolea, you need a strong, mature but semi-hard cheese like Gruyère or Gouda.

400g tin artichokes

2 cloves garlic

some olive oil

salt and pepper, to season

400g spinach

1 red onion

200g Coolea cheese (or similar)

8 flour tortillas or wraps

Drain the artichokes and rinse them for a few minutes under running cold water. Put them in a food processor with the garlic and blend in brief bursts to get a coarse purée. Add a few tablespoons of olive oil and blend again for a few seconds. You should have a thick, slightly chunky mash. Season with salt and pepper. Bring a pot of water to a boil, drop in the spinach and cook it for just half a minute, then lift it out and plunge it into a bowl of cold water. Squeeze all the water from the spinach and chop it coarsely. Halve the red onion, slice it very thinly and mix it through the spinach. Season with salt and pepper. Slice the cheese thinly with a vegetable peeler or a wide grater.

Place a wrap on a work surface and spread a generous layer of artichoke paste on it, covering most of the bread but leaving about 3cm at the near and far ends. Place a layer of spinach about one-third of the way up and cover it with a layer of cheese shavings. Fold the near end of the bread over the filling and roll it up quite tightly. Repeat with the rest of the bread and filling.

Brush a little oil on the sandwiches and grill them on a barbecue or griddle pan for a few minutes, turning at least once, until lightly coloured and warmed through.

Sauces and chutneys

Here are four sauces – well, two chutneys, a salsa and a sambal – which guests at our home always lash on to whatever they're served from the barbecue. Barbecues are by nature chaotic, and perfect food combining is not the priority. In any case, these are very versatile sauces. You may have your own, but one of these will add to your repertoire, and your reputation. If I must put a marker down, then the chilli, coconut and pistachio is my favourite.

Watermelon and ginger sambal

1kg watermelon
2 tablespoons sushi ginger or grated fresh ginger
4 spring onions
1 mild green chilli
rind and juice of 1 lime
salt, to season

Flick as many seeds out of the melon as you can and chop the flesh into small dice. Use a sharp knife to avoid squashing too much juice from the melon. Put the melon in a bowl, including whatever juice does escape. Slice the ginger thinly, chop the spring onions very fine, and slice the chilli thinly, discarding the seeds. Mix everything into the melon bowl, with the lime rind and juice, and season with a little salt.

Mango, lime and avocado salsa

1 large green mango
1 mild fresh red chilli
1 red onion, finely chopped
1 tablespoon olive oil
1 tablespoon grated fresh ginger
juice of 1 lime
1 avocado

Peel the mango, slice the flesh from the stone and chop it coarsely. Remove the seeds from the chilli and chop the flesh. Cook the red onion in a little olive oil for two minutes, then add the chopped mango, ginger and chilli, and cook for two minutes more. Put the salsa into a bowl and squeeze in the lime juice. Just before you serve the salsa, dice the avocado flesh and stir it in.

Sweet and hot pepper chutney

3 tablespoons olive oil
1 red onion, chopped into small dice
3 red peppers, de-seeded and chopped
3 yellow peppers, de-seeded and chopped
2 very ripe tomatoes, de-seeded and chopped
4 cloves garlic
6 dried bird's eye chillies
1 tablespoon cumin seeds, ground
2 tablespoons sugar
2 tablespoons white wine vinegar
salt, to season

Heat three tablespoons of olive oil in a pot and cook the red onion for five minutes, before adding the peppers, tomatoes, garlic, chillies and cumin. Cover and stew the vegetables for 30 minutes, stirring occasionally and checking to make sure they're not sticking, until the vegetables are very soft and the stew has a thick consistency. Add the sugar and vinegar and cook for ten minutes more. Season with salt.

Green chilli, pistachio and coconut chutney

150g fresh coconut, grated, or 100g desiccated coconut
4–6 fresh green chillies
4 cloves garlic
1 tablespoon black mustard seeds
200g pistachios
juice of 1 lemon
400mls tinned coconut milk

If using desiccated coconut, soak it in 400mls of warm water for 20 minutes.

Chop the chillies and garlic, and cook them in a little oil with the mustard seeds for a few minutes. Lightly roast the pistachios and chop them finely – but do not grind them to a powder – in a food processor. Add the nuts to the pan with the lemon juice, the grated coconut (and its soaking water, if using), and cook for one minute more. Add the coconut milk, bring it to a boil and remove from the heat. Leave to cool.

Autumn

blueberries

blackberries

mushrooms

aubergines

figs

pumpkins

leeks

Lemon verbena, ricotta and white chocolate pudding with blueberry compote

Blueberries are a mystery to me; bland and uninteresting raw, they make great jam and sauces and are wonderful in pancakes, tarts and cheesecakes. This pudding is as good or better, depending on your preference, with a compote of summer berries – the red, white and black currants that birds pinch from our garden before we get even a cupful – or with blackberries or raspberries. The recipe is actually all about the lemon verbena, a bush that grows at the back door of our house to mask the smell of our ageing dog, Paddy. The bush has an astonishing smell, part zest of citrus and part sherbet. Waving it in someone's face unfailingly gets an amazed reaction. I don't remember where the bush came from, but the dictionary says it is South American with sedative qualities! If that smell can put you to sleep, you're already dead. The shrub grows to about five feet high over the summer, then I gradually reduce it to a skeleton and next year it does it all again. God, I love that plant, though it may well be wishing that I would leave it to grow into a tree. Given all of that, it's amazing how many leaves it takes to flavour a custard. I suspect it's all volatile scent that's easily lost. When I tried reducing the quantity of leaves in this recipe, the pudding lost its flavour. The syrup holds the flavour better. It's unlikely that you'll find lemon verbena to buy, so all I can do is encourage you to plant it. If you never make a pudding, you will come to love the scent by your back door.

FOR SIX PUDDINGS:

150mls cream
30 lemon verbena leaves
300g white chocolate
200g ricotta
3 eggs
3 egg whites

350g caster sugar
300g blueberries

Warm the cream, without boiling, and pour it over 20 of the lemon verbena leaves in a bowl. Leave this to infuse until the cream has cooled.

Melt the chocolate in a bowl over hot water and leave it to cool a little.
Put the ricotta in a food mixer with the infused cream and beat them gently to soften the cheese. Add the eggs and egg whites and beat again to incorporate them. Fold in the chocolate.

Heat an oven to 180°C/350°F. Butter six small pudding moulds of 150mls capacity and place a circle of baking parchment in the base of each. Fill the moulds with the pudding custard and place them in an oven dish. Pour boiling water into the oven dish to come halfway up the moulds, and place the dish in the oven, to cook for one and a half hours. The puddings should be just set, not too firm or baked. It may take a little longer. Leave the puddings in their moulds for at least ten minutes, and in any case until you need them. They should be served warm or at room temperature.

While the puddings are cooking, make a syrup by putting 100g sugar in a pan with 100mls water and bringing it slowly to a boil. Drop in the remaining lemon verbena leaves and simmer for three minutes until you have a slightly thickened syrup.

Put 250g sugar in a small pan with the blueberries and a tablespoon of water. Bring this very slowly to a boil and simmer for five minutes until the fruit is soft.

Place the puddings on plates, discarding the parchment paper, and spoon a teaspoon of the lemon verbena syrup over each one, maybe a few drops more. Place some berries in their juices around each pudding.

Blackberry tart with Calvados ice cream

As the year turns and foods come back around into season, I try to look equally hard at the old standard recipes and new ways to work with them. I never do that with blackberries. For anyone over a certain age, the mere mention of blackberry picking is an instant key to a kaleidoscope of memories, triggering images, emotional throwbacks, longings and nostalgia. I could lead you, blindfold, from any point on the planet to the field where my strongest blackberry memories were formed. I recently heard a radio presenter holding forth about people buying blackberries in supermarkets instead of picking them from the hedgerows themselves. There's something in that; perhaps people are too busy going to garden centres and DIY stores on Sunday afternoons to notice the blackberries. But it is even more true that there are not so many hedges, brambles or blackberries to be found, and you practically need government clearance to walk on farmland. Where are we to pick our blackberries? The hedges in our small garden (and the neighbours' gardens too) in Cork city have a few brambles scattered through them. We scrounge a few blackberries every day during the season, enough to make a tart only by many days of steely-minded abstinence from casual picking – it doesn't happen every year! For the blackberries in the tart photographed here and the plate it was baked on, I have to thank my neighbour Mrs Mary Gamble, who picked the fruit on a long damp Sunday afternoon walk.

If you have a regular supply of blackberries, you'll have your own favourite recipes, probably including one for a tart you're very fond of. I hope you also eat huge bowls of berries tossed in sugar with a blob of cream on top, and that in good years you make jam. Which means, I suppose, that this recipe is actually for those of you who don't usually make blackberry tart, which must mean those of you who don't pick blackberries. Hey, get out there and pick blackberries!! It's going to be winter soon.

Calvados is an apple brandy traditionally made in Normandy in the north of France – blackberries and apples… that's as ancient and perfect as it gets.

FOR THE ICE CREAM:
1 cinnamon stick
300mls milk
5 egg yolks
125g caster sugar
300mls cream
2 tablespoons Calvados liqueur

Break the cinnamon stick and put it in a pan with the milk. Heat the milk to just short of boiling for one minute.

Whisk the egg yolks and sugar together until they are thick and pale. Still whisking, on low speed, pour in the milk through a sieve. Return this egg and milk custard to the pan and simmer, stirring all the time, until it is thick enough to coat the back of a spoon. Leave the custard to cool before adding the cream and the Calvados. Freeze using an ice cream machine.

FOR THE TART:

120g unsalted butter
240g plain flour
40g caster sugar
1 egg
1 tablespoon cornflour
500g blackberries
150g caster sugar
1 egg, beaten

Rub the butter into the flour, using your fingers or short bursts in a food processor. Transfer this to a bowl and stir in the sugar. Beat the egg lightly and add enough cold water to give 60mls of liquid. Stir this into the flour with a few quick strokes of a wooden spoon, then knead very briefly to get a smooth dough. Divide the dough into two flattened balls and chill them for an hour or more.

Heat an oven to 190°C/375°F. Roll one pastry ball to line a tart tin of 26cm diameter and 3cm high, leaving the pastry hanging a little over the edge. Sprinkle the cornflour over, through a sieve. Pile in the blackberries and sprinkle over the sugar. Roll out the second pastry ball to a diameter a few centimetres wider than the tart case. Brush the rim of the lower pastry with water. Use a rolling pin to pick up the second pastry and place it over the tart carefully. Press the edges together

and trim off the excess pastry. Press the rim of the pastry with a fork or the flat side of a knife to strengthen the seal. Brush the top of the pastry with beaten egg and make a couple of cuts in the top. Bake in the oven for 30 minutes until the pastry is browned and crisp, and the blackberry juices are bubbling up through the cuts. Leave the tart to cool for at least ten minutes, and serve it warm or at room temperature with the Calvados ice cream or simply a dollop of cream.

Field mushrooms in milk with herbs and garlic

I'm not really a mushroom lover. They simply don't get me excited the way fresh green produce does. Woodland mushrooms taste too much of the dark, dank places they grow in for my liking; though I make an exception for truffles, which I adore. Still, this embarrasses me a little sometimes, professionally speaking, because mushrooms are so much a part of restaurant culture, especially exotic and wild mushrooms.

Vegetarians in a restaurant are as likely to be offered 'wild' mushrooms as the ubiquitous goats' cheese, because they are perceived to be high-value items, something exotic you might not have at home. The restaurant trade is full of such profitable gems.

Confusingly, I can also claim to really like the taste of mushrooms – cultivated mushrooms, that is. Mushroom cultivation is an industry often derided, usually rightly, for churning out cheap, flavourless and chemically produced fodder. But there are exceptions. I love the oyster mushrooms we get from Forest Mushrooms in North Cork, for their delicate, elegant flavour. I like the dark-skinned organically cultivated 'chestnuts', or 'Paris browns' and their bigger cousins, the portobello; and I even like your standard cultivated supermarket mushroom when it's a little oversized with open gills, and fried in lots of garlic butter. I'm aware that what I like about these mushrooms is that their flavour is similar, though inferior, to that of the rarest mushroom of all, and my favourite by a long way, the 'common' field mushroom. Neither sophisticated, exotic nor expensive, and now no longer even common, it has changed in my lifetime from an abundant seasonal treat to a very rare one. This seems to be a consequence of modern farming methods, which have simply left nowhere for the mushroom to live. If you do find 'field mushrooms' on restaurant menus, do ask if they are from a field known to the cook or if they are simply large, open commercial mushrooms that have never seen a field. If the cook has indeed found the mushrooms in a field, it's unlikely he'll tell you where it is.

Those of you lucky enough to have access to field mushrooms in late summer/early autumn will have your own favourite way to eat them, but you might like to try this. Anyone else curious enough to try it might find that it works reasonably well with commercial mushrooms with open gills.

The essence of this dish is how my mother cooked mushrooms when I was a child. We knew of only one mushroom, the field mushroom, which popped up in late August and September in the fields left fallow between crops or used only for casual cattle grazing or hay harvesting. We cooked them in two ways – fried in butter or boiled in milk. This recipe involves a bit of meddling with the classic, which had neither herbs nor garlic. It is so simple that I'm still a little embarrassed to be writing it down, but I promise that it is divine to eat. Serve with buttered crusty bread.

FOR FOUR:

400g field mushrooms
1 litre milk
4 cloves garlic, sliced
small handful chopped herbs (one or more of parsley, thyme and lovage)
1 tablespoon chopped chives
salt and black pepper, to season

Break the large mushrooms into halves or quarters, leave the smaller ones whole. Put them in a pan with the milk, garlic and herbs, bring it to a boil and simmer for 15 to 20 minutes until the mushrooms are tender and the milk has taken on a light chocolate colour. Stir in the chives. Share out the mushrooms into shallow bowls, ladle the broth over them and season with lots of salt and coarsely ground black pepper.

Baked portobello mushroom with Cashel blue cheese, pecan crumbs and sage, and smoked paprika aioli

One of these mushrooms can make a substantial first course, and sometimes a main course. Portobellos come in very impressive sizes, and have an impressively weighty feel in the hand. When baked, as in this recipe, they become deliciously juicy, and the flavour and smell are intensely, well, mushroomy. They need to be, because there are a lot of flavours in this dish; all flavours that go very well with mushrooms in their own right, so it's simply a matter of balance – avoid any one being too dominant and you will get a blend that still lets the mushroom shine through.

Sage butter is my favourite way to use the herb, and there is always a jug of it in the Paradiso fridge. Cashel blue cheese is a firm, though not dry, cheese from Tipperary, and the piece I use here is from a matured round. Because there is so little cheese on each mushroom, using a mild or young 'blue' cheese will not have sufficient effect. Buy the cheese, and any cheese for that matter, from a cheese shop where you can see, and taste, what you are buying. A Gorgonzola or similar would be very good here too.

Smoked paprika should taste of the peppers it was made from, with quite heavy smoky undertones. At the moment, I have two varieties, both Spanish: one is sweet, made from sweet peppers, and the other is hot, made from hot peppers. Both are defiantly as they advertise themselves, and, rather than choose between them, I mix them for a wonderful blend that gives a smoky, sweet flavour but with a respectable kick of heat too. Amazing stuff. Spanish paprika is the best I've come across, though I'm sure there are Hungarians and Turks who would argue that one with you. If you make this aioli with cheap paprika, 'produce of more than one country', you will get nothing more than a lovely red emulsion. I have listed lemon juice as an ingredient in the aioli, but I don't always use it – remember this is not a mayonnaise, and how acid, or not, you want it to be is totally up to you, and what you're eating it with. Taste the aioli and decide if you would like a few drops of lemon in it; try that and think about more – let your own tastebuds decide.

FOR FOUR:

4 cloves garlic

1 egg

1 egg yolk

1 teaspoon Dijon mustard or similar

250mls olive oil

1 teaspoon smoked paprika

salt and pepper, to season

juice of half a lemon

450g butter

1 bunch sage leaves

30g pecans

30g day-old bread

4 large portobello mushrooms

50g mature Cashel blue cheese, or similar

First make the aioli. Cut the ends off the garlic cloves and roast the cloves in a low to medium oven until the garlic is soft, then squeeze the garlic from its skin. Put the garlic in a food processor with the egg, egg yolk and mustard, and blend for one minute. Pour in the olive oil in a slow stream until the aioli thickens, then add the paprika and some salt and pepper. Taste it, and add some lemon juice to your own taste. Clarify the butter to remove the milk solids (see the method on page 60). Put it back in a clean pan with most of the sage leaves, leaving a few, and bring it to a boil. Leave this to cool and for the butter to absorb the sage flavour. Put the pecans in a food processor with the bread and process to get a breadcrumb texture. Spread this on an oven tray and toast it in a medium oven until crisp, tossing occa-sionally to ensure even cooking. When it is crisp, put it in a bowl, chop the remaining sage leaves and stir them in.

Brush the mushrooms with the sage butter, sprinkle with a little salt and bake them in a moderate oven for eight to ten minutes until they are tender – check by piercing them with a knife. Crumble some cheese over each, sprinkle on some of the pecan crumbs, and put the mushrooms back in the oven for a few minutes more until the cheese begins to melt. Serve one mushroom each with some smoked paprika aioli.

Oyster mushroom ravioli with a truffled lovage cream and peas

The filling in these ravioli is a very simple one because I want it to taste of the delicate flavour of the oyster mushrooms and it needs to be simple to live with the richly flavoured sauce. Lovage isn't a very widely available herb, which is surprising given its exciting flavour and the fact that it grows easily in bushes of long stems with large wide leaves. In appearance it is a bit like a celery plant gone wild, and that's a fairly good description of its flavour too: it's celery, but it's more than celery – celery exaggerated, celery from *Alice in Wonderland*. Perhaps if it were a little more timid it would be more popular. It is fantastic with potatoes and eggs; it can turn a stodgy comfort soup into something refreshing and lively, and is a delightful flavour to come across in a salad of mixed greens. Always add lovage at the very end of cooking, to preserve its exuberant qualities.

I use truffle oil to add a tiny high note to the lovage cream, a hint or suggestion of another flavour. Be very careful not to use it to drown the flavours of the dish. Truffle oil, as it is available in shops, is usually a light oil such as sunflower that has been flavoured with essence of white truffles. Disdained by those who have access to, and the wallets for, real white truffles of Alba, white truffle oil is a remarkably good product, and an incredibly cheap one given how few drops it takes to flavour a meal. It can be lethal in the hands of a heavy-handed chef desperate to add value to your expensive dinner. The flavour is so heady it is almost more scent than taste; it will certainly be the first thing you smell in a dish, but it shouldn't be the only thing you taste; I like it best when it is so elusive that it is a mere suggestion of a scent floating in the heavy air above your plate. Go easy with that bottle, boys and girls. While it may originally have been a whimsy to put the slightly unseasonal peas in the dish, I love the fresh contrast they bring to it.

FOR FOUR STARTERS:

1 tablespoon butter

150g oyster mushrooms, chopped finely

2 cloves garlic, chopped finely

1 tablespoon white wine

salt and pepper, to season

2 tablespoons very fine breadcrumbs

2 sheets fresh pasta, approx 16cm x 60cm

150mls light stock (see page 276)

150mls white wine

400mls cream

salt and pepper, to season

4–6 lovage leaves

white truffle oil

50g peas

Melt the butter in a wide, shallow pan and cook the mushrooms and garlic over high heat for two minutes. Add the wine and cook for one minute more. Remove from the heat immediately, season with salt and pepper, and leave to cool before stirring in the breadcrumbs.

Lay the pasta on a work surface and cut out twenty four circles of eight centimetres in diameter. Take a rounded teaspoonful of the filling. Roll it into a ball and place it in the centre of one of the circles of pasta. Brush the visible part of the pasta circle with water and place one of the larger pieces on top. Now press the edges together firmly while, at the same time, taking care not to leave any air pockets inside the parcel. Repeat this with the rest of the circles – you need three each for a starter, more for a main course.
Bring the stock and wine to a boil in a pan, and simmer until the volume is reduced by half. Add the cream and simmer for a few minutes until the sauce thickens to a nice

pasta-coating consistency – try some on the back of a wooden spoon to get an idea. Season carefully with salt and pepper. Keep the sauce warm, or make it before you start to cook the ravioli and reheat it gently. Just before you serve, chop the lovage and add it to the sauce, then shake in a little truffle oil – one or two drops per person is enough.
To cook the pasta, bring a large pot of water to a boil and drop in the ravioli. If you think the parcels might be overcrowded, do two batches. As with all pasta, the only way to decide that it's cooked is to test it, so nick a tiny bit off one of the ravioli and taste it. Remove the ravioli with a slotted spoon and put them in a bowl with a little olive oil to prevent them sticking to each other. If you do two batches, tip the first one back into the pot just as the second batch is cooked and remove the lot in half a minute.

Serve three ravioli per portion with some cream poured over each. Scatter a few lightly cooked peas on each portion.

Pan-fried mushrooms in sage and cider cream with a potato, parsnip and wild rice cake, and beetroot relish

This recipe works with most mushrooms, so use your favourites. I usually make it with mild oyster mushrooms, sometimes mixed with those lovely dark-skinned organic chestnut mushrooms. If your preference is towards wild woodland mushrooms or shiitakes, some of those in a mix would be fine too. Just don't invite me round.

If you have sage butter in your fridge, as in the earlier recipe for portobello mushrooms, use that to fry the mushrooms and you will need fewer or no sage leaves.

It's important to fry the mushrooms over a fairly high heat, so if you have doubts about the capacity of your pan or cooker elements, fry the mushrooms in two batches, then return them to the pan before adding the cider.

The potato cakes came about during one of my occasional attempts to find a rosti recipe that would work consistently in the restaurant without driving me crazy every second or third time I used it. It's a personal weakness I come back to every now and again, then walk away from, telling myself it really doesn't matter, life's too short, etc etc. Eventually I decided to limit myself to trying to make a potato and parsnip cake recipe that didn't need eggs to stand up, but wasn't just sculptured mash. This is it, and I'm not going back to rosti again. The texture of the cooked potatoes is important: use a medium floury potato such as a rooster, which will hold its shape but has some starch; chop the cooked potatoes with a knife to get a 'coarse mash' – that is, a mixture of various-sized lumps of potato. There is no scientific way to achieve this better than randomly chopping with a knife. The cakes are flavoured with fresh thyme and rosemary oil. The oil in the cake mix will help the insides of the cakes to cook rather than simply heat through. However, if you don't make the rosemary oil, use plain olive oil and another herb such as parsley, chives or lovage, as raw rosemary can be too overpowering.

This is a very rich meal, so I would add some fresh greens for light relief. It's a personal thing, and you may prefer your rich, creamy dishes uncompromised. If you are of my tendency, you could serve a separate side dish of cooked green beans or broccoli, but my favourite is to wilt some greens – kale, spinach or cabbage – in olive oil and water, and to serve a little pile under each potato cake.

The beetroot relish is sweet, with the distinctive taste of caraway, so use just a little blob for each portion. The recipe is for more than you will need but it will keep well for a week or two.

FOR FOUR:

olive oil

500g beetroot, washed and grated

500g red onions, halved and thinly sliced

1 tablespoon caraway seeds

half teaspoon nutmeg

100mls balsamic vinegar

100g brown sugar

large pinch cayenne pepper

a little salt

100g wild rice

500g rooster potatoes, or similar, peeled and quartered

200g parsnips, peeled and grated

2 sprigs fresh thyme

2 tablespoons rosemary oil (see page 18)

salt and pepper, to season

400g mushrooms

4 tablespoons butter

4 cloves garlic, chopped

8 sage leaves

150mls dry cider

300mls cream

Heat some olive oil in a pan and put in the beets, onions, caraway seeds and nutmeg. Cook, stirring often, until the onions are soft, then add the balsamic vinegar and sugar, and simmer for at least 20 minutes, until the vegetables are very soft and the liquid has become thick and syrupy. Season with the cayenne pepper and a little salt. Leave to cool.

Cook the wild rice at a simmer in boiling water until it has softened, about 40 minutes, then drain it. Steam the potatoes until just done, then chop them into a coarse mash. Add the parsnips to the potato with the wild rice, thyme, rosemary oil and some salt and pepper. Stir gently to combine everything without breaking the potato any more. Place four metal rings, 9cm in diameter and 3cm high, in a wide frying pan. Brush them and the pan with oil and set it over a low

heat. Pack the rings with the cake mix to begin cooking gently. After about five minutes, flip the cakes to cook on the other side. You may need to flip them a few more times, and to shuffle the cakes around the pan, to cook them evenly. They should cook all the way through, and become crisp and lightly browned on the outsides.

While the cakes are cooking, slice or tear any large mushrooms in half, leaving the small ones whole. Melt the butter in a wide pan, turn the heat to high and toss in the mushrooms and garlic. Cook, stirring, over high heat, until the mushrooms begin to colour, adding more butter if they seem too dry. Slice the sage leaves, add them to the pan with the cider and boil it on high for two minutes, then pour in the cream. Bring it back to a boil and simmer for one minute. Serve immediately.

Aubergine, tomato and goats' cheese galette with a balsamic-tomato emulsion

This was one of my first aubergine dishes, and one that I am very fond of, but in thought more than use. I gave it up for a long time because, as the restaurant got busier and busier, it became a nightmare to produce in large volumes night after night. John Healy, who was cooking with me in Paradiso at the time, became very fond of the dish, in his perverse way, and he would cook it for me occasionally when he invited us round to his lovely home for dinner. What a treat that was, to have John Healy cook dinner for you. I miss him, but he's in Auckland now, gardening and studying the fine art of jewellery. If you come across him, try to wangle an invitation to dinner. I recently rediscovered the dish when I cooked at home for some friends, and it was a lovely meal to prepare. I think the scale of four portions suits it, maybe six at most; any more and there will be some gnashing of teeth and a fine old mess.

The galettes are very simple constructions of very compatible ingredients, and the success of the dish depends on careful preparation. Slice the tomatoes and cheese as thinly as you can, construct the layers neatly and evenly, and, above all, remember that the finished galettes need only be warmed through, not baked. Too long in the oven and the cheese will run off, and the whole balance of the dish will be lost. Balance is the key – no one ingredient should dominate, especially not the cheese.

The balsamic emulsion, as with all dishes using balsamic vinegar, needs a good vinegar – a very good vinegar, in fact: it needs the fruitiness and the rich, concentrated sweetness as much as it needs acidity. It also needs a good strong blender. If your sauce separates after a while, simply blend or whisk it back together just before you use it. Serve some lightly cooked greens to balance the richness of the galettes. It should store fine in the fridge for a week or so.

FOR FOUR:

4 aubergines
olive oil, to coat
4–6 large tomatoes
300g goats' cheese, from a large log
4 tablespoons olive tapenade (see page 108) or use a shop-bought one
1 bunch basil leaves
black pepper, to season

1 clove garlic
200mls olive oil
80mls tomato passata
60mls balsamic vinegar
salt and pepper, to season

Shave a slice off two long sides of each aubergine, then lay the aubergines on a cut side and slice them horizontally into four flat slices from each aubergine. Brush the slices lightly with olive oil and roast them in a hot oven, about 190°C/375°F until lightly coloured, but fully cooked. Slice the tomatoes very thinly and discard the seeds. Slice the cheese very thinly too – it may help to have it very well chilled before you attempt this. If the cheese does fall apart, don't worry – you can use it in a patchwork way just as well as in neat slices.

Choose sets of four well-matched slices of aubergine, or better still reunite the original aubergines. Set aside the best-looking ones to be the top slices. Spread a thin layer of tapenade on each of the bottom slices, then cover this with a layer of tomato slices, then cheese slices, then torn basil leaves. Season with black pepper but no salt. Place another slice of aubergine on top, press it gently and repeat the tomato, cheese and basil layers. Put on another slice of aubergine and repeat the process. Finally put the top slices on and press gently.

When you are ready to serve the galettes, place them on an oven tray lined with baking parchment, and bake them in the oven at 160°C/325°F for 15 to 20 minutes. Remember that you are just trying to warm the galettes rather than bake them. They are done when the cheese has softened but has not quite started to run.

While the galettes are warming, make the sauce. Crush the garlic and put it in a jug with the rest of the ingredients. Use a hand blender to blend everything to a thick emulsion, then season it well with plenty of black pepper and a little salt.

Serve one galette per person, with a thin stream of balsamic emulsion poured around each.

Fresh linguine with aubergine-tomato relish

More often than not, aubergines with pasta suggests to me roasted slices of aubergine tossed with a dried pasta like penne or rigatoni in olive oil with, say, chillies, garlic, basil if I've got it, leeks maybe, and some fresh greens such as rocket, spinach or kale. Occasionally, and this is a very private thing, I like to use this rich aubergine relish as a sauce for fresh pasta. Private, in that the relish is rarely used for pasta in Paradiso except by me. I like to take a little from the fridge on a Sunday evening to make a pasta sauce at home. As you can tell by the spicing, the relish has roots in both eastern and western cooking, and can easily be adapted to either. I have used it as the base for a stew, a sauce for tarts, rice cakes and frittata, a topping for Indonesian pancakes, part of a filling for a dolma dish as well as an accompaniment to another dolma. This, I think I'm trying to say, is a very versatile relish. The ingredients here constitute the full-on version, with the leanings of both east and west left in, while in practice I would often vary the recipe depending on the main use for the relish at the time. For example, if I am serving it with a late summer frittata of squash and feta, I will leave out the ginger and add some fresh herbs at the end, probably basil or oregano; if it is to be served with an Indian-oriented rice cake, I might take out the rosemary and add some whole cumin seeds. Either way, I will still take some home on a Sunday night and eat it with fresh pasta.

The recipe makes much more than you need to feed four people, but it keeps for days in the fridge, and how else can you discover its wonderful versatility unless you have a stash of it in the fridge?

FOR FOUR:

500g aubergine
olive oil
2 sprigs rosemary
2 onions, chopped finely
4 cloves garlic, chopped finely
2 teaspoons grated fresh ginger
2 teaspoons coriander seeds, ground
4 dried bird's eye chillies, ground
2 sprigs thyme
5 fresh tomatoes
120mls red wine
2 teaspoons tomato purée
salt, to season

120g fresh linguine per person
Parmesan, to serve

Chop the aubergine into small dice, put them in an oven dish and toss them in enough olive oil to coat them. Add the whole rosemary sprigs, and roast the aubergine in a moderate to hot oven, stirring occasionally, until the aubergine is browned and cooked through. Discard the rosemary stalks.

Heat two tablespoons of olive oil in a pan and cook the onion for five minutes, then add the garlic, spices and the leaves from the thyme sprigs. Cook for two minutes more. Chop the tomatoes into small dice and add them to the pan with the red wine and the tomato purée. Bring it to a boil and simmer for 20 minutes or more, until the sauce is reduced and thickened. Add the roasted aubergine and cook for a further ten minutes, stirring occasionally to ensure the sauce is thickening but not sticking. Season with salt.

Bring a large pot of water to a boil and cook the linguine for a few minutes until just tender. In a wide pan, gently heat two tablespoons of aubergine relish and one of olive oil per person. Drain the pasta, add it to the aubergine relish, and stir to coat the pasta. Serve with some finely grated Parmesan.

Aubergine wraps of pinenuts, spinach and Coolea cheese with a fresh tomato, thyme and caper sauce

I've called these things many a name in their day – today, they're wraps, but they've also been mere 'parcels', 'open ravioli' (a tad pretentious), 'foldovers' (literal, I'll use that again) and a few others; every name will cause someone to wrinkle up their nose and say 'but they're not…'. It's an occupational difficulty of having ditched the formal French food vocabulary, and can sometimes make a minefield of communicating what a dish on a restaurant menu actually is.

As delicious and perfectly matched as the flavours in these wraps are, the dish is really all about texture; and the texture depends on the cheese. When it works really well, the layers of shaved cheese melt – no, soften – into a luscious pillow that melts in the mouth. The roasted aubergine slices are wrapped around a mound of spinach, which is crammed with pinenuts and sweetened with the intensity of dried tomatoes. Now, if you grate the cheese and stir it through the spinach too, you will have all the flavours of the dish; but it won't be the same. You could spend the best part of a long wet evening thinking about the mysteries of that, and the melting properties of fine cheeses. In fact, this dish was created to try to grasp at that perfect moment in the melting of mature Coolea cheese. As I mentioned earlier it is a Gouda-style cheese made in Coolea in mid-Cork, a fun sandwich cheese at any stage of its life but a thing of sublime beauty at a year and a half old. All good Gouda melts beautifully, but there is a stage in the melting where the cheese has left its raw state behind, when it is warm and soft but hasn't yet become runny or stringy, and hasn't quite taken on the flavour of cooked cheese. There – catch it just there! Now do that with a cheese with the rich and complex flavour of mature Coolea… mmm… heaven. If you can't get Coolea, search out a good mature Gouda and keep going back for more – cheesemakers thrive on devoted fans.

I would usually serve these wraps with some grounding, earthy carbohydrates such as parsnip chips, or a simple potato, polenta or risotto dish.

The wraps can be made up and left to sit for an hour or two while you get on with the rest of the meal, and the final cooking will then only take ten minutes.

FOR FOUR:

4 medium aubergines
olive oil
400g spinach
60g pinenuts
2 tablespoons olive oil
4 sundried tomatoes
salt and pepper, to season
160g mature Coolea cheese or similar

6 tomatoes
2 cloves garlic
2 teaspoons small capers
2 sprigs thyme
3 tablespoons olive oil

Cut a slice from two sides of each aubergine, then cut the remaining flesh into three slices from each aubergine, four if they're very fat. You will need a few extra slices to allow for burning, accidents and sheer greed. Brush these slices lightly with olive oil and roast them in a hot oven until fully cooked and lightly coloured.

Bring a large pot of water to a boil, drop in the spinach and cook it for one minute, then remove it to a bowl of cold water to stop the cooking. When it is cooled, squeeze as much water as possible from the spinach and chop it coarsely. Toast the pinenuts lightly and chop them with a knife – you want them to be roughly chopped but not ground, and a food processor will make too much powder even if you're careful; another efficient method is to break them with a rolling pin. Chop the sundried tomatoes very finely and stir them into the spinach with the pinenuts and olive oil, and season it well with salt and black pepper.

Use a vegetable peeler to slice the cheese into thin shavings.

Place the aubergines on a work surface, best-looking sides down. Place some of the spinach-pinenut mix on one half of each slice, cover it with some shavings of cheese and fold over the other half of the aubergine to cover the filling. Place the aubergines on a parchment-lined oven tray and bake them in the oven, at 180°C/350°F, for ten minutes or so, until the cheese has just melted into soft pillows, but hasn't become runny. Serve the wraps immediately.

To make the sauce, first peel the tomatoes. Cut a small cross into the base of each tomato and drop them into boiling water for a few seconds, then plunge them into cold water. The skins should slip off easily. Cut the tomatoes in half, scoop out the seeds and cut out any green stem. Chop the remaining flesh into small dice and put them in a small pan. Chop the garlic finely and add it to the pan with the capers, the leaves from the thyme sprigs and the olive oil. Heat the sauce gently until boiling, then simmer for one minute. Serve immediately.

Aubergine, potato and fennel stew with red wine, thyme and chillies, and goats' cheese gougères

I first made this on one of those lovely autumn days that can cheer up a nation and make it forget an endlessly disappointing summer. We were coming home from a few days' kayaking, walking and drinking in West Cork with Bridget's parents and a few other globetrotting New Zealanders. I headed home before the others to get some dinner ready while they took in a few beaches on the way, as is the way of the kiwi. It had been on my mind to do something impressive for ma and pa, something I could serve with braised fennel, which I love to cook, but when I realised how many were coming home, and how hungry they were likely to be, the menu changed to something more substantial. In such circumstances, there's nothing to beat the old double-starch routine: in this case a stew containing potatoes served with lots of grilled crusty bread. Instead of making something elegant with aubergines and serving it with a sauce, potatoes and braised fennel, I cooked the vegetables and made a sauce to stew them in. Both the aubergines and the fennel are cooked in quite a bit of olive oil, which makes the stew very rich.

The stew is put together like a lot of stews I do, in that the vegetables are prepared separately and brought together in a sauce for a relatively short time. The idea is to have a full-bodied background of rich, deep flavours, while the vegetables in the stew retain their own distinct taste and texture. The aubergine and fennel also add to the flavour of the sauce, but I have deliberately chosen a firm potato that will hold its shape, in contrast to how potatoes often work to thicken the sauce in stews. The variety here is Nicola, a French potato I think, which I use a lot. It has a lovely yellow flesh with a rich, sweet flavour, clean thin skin, and is somewhere in the middle of the starch scale, making it suitable for just about everything, even a passable, though not Irish-mammy-standard, mash. If you make the stew well ahead of dinner, put the vegetables into the sauce but don't simmer it. Instead, simply reheat it gently when you need to.

Although I think of the sauce as primarily a wine- and herb-flavoured one, I throw in some chillies – just enough to add their mouth-warming quality to the rich, comforting nature of the stew. I also like the way chillies work with some herbs, especially thyme as here, but also basil, mint, fennel and coriander. Indeed one of my favourite stews from my early cooking days was a Caribbean-style dish flavoured with coconut, chillies and lots of fresh thyme. I must dig that one up again now I've remembered how good it was.

Use a fruity red wine for the sauce, a Merlot perhaps, or a Sangiovese or even an easy-drinking Portuguese from periquita grapes, as I used the first time I made it. I also drank the rest while the stew cooked, but that's not always necessary.

Although originally served with bread, the stew is a little more elegant with the choux pastry gougeres in this recipe. The gougères are best made to order, but they freeze well and can be reheated in a moderate oven. Any goats' cheese will do, but the drier and harder it is the better, to avoid making the pastry too wet.

FOR THE STEW:
3 fat bulbs fennel
150mls olive oil
*500mls vegetable stock
(see page 276)*
2 large aubergines
*500g potatoes, roosters,
Nicola or similar*
6 tomatoes
6 cloves garlic, sliced
2–4 fresh chillies, sliced
2 sprigs thyme
300mls red wine
salt, to season

Trim the greens off the top of the fennel bulbs, and slice a thin sliver off the root end, then slice the bulbs into quarters. Place them in a pot with 100mls of olive oil and 200mls stock, bring it to a boil and simmer for five minutes before transferring the contents of the pot to an oven dish (it would be even better if you start with a pot that can go in the oven). Cover the fennel loosely with parchment and place it in the oven at about 180°C/350°F. It should take about an hour for the fennel to become tender, but check occasionally that there is enough liquid, and you may need to turn some of the fennel pieces.

Slice the aubergines in quarters lengthways, then into large chunks. Toss these in olive oil in an oven dish and roast them in the oven for about 15 or 20 minutes, until soft and browned, turning them occasionally, but being careful not to break the pieces.

Wash the potatoes, but leave the skins on, and chop them into pieces about the same size as the aubergine. Steam the potato pieces until just tender.

Halve the tomatoes and slice them thickly. Heat some olive oil in a large pan and add the tomatoes, garlic and chillies. Cook them for a few minutes until the tomato softens a little, then add the whole thyme sprigs, the wine and the other 300mls of stock. Season with a little salt, bring to a boil and simmer for 20 minutes. Add the fennel in all its oily juice, the aubergines and potatoes, bring it back to a boil and simmer again over very low heat, covered, for 15 minutes. Check the seasoning before serving.

Serve generous portions of the stew surrounded by a few gougères (see below).

FOR THE GOUGÈRES:
170mls water
60g butter
2 eggs
80g goats' cheese

Put the flour in a food processor. Bring the water and butter to a rolling boil in a small pan and tip it quickly into the flour, with the motor running. After 30 seconds crack in one egg, wait 30 seconds again before adding the second egg, then add the cheese after a further 30 seconds. Once the cheese is incorporated into the dough, use a spatula to put the dough into a piping bag. Pipe small mounds of the dough on to parchment-lined oven trays, then put the trays in an oven at 190°C/375°F. After eight minutes, turn the oven down to 180°C/350°F, and turn any gougères that are cooking unevenly. The gougères should have puffed up to almost twice their size. Cook for another five minutes, or more, until they are firm and dry. Serve warm.

Roasted aubergine rolls with sheep's cheese and almond stuffing, and a Turkish pepper sauce

In the manner of the old truism about skinning cats, there's more than one way to stuff an aubergine. This variation on the theme uses two different-sized slices of roasted aubergine to hold a simple, classic filling of sheep's cheese, almonds and fresh coriander. I originally used the filling to stuff a halved aubergine, which was first roasted, then stuffed, and then the skin was carefully peeled off before the stuffed aubergine was roasted again. I did it for all those timid folks out there who leave aubergine skins on their plates, which drives me crazy; but the other cooks mocked its bald appearance and made rude remarks at it. Sometimes, the flesh would turn a dark grey between roastings, not an attractive colour in the food world, and in the end I had to admit it probably wasn't the most beautiful aubergine dish we'd ever done. If I crack the colour thing, I'll be back to it, though.

Anyway, this recipe is as much about the pepper sauce as the aubergine. There was a little mischievousness in naming it Turkish pepper sauce: when people asked what it was that made the sauce Turkish, I could say 'it's made from Turkish peppers'. And that is exactly what it is, or at least what it originally was – sauce made from Turkish peppers. The first time I put it on the Café Paradiso menu, I simply used olive oil and water to dilute the powerful pepper sauce that Sevinc brought back from a trip home.

Sevinc says her mother's sauce is a little heavy on texture because she doesn't peel the peppers, which makes her a lazy housewife where she comes from, but every culture has its own judgement system and, in mine, anyone who makes vats of pepper sauce is a hero. Her method I find hard to write down, because I find it hard to believe. Take some ripe peppers, Turkish ones that are hot and sweet from the sun, chop them, season with salt and place them in a large vessel. Cover the peppers with a few layers of muslin and put the vessel out in the sun for a few days – as long as it takes. Stir the peppers occasionally, and discard any from the top that may be going off instead of cooking… honest. When the peppers are sun-cooked, bring them indoors, stir in some olive oil and pack the sauce into jars. Try that in Ireland and you'll end up with peppers floating in barrels of rain. In attempting to duplicate the flavour using Spanish peppers and indoor cooking equipment, I've added chillies for heat and smoked paprika for that sun-roasted effect. Serve the aubergines with a green vegetable – green beans perhaps – and some potatoes or a grain dish such as couscous or basmati rice.

FOR FOUR:

2 sweet red peppers

2 teaspoons sweet paprika

4 dried bird's eye chillies, sliced

2 cloves garlic, sliced

200mls olive oil

100mls water

2 large aubergines

olive oil

1 red onion

2 cloves garlic

1 tablespoon cumin seeds

30g breadcrumbs

60g almonds

200g sheep's cheese, such as Knockalara, or use feta

1 small bunch fresh coriander

Blacken the skins of the red peppers under a hot grill or over a flame, then put the peppers into a paper bag until cool enough to handle. Peel off the skins and scrape out the seeds. Put the flesh into a pan with the paprika, chillies, garlic, olive oil and water. Boil for two minutes, then blend with a hand blender until the sauce is emulsified. Leave the sauce to cool and dilute to a pouring thickness if it seems too thick. Check the chilli heat and add a little more if you think fit.

Cut a slice from opposite sides of each aubergine, then slice the remaining flesh into four slices from each aubergine. Brush the slices lightly on both sides with olive oil and roast them in the oven until soft and lightly coloured.

Finely chop the red onion and garlic, and fry them in a little olive oil with the cumin seeds, until soft. Add the breadcrumbs and cook for one minute more. Toast the almonds briefly in the oven and chop them quite finely. Crumble the sheep's cheese and chop the coriander, then gently mix these with the almonds and the cooked onion.

Place the four smallest aubergine slices on a work surface. Place some filling down the centre of each, piled about 2cm high but leaving an edge of almost 1cm all around. Place one of the remaining slices of

aubergine over each, best-looking side up, and press it down all round the edges to enclose the filling. Place the filled aubergine on an oven tray lined with baking parchment, and bake them in a moderate oven for 10 to 15 minutes.

Serve one aubergine roll per person, with some of the pepper sauce at room temperature poured over.

Salad of grilled figs with pecans, rocket and watercress, mascarpone and a vanilla-citrus dressing

There's always a little battle of tug-o'-war in the Paradiso kitchen when the figs arrive. My supply is from a French organic grower, through an importer, so the figs are expensive, the season is brief and the supply a little erratic. Not through anyone's fault, it's just that ripe figs are fragile and don't travel well. Because of these factors, especially the cost, I only use figs when they are irresistibly good. There is sometimes an early supply of green figs in summer, which has never impressed me much, so I ignore those. Then in early autumn come the dark purple figs with deep-red flesh, just barely firm enough to be handled, perfectly ripe and sweet. Now that we're happy to pay for the figs, the issue is whether we can get enough to put a sweet and a savoury dish on the menu or if we'll have to compromise on one; if it's to be one, who gets the figs? Oh, I can pull rank on the pastry cook, but I've never liked the side-effects of pulling rank – it always comes back to haunt you. Sometimes I'm allowed to get my way and, if I do, I serve the figs in some variation of this salad – grilled, with some peppery leaves, a sweet-spiced dressing and mascarpone. Little dollops of mascarpone, dipped in olive oil, are lovely with salad greens, and with figs.

We get our watercress from Hollyhill Farm in West Cork, where it is not so much grown as managed and monitored in a pond fed by a running stream. Most years, when the heat of the summer is fading, there is a second crop that can survive until the first frost. If you have access to such a crop, lucky you; otherwise use rocket leaves or any mildly bitter or peppery leaves such as endive or mizuna.

FOR FOUR:

1 vanilla bean
rind of 1 orange
juice of half an orange
juice of 1 lemon
1 teaspoon fresh thyme
200mls olive oil
2 tablespoons pecans
150g rocket
150g watercress
10–12 ripe purple figs
80g mascarpone

Slice the vanilla bean in half lengthways and scrape the pulpy seeds into a jug or jar. Add to this the orange, lemon, thyme and olive oil, and use a hand blender to emulsify the dressing. Alternatively, put a tight lid on the jar and shake it vigorously until the dressing emulsifies. If it separates again later, simply shake it again just before you use it. Lightly toast the pecans in a moderate oven, leave them to cool and toss them with the salad leaves.

Heat a heavy frying pan or griddle pan to fairly hot and brush it very lightly with olive oil. Slice the figs in half and cook them briefly, cut sides down, until lightly singed – 20 or 30 seconds should be enough.

Toss the leaves in a little of the dressing and share them out on to individual plates. Arrange the figs on the salads. Use a teaspoon dipped in olive oil to drop a few blobs of mascarpone on each salad plate, then drizzle a little more dressing over everything and serve.

Cardamom and orange-roasted figs with amaretto semi-freddo

When you cook figs, think of where they come from and the images in your head will suggest the flavours that figs are happiest with. Warm exotic spices, citrus, almonds, honey… the recipes write themselves and, if only they would cook themselves, we'd never leave the table.

Semi-freddo is nothing more daunting than almost-frozen ice cream, though in restaurants it is more likely to be frozen ice cream that has been allowed to soften a little in the fridge before serving. For me, fresh – that is, before storage freezing – is the best way to eat ice cream. Freezers don't preserve food in perfect condition for even a short time; something is always lost in the process. Ever since working in an ice cream shop in New Zealand that made its own ice cream every day, I've had a thing about fresh ice cream. The best ice cream I've ever eaten was scooped with my fingers from the 20-litre churn we used; next day the ice cream was a frozen product, its irresistible magic gone.

FOR FOUR:

300mls milk
3 egg yolks
60g caster sugar
200mls cream
2 tablespoons amaretto liqueur

8–12 figs
6 cardamom pods
2 tablespoons unsalted butter
rind and juice of 1 orange
1 tablespoon honey or sugar

Heat the milk to just short of boiling for one minute. Whisk the egg yolks and sugar together until thick and pale. Still whisking, on low speed, pour in the milk through a sieve. Return this egg and milk custard to the pan and simmer, stirring all the time, until it is thick enough to coat the back of a spoon. Leave the custard to cool before adding the cream and the amaretto. Churn in an ice cream machine until almost set.

Serve what you need from the machine, then churn the rest until fully frozen and store in the freezer

Heat an oven to 180°C/350°F. Make a deep cross cut in the figs, to halfway down. Split the cardamom pods and crush the seeds, discarding the pods. Put the butter in an oven dish with the orange, the cardamom seeds and two tablespoons of water. Put the dish in the oven until the butter has melted, then stir everything together. Stand the figs in the dish and use a spoon to baste them with the liquid. Put the dish back in the oven for 15 minutes, until the figs are hot and the juice bubbling. Carefully remove the figs and put them on serving plates. Stir the honey or sugar into the juice and spoon it over and around the figs.

Place a small dollop of semi-freddo in the opening of each fig.

Pumpkins

I fell in love with pumpkins on my first trip to New Zealand. I fell in love with lots of things then, but pumpkin has been a stayer. There was always a pumpkin in the cupboard, or more likely half of a huge one, wrapped in newspaper. We ate pumpkin almost every day, but rarely did anything fancy with it. No matter what fabulous dishes were served, roast pumpkin would be a side dish; more than that, it was the staple, the starch, and in many ways the real centre of the meal. The quality of the pumpkin would be discussed and fretted over. This is very similar to how the Irish eat potatoes, so I knew the rituals.

Even now, despite the endless variety of pumpkin dishes we cook in the restaurant, at home we usually prepare pumpkin the classic way by chopping it into chunks, tossing them in butter, or a mix of butter and olive oil, and roasting them in the oven. This basic method is very flexible and can be adapted to complement the rest of the meal. Pumpkin roasted in butter and olive oil is so comforting, so melt-in-the-mouth, that it is a perfect carrier of herbs or spices. Rosemary is excellent, whole sprigs tossed in at the start of cooking; sage is always good with pumpkin, but added later in the cooking; the same goes for thyme, which is even better paired with some lemon rind. Mind you, I tend to add spice to roast pumpkin more than herbs – I have a thing about spiking comfort food with a kick – and I generally prefer to

use just one or two spices at a time. Chillies, chopped or ground, can be added to the roasting at an early stage; whole cumin seeds or chopped coriander seeds are very good with chillies, while cumin seeds alone is one of my favourites – but then I love almost anything with cumin seeds; ginger is wonderful with pumpkin, added late in the cooking, and, again, some lime or lemon rind is good with the sweetness of ginger. Always add a generous pinch of salt – pumpkins, like all starchy foods, need salt. I couldn't possibly exaggerate how important pumpkins and squashes are to my cooking in Café Paradiso. It would surely strain my imagination beyond capacity to produce lunch and dinner menus through the long autumn and winter without pumpkins. More than that, it would depress me to have to live without them.

When I returned to Ireland, there wasn't a pumpkin to be seen, except for the monstrous Hallowe'en varieties that have too little flavour and too much water content to be of any interest as food. Life took a major upward swing when we found Hollyhill Farm, a small organic vegetable farm, or it found us, more correctly. The farm is currently owned by a New Zealand/Irish couple who know their pumpkins and who even produce New Zealand's favourite variety, the Whanga Crown. When Café Paradiso opened, I was still either roasting pumpkins or making soup of them. With my own kitchen and a steady supply, I came to see pumpkins as hugely inspirational raw material. Because of the way I work – whereby dishes are always focused on one vegetable; and how that vegetable is initially prepared, cut and cooked can form the idea for the dish – pumpkins open up a very wide range of options and creating dishes from them seems so full of possibilities. With pumpkins, there are so many ways to start. The colour alone is reason enough to include pumpkin as an element on a plate, as are the possibilities of texture and structure. Large, roughly chopped pieces with their skin on make fine dramatic roast pumpkin; peeled and chopped into small dice, the pumpkin can be roasted or steamed and made into frittata, pies, gratins, pancake or dolma fillings, as well as risotto and pasta; grated or chopped as thin as matchsticks is a good shape for spring-roll fillings or fried fritters; sliced in thin wedges makes pumpkin one of the best vegetables to cook as tempura, while a thicker slice coated in crumbs or batter makes a more substantial fried snack. Some squashes, the firm but less floury varieties like butternut, can be sliced and stir-fried. Steamed pumpkin can be mashed, or puréed in a food processor, which will be wetter. Puréed is best for soups, sauces and sweet dishes, while gently mashed gives a dry, fluffy finish that makes wonderful gratins, gnocchi, ravioli, kofta and, well, mash.

I hope my use of the words 'pumpkin' and 'squash' isn't too confusing. I think of pumpkins as having dense and floury orange flesh, autumn vegetables that store well into the winter; and squashes as being summer vegetables, lighter in texture and less intensely flavoured, grown to be eaten freshly picked. I'm not sure my use is always technically correct, but I know what I mean, my staff know what I mean and the floor staff in Paradiso are very patient at translating to the public. In essence, if it behaves like a pumpkin it is a pumpkin – except the butternut, which is dense and orange-fleshed but is always called a squash! I think my definitions are consistent with usage in New Zealand, where I learned the language of pumpkins. For a more technical view of the matter, have a look at the *Oxford Companion to Food*, by Alan Davidson. The gist of his pumpkin section seems to be that only big orange-coloured vegetables like the Hallowe'en pumpkins are actually 'pumpkins'; but then he allows that 'pumpkin' is a kind of pet name anyway, and furthermore, all winter squashes can be and are called 'pumpkins'. Follow that? So, at least we're agreed that everyone is confused on the matter.

There must be thousands of varieties of pumpkin out there, and I can't claim to have used more than ten. Whanga Crowns are a class act among pumpkins and would be most connoisseurs' favourite. Crowns are usually large, 4–10kg, with a hard but thin, smooth, grey skin and vivid orange flesh that is sweet, rich and floury but not mouth-dryingly so. Their crowning glory, as it were, is that they are almost solid,

with a relatively small seed cavity, making them wonderful store food. There is little worse than a pumpkin that is all thick skin and stringy seeds. Two other large varieties that have stored very well for us are the Australian Queensland blue, which is actually grey-green in skin colour and has very dense, dry flesh; and Sweet Mama, American I think, dark green and with good orange flesh. Both, however, have an annoying tendency for the skin colour to bleed an inch or so into the flesh, causing a lot of waste when colour is an important part of the dish.

The most conveniently sized pumpkins are the smaller, more user-friendly, varieties such as the orange-skinned Japanese varieties, like hokaido, hobacha and uchiki kuri, as well as the butternut squash. These come in sizes of 1–2kg, which makes them more suitable for supermarkets and domestic pantries.

One final thing: peeling pumpkins isn't always necessary, as the skin softens when roasted and is often deliciously edible in the way that potato skins are. However, if a recipe calls for peeling, do it very carefully, as it often requires force and can be dangerous. The best way to peel a pumpkin is to chop it into halves, quarters or even smaller pieces and to use a sharp knife to slice the skin off, always pushing the knife away from you and down.

Roasted butternut squash with chickpeas and cumin

Roasted butternut squash holds its shape better than any other squash or pumpkin, which is why it is so popular in restaurant kitchens. That and its wonderfully rich orange colour. Although not as dry in texture as some of the other orange-fleshed pumpkins, butternuts still have an intense, sweet flavour. It isn't my favourite, but butternut certainly has its place and its uses. This dish, a simple variation on roast pumpkin, is one of them. The roasted squash is doused, just before it finishes cooking, in an oily combination of chickpeas and spices. The quantities don't really matter, how spicy you make it is up to you, but the proportions do – there should be just a scattering of chickpeas through the squash. I serve squash this way as a side dish to mildly spiced cabbage dolmas or spring rolls.

FOR FOUR:

1 small butternut squash, approx 1kg

olive oil

4 scallions

1 fresh red chilli

4 tablespoons cooked chickpeas

1 tablespoon cumin seeds

150mls vegetable stock or water

large pinch salt

1 small bunch fresh coriander

Peel the squash, slice it in half and scoop out the seeds. Chop the flesh into two-bite pieces, toss them in olive oil in an oven dish, and roast them in a moderate to hot oven until tender and beginning to caramelise at the edges.

Slice the scallions into long diagonal pieces; slice the chilli into thin rounds. Put these in a pan with the chickpeas and the cumin seeds. Add two tablespoons of olive oil and 150mls of stock or water, and a large pinch of salt. Bring this to a boil, simmer for one minute, then pour the contents of the pan over the roasted squash. Return the dish to the oven for five minutes. Stir in the fresh coriander before serving.

Spinach ravioli of pumpkin, basil and Gabriel cheese with lemon and black peppercorn butter

For these ravioli, and for most dishes that involve mashed pumpkin, it's important to start with the right pumpkin: one with dry flesh of an intense orange colour and sweet, rich flavour. To get the best of that flavour, I cook the pumpkin without water, by roasting it, and mash it gently by hand to get a dry, fluffy texture. All going according to plan, the ravioli filling will be no more than pumpkin flavoured with basil, snuggled up to some Gabriel cheese, needing no eggs, breadcrumbs, flour or anything else to bind or hold it together. The cheese is draped over the pumpkin mash in thin shavings, so that, when the ravioli are cooked, the cheese will melt into a lovely soft, distinct layer over the pumpkin. As well as the textural effect this gives, I like the way the flavours remain distinct yet together, rather than blended into one. The sharp, peppery flavour of mature Gabriel works very well with pumpkin, as will any full-flavoured and mature Gouda- or Gruyère-type cheese.

The sauce is a very simple one of clarified butter flavoured with lemon and a few cracked peppercorns. Don't grind the peppercorns or the whole dish will be too uniformly spicy – rather, split them (or buy cracked peppercorns), to provide the occasional thrill.

FOR FOUR STARTERS:

500g pumpkin flesh
olive oil
1 small bunch fresh basil
salt and pepper, to season
100g Gabriel cheese, or similar

2 sheets fresh spinach pasta, approx 16cm x 60cm

12 black peppercorns
80g clarified butter (see page 60)
rind and juice of 1 lemon

Peel the pumpkin carefully, scoop out the seeds and chop 500g of the flesh into large pieces. Toss these in a little olive oil and roast them in a hot oven until soft and lightly coloured. Mash the pumpkin with a fork or potato masher to get a smooth but dry mash. Don't overbeat the pumpkin or the mash will become too wet to stay inside the ravioli.

Chop the basil and stir it into the pumpkin mash. Season with salt and pepper. Use a vegetable peeler to shave thin slivers from the Gabriel cheese.

Lay the pasta on a work surface and cut out two sets of circles, one slightly larger than the other, 12 of each size. From the size of pasta sheet given, one circle of 8cm and one of 7cm would be perfect, but do whatever best suits the pasta size and your cutting equipment. Take a smallish amount of the filling, small but as much as you think the parcel will hold – perhaps a teaspoonful – roll it into a ball and place it in the centre of one of the smaller circles of pasta, and press it gently to flatten it a little. Place three or four of the cheese shavings over the pumpkin. Brush the visible part of the pasta circle with water and place one of the larger pieces of pasta on top. Now press the edges together firmly while, at the same time, taking care not to leave any air pockets inside the parcel.

Repeat this with the rest of the parcels – you will need three each for a starter, more for a main course.

Make the lemon-black peppercorn butter before you cook the ravioli. Crack the peppercorns by laying them on a chopping board and pressing them with a rolling pin or the flat side of a knife, so that the peppercorns crack into large pieces but don't crumble to powder. Put the cracked pepper in a pan with the butter, lemon rind and juice. Heat it gently just before you serve the ravioli.

To cook the pasta, bring a large pot of water to a boil and drop in the ravioli. If you think the parcels might be overcrowded, do two batches. As with all pasta, the only way to decide that it's cooked is to test it, so nick a tiny bit off one of the ravioli and taste it. Remove the ravioli with a slotted spoon and put them in a bowl with a little olive oil to prevent them sticking to each other. If you do two batches, tip the first one back into the pot just as the second batch is cooked and remove the lot in half a minute.

Serve the ravioli on warm plates and spoon a generous amount of the butter over each portion.

Pumpkin gnocchi with spinach in a roasted garlic cream

We make gnocchi from either potatoes or pumpkins and so, having never tried to make the semolina flour-based version, I tend to think of gnocchi as a vegetable dish more than a pasta. Granted, it is necessary to add some flour to hold the show together… and the pieces of dough are boiled in water and served in a sauce… very pasta-like behaviour, yet I persist in my possibly skewed thinking. This attitude lost me most of my credibility one lunchtime in a fabulous and famous Italian restaurant in London when, while negotiating the short menu to concoct a vegetarian meal, I ordered a salad, then a starter of potato gnocchi in walnut and sage sauce, followed by a pasta dish in olive oil. I was pleased with myself and excited about the meal ahead, but the waiter was aghast and felt he had to save me from the inevitable disaster of lunching on serial pasta dishes. I argued that I was having a potato dish and a pasta dish made mainly from wheat; he pointed out, helpfully and sincerely for my benefit, that they were both in the section headed 'pasta' and were therefore pastas. Like all good waiters, having done his best, he gave me what I wanted without conceding his position. But I would bet my good leg that he had to argue my case for me in the kitchen and that there were a few eyebrows thrown skywards. Bloody English, he probably thought; I should have explained that I was Irish and that we never eat a meal without potatoes and that if they weren't available boiled in their skins we'd make do with gnocchi.

Still without conceding the argument, another thing that gnocchi has in common with pasta is that it can be served in a cream sauce or an olive oil-based one. I do a few different pumpkin gnocchi during the season and I serve some in robust, almost stew-like sauces with tomatoes, greens and olive oil; and sometimes I use rich but simpler cream sauces like this garlic cream.

If it is important to start with a pumpkin of dry, orange flesh when making ravioli, it is even more so for gnocchi. The gnocchi are made from a dough of mashed pumpkin and flour, flavoured with grated Parmesan and anything else you fancy; and the intention should be to use as much flour as is needed to hold the dough together, but to use as little as possible! Which is why you should take the measurements in this recipe as a guide only. It helps, too, to mash the pumpkin gently and to incorporate the flour with a light touch – think pastry making rather than bread kneading. Rough handling can make the dough wetter and in need of more flour, and can cause a tough finished texture.

Gnocchi need to be cooked soon after being made but uncooked ones keep well in a freezer if tossed in flour – rice flour is better for this than wheat flour, as it is much less inclined to be incorporated into the gnocchi.

Serve this gnocchi dish as a starter, and follow it with whatever you feel like, bearing in mind that gnocchi is quite a filling dish… like pasta.

FOR FOUR:

500g pumpkin flesh
salt and pepper, to season
100g flour
80g Parmesan

8 cloves garlic
olive oil, to coat
100mls light stock (see page 276)
100mls white wine
300mls cream
1 tablespoon chopped chives

100g spinach

Chop the pumpkin flesh into chunks and roast them in a moderate oven until tender, then mash them carefully with a potato masher, to get a lump-free mash but without over-pounding the pumpkin, which will cause it to become too wet. Season the pumpkin well with salt and pepper, then leave it to cool completely before carefully folding in half the flour. Mix in the flour by hand, then test whether the dough is firm enough to roll. If not, add some more flour until it is, bearing in mind that the less flour you use the better your gnocchi will taste. When you feel that the dough is right, fold in 60g of the Parmesan. If you have had to add more than 100g of flour, you may want to also add extra Parmesan and more seasoning. Roll a small piece of dough into a ball and drop it into boiling water to check the texture. If the ball holds its shape and floats to the surface after a few minutes, it is cooked and your dough is ready to use. Tear off a piece of dough and use your hands to roll it into a long tubular shape, about the thickness of your finger, then cut it into pieces 2–3cm long. Keep the gnocchi tossed in rice flour to avoid them sticking together.

To make the sauce, slice the ends off the garlic cloves, coat them lightly in olive oil and roast them gently in a low to medium oven, about 150°C/300°F, until the garlic is completely soft. Squeeze the garlic from its skin and put it in a jug with the stock and white wine. Use a hand blender to purée these and pass the purée through a sieve into a pan. Bring this to a boil and simmer until the volume is reduced by half. Add the cream and simmer again for a few minutes until the sauce thickens to a nice pouring consistency – try some on the back of a wooden spoon to get an idea. Season with salt and pepper. While the gnocchi are boiling, reheat the sauce and add the chopped chives to it.

Bring a large pot of water to a boil and drop the spinach in for a few seconds, then remove it to a bowl of cold water. Squeeze the water from the cooked spinach and chop it coarsely.

Drop the gnocchi into the boiling water, but don't overcrowd them – do a second batch if necessary. The gnocchi are done when they float to the top. Remove the cooked gnocchi with a slotted spoon. Place a generous portion of gnocchi on each of four plates, and pour some of the garlic cream over each. Place a few pieces of spinach on each plate and scatter the remaining Parmesan over. Finish the gnocchi by cooking them under a hot grill until the Parmesan melts, then serve immediately.

Butternut squash soup with lime and a coconut-peanut relish

Using butternuts instead of a dry pumpkin such as a crown or hokaido gives a finish that is more velvety than starchy, and can make a soup that is more elegant than substantial. Using a high proportion of onion in a potentially starchy soup like pumpkin or potato can also help to reduce the wallpaper-paste effect.

I use the coconut-peanut relish to provide contrast with the soup; whereas the soup is smooth, mellow and lightly spiced, the relish has bite, both in its texture and in its spicing, which should be hot if you have used hot chillies. If your chillies aren't hot enough, add a few dried hot chillies as well – it's important that there is a contrast between a mild soup and a hot relish, as there should be between a fiery hot soup and a cooling relish or cream. Lime juice is squeezed over the soup at the table for the same reason, as a sharp but pleasant contrast to the sweetness of the squash. If you like the relish, you will find that it is delicious with a lot of lightly spiced food, especially Indian and South Asian snacky things like fritters, pancakes, kofta and so on. Make the relish early on the day you need it, or a day before. It isn't a great keeper, however, so try to use it up in a couple of days.

FOR FOUR:

50g desiccated coconut
100g peanuts
2 hot red chillies, fresh
2 cloves garlic
juice of 1 lime
1 tablespoon sugar
large pinch salt

3 onions, chopped
1 medium butternut squash, about 1.2kg
1 tablespoon cumin seeds
1 tablespoon coriander seeds
1 dried bird's eye chilli
6 cloves garlic
1 tablespoon fresh ginger, grated
1.5 litres vegetable stock (see page 276)
200mls coconut milk
2 limes
large pinch salt

Soak the desiccated coconut in 200mls of hot water for 20 minutes. Roast the peanuts lightly in a low to medium oven, until lightly coloured, then chop them finely, almost but not quite ground.

Chop the chillies and garlic finely, and fry them in a little oil for two minutes. Add the peanuts for one minute, then add the coconut in its water, the lime juice and sugar, and a large pinch of salt. Bring this to a boil and simmer for two minutes. Put the relish in a bowl and leave it to cool. It should be slightly moist

Heat a little oil in a large pot and put in the onions to start cooking. Peel the squash, slice it in half and scoop out the seeds. Chop the flesh into chunks and add these to the pot once the onion has softened, and cook both together for five minutes. Toast the cumin, coriander and chilli in a small pan for a minute, then grind them finely and add them to the soup pot, along with the whole garlic cloves and the grated ginger.

Cook for two minutes before adding the stock. Bring this to a boil and simmer, covered, for 30 minutes or so, until the squash is soft and beginning to break up. Add all but two tablespoons of the coconut milk, the rind and juice of one lime and a large pinch of salt. Simmer for one minute more, then blend the soup to a smooth purée.

Ladle the soup into bowls and put a teaspoon of the relish on each. Swirl some of the remaining coconut milk into the soup and, finally, squeeze some fresh lime juice over.

Honey-roasted butternut with avocado-lime salsa, and green curry of cauliflower and beans

In general, squashes and pumpkins are large vegetables of haphazardly almost-round form. There are exceptions and, if I find any smaller squashes with interesting shapes, I try to maintain some element of that shape in the cooking. The simplest examples are those that are small enough to be stuffed whole or in halves, or the spaceship-like pattypans. The shape of butternut squash, with its elegant oval upper half ending in a round, bulbous base on which it sits, seems a partly dramatic and partly comic appearance, sometimes both and sometimes just one.

Slicing the squash into long wedges, as in this dish, preserves the dramatic element, even if it loses the comic. I'm not sure I'm ready for comic food anyway. Here, the butternut is cooked very simply, roasted with a glaze of honeyed butter, which gives a lovely caramelised sheen to it. The honey does boost the natural sweetness of the butternut, and that's why we serve it with an avocado salsa heavily laced with lime.

The green curry has a degree of sweetness too, though coconut milk is nothing like as sweet as the concentrated creams you can get in tins or pressed blocks. Mostly, the curry is a combination of hot chillies and ginger with lots of fresh herbs, coriander and basil, and it is the herbs that give it that lovely fresh and vibrant quality. The curry recipe is a combination of a few I found in the Café Paradiso notebooks when trying to pin down one definitive version to be used in the restaurant. It seems like we use a new variation every year, under the influence of travelling cooks and glossy magazines, so I'm making no claims of authenticity or correctness. It's a damn fine curry, though.

Serve some simple boiled basmati rice with this dish, to mop up the curry and prop up the roasted butternuts.

FOR FOUR:

1 large butternut squash, about 2kg, or 2 smaller ones

2 tablespoons clarified butter (see page 60)

1 tablespoon clear honey

1 leek, white part only

2 teaspoons cumin seeds, ground

1 teaspoon fennel seeds, ground

60g fresh ginger

5 bird's eye chillies

1 bunch fresh coriander

1 bunch Thai basil, or any basil

400mls coconut milk

1 small cauliflower

200g runner beans

4 scallions

salt

1 clove garlic

1 lime

1 avocado

1 tablespoon olive oil

Peel the squash with a vegetable peeler, slice it into quarters lengthways, and scoop out the seeds. Slice each quarter in half again lengthways to get eight long wedges. Melt together the butter and honey, brush the squash wedges with it and place them in an oven dish. Roast the squash in a moderate oven, at about 180°C/350°F, until tender and lightly browned, turning them once or twice to cook evenly.

Chop the white of the leek and put it in a food processor with the cumin and fennel seeds, the ginger and chillies. Blend to a smooth paste and remove it to a container. Put the herbs in the processor and chop them finely, then add the coconut milk and blend to get a nice green milk.

Break the cauliflower into florets, then slice these into halves or quarters. Slice the beans and scallions into long diagonal pieces. Heat some oil in a wok or large frying pan and fry the cauliflower for a minute before adding the green beans. Cook these together for two minutes before adding the scallions and the paste. Continue to fry for two or three minutes, then pour in the herbed milk and a pinch of salt. Bring the milk to a boil for one minute, then serve immediately.

Crush the garlic clove and put it in a small bowl with the finely grated rind and juice of the lime and a pinch of salt. Dice the avocado flesh and stir it in with one tablespoon of olive oil.

Serve the curry with some basmati rice, and lean two wedges of butternut squash on each portion. Spoon some avocado-lime salsa into the well of the squash.

Roast pumpkin, onion and feta tart in walnut filo pastry with cucumber and yoghurt sauce

There was always going to come a point in this book where I would have to eat my words on the subject of filo pastry, and this is as good a recipe as any to take a stand on. While acknowledging that it is one of the most useful materials in the professional catering world, it is its very convenience that also makes it responsible for some lazy, bland cooking. At least the words that need to be temporarily swallowed are not mine but those of an unidentified Turkish cook whom I quoted earlier as praying that 'creative' chefs be kept away from filo pastry. Okay, I agree most days and for most dishes, but the thing is that this is a wonderful pie in the honourable tradition of pies, and I have tried to make it with other pastries but none works as well as filo. I think the only other one that would work is that old English 'hot-crust pastry' that we used in Cranks in the early 1980s to make a wonderfully earthy pie, almost 10cm high and filled with root vegetables and winter herbs. Even so, the semi-open top of this pie can only be achieved with filo. The effect justifies the means, perhaps? I scatter some coarsely ground walnuts between the sheets of pastry, partly for their flavour and partly to help the pastry to stay separate and crisp. After that the filling is a simple matter of pumpkin and feta cheese laced with what I think are my top-drawer spices, the ones I would take to a desert island and which, by an extraordinary coincidence, go very well with pumpkin. So I guess I'd take a pumpkin plant as well.

FOR ONE TART
(ENOUGH FOR SIX):

800g pumpkin flesh
600g onions
olive oil
6 cloves garlic, coarsely chopped
2 teaspoons cumin seeds
2 teaspoons coriander seeds, ground
1 fresh chilli
240g feta cheese

80g butter
1 packet filo pastry

80g walnuts, coarsely ground
4 eggs
150mls cream

Chop the pumpkin flesh into dice of about 2cm, toss these in a little olive oil and roast them in a moderate oven until soft and lightly coloured.

Slice the onions in half, then into short, thickish slices. Heat a little olive oil in a pan and cook the onions and garlic together for ten minutes, stirring often, until the onion is very soft. Add the cumin, coriander and chilli, and cook for another five minutes, then stir this into the roasted pumpkin. Crumble the feta into pieces roughly the same size as the pumpkin and fold it in gently.

Melt the butter, and butter a 26cm spring-form tin. Lay a sheet of filo pastry on a worktop, with a long side facing you as the bottom edge. Cut it into three pieces from top to bottom. Brush the pastry with butter, scatter some ground walnuts over half of each piece and fold them in half to get three long strips. Place one in the tart tin, starting at the centre, coming up the side and over-hanging the top. Place the second strip in the tin in the same way, slightly overlapping the first. Continue with the third piece, then repeat with more pastry until the tin is fully lined. Pile in the filling and pack it gently.

Beat the eggs with the cream and pour this custard over the filling. Fold the overhanging pastry over the top of the tart, folding the strips back on themselves once or twice and leaving the centre of the tart uncovered. Brush any unbuttered pastry with butter and place the tart on an oven tray in a moderate oven, 180°C/350°F, for 40 minutes or so, until the filling is set and the pastry lightly coloured. If possible, cook this in an oven without a fan to avoid burning the pastry. Leave the tart to sit in the tin for ten minutes before removing the side of the tin and slicing the tart carefully.

1 medium cucumber

2 scallions

2 cloves garlic

2 tablespoons chopped
fresh coriander

1 tablespoon chopped
fresh mint

400mls thick plain
yoghurt

salt and cayenne pepper,
to season

Slice the cucumber in half lengthways and
scoop out the seeds. Roughly chop the
cucumber and the scallions, and put them in
a food processor with the garlic and herbs.
Add three tablespoons of the yoghurt and
blend until you get an almost-smooth purée.
Use a spatula to move this to a bowl or jug
and stir in the rest of the yoghurt. Season
with a little salt and a small pinch of cayenne
pepper.

Gratin of roast pumpkin, leeks, sweetcorn and hazelnuts with a Gabriel cheese cream

There are dishes that are wonderful to eat but that could never be sold in restaurants, usually for aesthetic or legal reasons. At the opposite end of the spectrum, there are dishes that could exist only in restaurants and have no function in the real world. The ultimate embodiment of this is the very famous restaurant in Spain that contorts a little food and a lot of air into mindbendingly brilliant creations held together with gelatine, egg white, ice, sugar, water, magic spells and what-not; and where the clientele are mostly other chefs and bored gourmets in need of impressing while the public stubbornly go on eating for pleasure and good company.

Further in on the scale, the scene is a bit blurry and dishes overlap and slip from one side to the other, and get adapted to make them work in the other setting. Some domestic dishes are never as good in a restaurant, usually because they have to be prepared in a different way; some restaurant dishes don't turn out quite so well at home.

Occasionally, the way a restaurant adapts a simple dish from home can actually improve it. I think this gratin is one. At heart it's a basic domestic crumble, where the vegetables are bound with a sauce in a large oven dish, covered with a crust and baked in the oven. Which is where the rings come in. You will need four steel rings of about 8cm diameter and 3cm high.

The rings are indeed a restaurant affectation, their prime function being to hold individual portions in a uniform shape that looks good on a plate. But cooking individual portions for a shorter time, and cooking the sauce separately, also allow the elements and the flavours of the dish to be held together yet remain distinct in flavour. All going well, the dish is no longer a simple one-taste comfort food, it is more sophisticated both in its appearance and flavour. The crust, the vegetables and the rich Gabriel cheese sauce get along all the better for being distinct.

Serve a vegetable dish with the gratin – one that looks good on the plate. Some green or broad beans cooked with tomato and garlic are good, maybe some fried cabbage or other greens, or, as we often serve in Paradiso, little spoonfuls of braised lentils or cannellini beans as on page 252.

80g hazelnuts

40g fine breadcrumbs

2 tablespoons melted butter

1 tablespoon chopped chives

salt and pepper, to season

120g Gabriel cheese, grated

400g leeks

4 cloves garlic, coarsely chopped

2 tablespoons butter

half glass white wine

1 teaspoon Dijon mustard

2 sprigs thyme

120mls cream

600g pumpkin flesh

olive oil

2 ears of sweetcorn

50mls vegetable stock (see page 276)

50mls white wine

200mls cream

Roast the hazelnuts in a low to medium oven for 30 minutes or so, until they are toasted through but only lightly coloured. Rub the nuts in a damp towel to remove the skins, then break them gently under the side of a knife or a rolling pin. You should get halves and quarters of hazelnuts in the mix as well as smaller pieces. Stir the nuts into the bread-crumbs with the melted butter and chives, and season well with salt and pepper. Finally, add 40g of the grated Gabriel cheese.

Wash the leeks carefully, and cut them in half lengthways, then across into slices about 1cm thick. Melt the butter in a large pan, and cook the leeks and garlic in it, over high heat, until the leeks are just tender but still bright green. Add the wine, mustard and thyme, and cook for three minutes more, then add the cream and boil it for two minutes. Pour the leeks into a wide bowl to cool.

Peel the pumpkin, unless the skin is very thin, and chop the flesh into dice of about 1.5cm. Toss the pumpkin pieces in a little olive oil and roast them in a moderately hot oven until the pumpkin is tender.

At the same time, boil the sweetcorn until tender, then use a sharp knife to scrape the kernels from the core. Break up the very big pieces but don't fret about breaking it all down to individual kernels.
Gently stir both the pumpkin and the sweet-corn into the leeks.

Place your four steel rings on an oven tray lined with baking parchment. Fill each with the leek and pumpkin stuff, gently pressing it in. Spoon some of the hazelnut crumble over each one and press it down firmly. Bake the gratins in an oven at 190°C/375°F for 15 to 20 minutes. The top should be lightly browned and the filling heated through.

At the same time, bring the stock and white wine to a boil in a small pan, and boil for two minutes before adding the cream. Bring it back to a boil and simmer for two minutes before stirring in the Gabriel cheese and a little salt and pepper. Allow the sauce to boil for just a few seconds before serving.

Use a serving slice to lift the gratins on to individual plates, then lift off the rings. The gratins should hold up fine without the support. Pour the Gabriel cream around each gratin and serve. If you are serving a vegetable, put three small spoonsful around each portion.

Baked pumpkin, cashew and yoghurt curry

Pumpkins take on spices beautifully, especially in slow-cooked dishes like this simple curry. Eat the curry with rice or Indian bread for a simple meal but, if you can, make at least one other dish. A tomato-based dish with lots of chillies will give the contrast you need.

The pumpkin is boiled briefly before baking, partly to speed the cooking but mostly because the warm and slightly softened pumpkin pieces will absorb the spices better.

FOR FOUR:

100g whole cashews

1kg pumpkin flesh

1 medium leek

1 tablespoon olive oil or butter

3–4 fresh green chillies

1 tablespoon grated fresh ginger

1 tablespoon cumin seeds, ground

1 handful fresh coriander, chopped

500mls plain yoghurt

200mls cream

large pinch salt

Heat an oven to 150°C/300°F, and roast the cashews for 15 minutes or so until lightly coloured but cooked through.

Peel the pumpkin and chop the flesh into large pieces. Drop these into boiling water for three minutes until partly cooked.

Slice the leek in half lengthways, wash it well, and chop it into thickish slices. Heat a tablespoon of oil or butter in a large, wide pan and cook the leeks for three minutes. Slice the chillies thinly and add them to the leeks with the ginger and cumin, and cook for one minute more. Add the part-cooked pumpkin, the cashews, fresh coriander, yoghurt, cream and a large pinch of salt, and stir gently to combine everything. Transfer everything to an oven dish and place in the oven at 150°C/300°F to cook slowly for 30 to 40 minutes, until the pumpkin is tender and the yoghurt sauce has become drier.

Chickpea, leek and rosemary soup with a hot pepper salsa

Leeks make such a wonderful base for soup that everybody's got a leek soup of one kind or another. Most of them are a variation on the classic and almost unbeatable leek and potato soup, which, up until recently, you could find in every bar, bistro and fine restaurant the length and breadth of Ireland, given a run for popularity only by the worryingly non-committal 'vegetable soup'. Although occasionally you might have come across a mean-spirited one that was all cheap potato and cheaper water with a mere hint of leek, the soups were (and still are) generally well made from raw ingredients by people who understood leeks and potatoes. Leek and potato soup on a blackboard menu outside a pub meant comfort, warmth and nourishment against the rain and cold. Okay, sometimes it never came off the menu, even in the summer, and you might have suspiciously wondered where the leeks came from then. Now, 'leek and potato' is gradually being replaced by soups thought to give a more modern image, notoriously 'tomato and basil'; and I can assure you that the mild surprise of finding leek and potato soup in summer is nothing to the horror of finding 'tomato and basil' after a long trudge in the misty Irish countryside in winter. If it's not made with tinned tomatoes and dried basil, it's sure to be green Dutch tomatoes and, well, nothing else. Grown, bearded and muddied men crying into their watery tureens is an awful sight.

As well as their old friend, the spud, leeks also make great soup with carrots, parsnips or turnips. There is a lovely soup I made for years in another restaurant, which went by the slightly pretentious name of 'Crème Andalucia'; it was a variation of a Spanish leek, tomato and potato soup, which had been given a French twist with the addition of tarragon and cream. It was fantastic, and a huge hit, but I left the recipe behind and have never tried to make it since.

Leeks have a lot of natural sweetness, which can be too much if combined with another sweet ingredient like carrots or parsnips, in which case it is a good idea to add a little lemon juice at the end of cooking; or swirl some soured cream or yoghurt into the bowls of soup for balance.

The almost automatic tendency to add potato to leek soups can give the impression that leeks make thick, comforting soup. This is not necessarily true – indeed, a simple leek soup with white wine, herbs and a little cream or olive oil can be a very elegant and light first course. This recipe for chickpea, leek and rosemary soup can go either way, though I prefer to rein in its comfort-food tendencies by keeping the proportion of leeks to potato and chickpeas high. It started life as a very simple chickpea and rosemary soup, which was surprisingly delicious, even if poor-sighted customers of Café Paradiso occasionally thought they were being promised a herbed broth of fowl bones.

The soup is only partly blended, which is achieved by removing some of the vegetables before blending and putting them back into the blended soup. This is one of many tricks I use to give texture to soups without spending hours chopping kilos of vegetables into tiny pieces. As much as I, in my caterer's hat, like to sell easily made blended soups, I know that, as a consumer, I get bored after a few identical spoonfuls, and only a ferocious hunger could make me go on. If I don't leave some

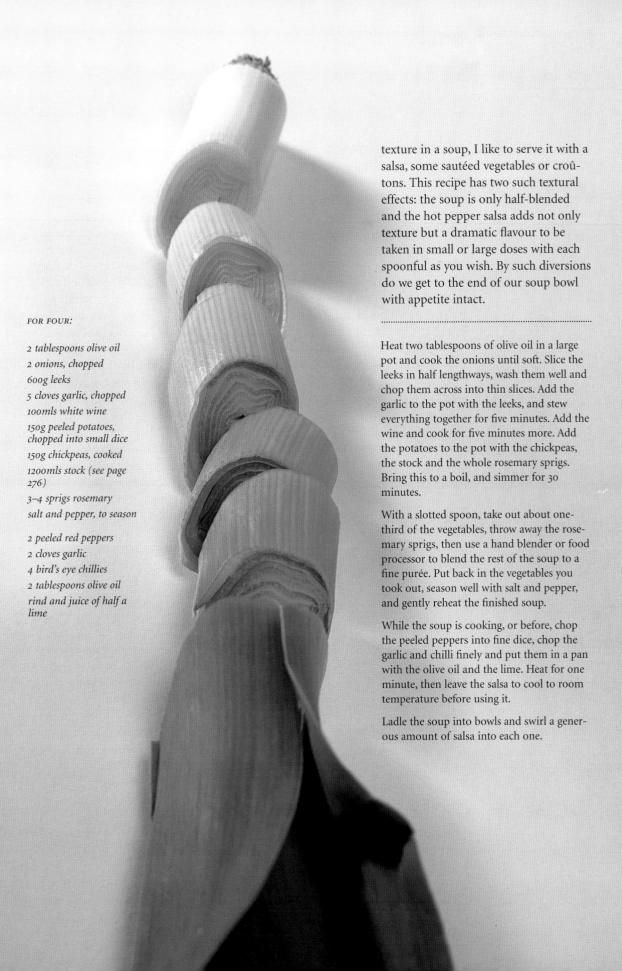

texture in a soup, I like to serve it with a salsa, some sautéed vegetables or croûtons. This recipe has two such textural effects: the soup is only half-blended and the hot pepper salsa adds not only texture but a dramatic flavour to be taken in small or large doses with each spoonful as you wish. By such diversions do we get to the end of our soup bowl with appetite intact.

....

Heat two tablespoons of olive oil in a large pot and cook the onions until soft. Slice the leeks in half lengthways, wash them well and chop them across into thin slices. Add the garlic to the pot with the leeks, and stew everything together for five minutes. Add the wine and cook for five minutes more. Add the potatoes to the pot with the chickpeas, the stock and the whole rosemary sprigs. Bring this to a boil, and simmer for 30 minutes.

With a slotted spoon, take out about one-third of the vegetables, throw away the rosemary sprigs, then use a hand blender or food processor to blend the rest of the soup to a fine purée. Put back in the vegetables you took out, season well with salt and pepper, and gently reheat the finished soup.

While the soup is cooking, or before, chop the peeled peppers into fine dice, chop the garlic and chilli finely and put them in a pan with the olive oil and the lime. Heat for one minute, then leave the salsa to cool to room temperature before using it.

Ladle the soup into bowls and swirl a generous amount of salsa into each one.

FOR FOUR:

2 tablespoons olive oil
2 onions, chopped
600g leeks
5 cloves garlic, chopped
100mls white wine
150g peeled potatoes, chopped into small dice
150g chickpeas, cooked
1200mls stock (see page 276)
3–4 sprigs rosemary
salt and pepper, to season

2 peeled red peppers
2 cloves garlic
4 bird's eye chillies
2 tablespoons olive oil
rind and juice of half a lime

Leek and blue cheese tartlet with roasted cherry tomatoes

Up to mid-autumn, the focus tends to be on freshly picked or dug vegetables, and all energy and attention is concentrated on getting them in their prime and using them at their best. As these fresh foods fade away, the emphasis switches to vegetables that store well or grow slowly, leaving a wide window of time in which to harvest them. Then, leeks gradually become the most versatile and most used vegetable. From late autumn through the freezing winter and into spring, the leeks sit in the ground, ready and waiting to be picked. Eventually, at the first warming of the ground, any leeks still in the ground bolt, their cores becoming woody and unusable. Chances are that, by then, you've just about had enough of them. That's an element of seasonal eating I enjoy – the putting away until next time of a vegetable you love but have gorged on for long enough.

During this time, leeks find a role in so many dishes, often combined with other vegetables, sometimes used almost anonymously as though they were onions. We cook them with pasta and noodles, in omelettes and fritters. They're used in soups, stews, stir-fries – in fact, just about any dish using two or more vegetables is likely to include a leek or two.

Occasionally, it's all about the leeks. The natural sweetness of leeks gives them a great affinity with cheeses. I particularly like them with lightly smoked Gubbeen, the rich and peppery Gabriel, goats' cheeses of all styles and ages, and the softly melting Goudas and Gruyères. But it's the simple sweetness and acidity balance, I think, that makes a nice creamy mature blue cheese as good a partner for leeks as you'll get. That's all there is to this tart – a perfect combination of leeks and mature Cashel blue in a crisp buttery pastry. I serve it sitting on sweet, roasted cherry tomatoes balanced with a touch of balsamic vinegar, and a few peppery leaves of watercress or rocket, whichever is available. I have sometimes served a pesto with it but it's a sauce too far, to be honest. Keep it simple, the flavours are perfect.

FOR SIX TARTLETS:

150g plain flour
large pinch salt
75g cold butter
40mls cold water

400g leeks
2 cloves garlic, chopped
1 tablespoon butter
half teaspoon Dijon mustard
1 tablespoon chopped chives
salt and black pepper, to season
100g blue cheese

400g cherry tomatoes
drizzle of olive oil
2 teaspoons balsamic vinegar

Sift the flour and salt together. Cut in the butter. A food processor does this very efficiently, but remove the pastry to a bowl before stirring in the water with a few quick strokes. Shape it into a ball with your hands, flatten it gently and chill for at least half an hour. Roll the pastry and cut out circles to fit six small tartlet cases of about 7cm diameter. Prick the pastry cases all over with a fork and chill them again for 30 minutes, then bake them for eight to ten minutes at 180°C/350°F until crisp. Check after five minutes in case the pastry has puffed up in places; if it has, press it gently back in place while it is still soft.

Slice the leeks in half lengthways, and wash them well, then slice them thinly. Melt the butter in a wide pan and cook the leek and garlic over high heat for about five minutes, until the leek softens but retains its colour. Add the mustard and the chives and cook for one minute more. Season with coarsely ground black pepper and a small pinch of salt.

Fill each pastry case three-quarters full with the leeks, without packing too hard. Crumble some blue cheese on top and bake the tartlets at 180°C/350°F for eight to ten minutes, until the leeks have warmed through and the cheese has melted.

Halve the cherry tomatoes, put them in a small oven dish and sprinkle over a little olive oil and some salt and pepper. Roast the tomatoes in the oven for eight to ten minutes, until softened a little. Add the balsamic vinegar for the last minute of cooking.

Spoon a pile of roasted tomatoes in their juice on each plate and place a tartlet on top.

Corn pancakes of leek, parsnip and Gabriel cheese with a cherry tomato-fennel salsa

We've been using these corn pancakes for a few years to wrap various fillings. They're made from a variation on a classic crêpe batter, with a few spices thrown in and most of the wheat flour replaced by maize meal. You may know maize meal, which is very finely ground maize or corn, as corn meal; you may even know it as corn flour, but calling it that will only lead to confusion with the very fine white starch powder used for thickening, also derived from corn, and known as cornflour. Besides its colour and flavour, the reason I use maize meal is the way it helps the pancakes to become crisp in the oven.

Leeks and parsnips make good soup, so it makes sense that they would get on well in other dishes, and they work very well here with the strong, peppery Gabriel cheese. The way the leeks are cooked for the filling is a method we use for a lot of leek dishes. The chopped leek is cooked over very high heat so that it goes soft in a short time but without leaking too much liquid or losing its lovely pale green colour, which it will do if a large volume of leek is stewed slowly. The leek is then quickly flavoured with thyme, mustard and wine, and then bound together with some cream. The technique was perfected by John Healy, who used to put a large pot on a very hot flame and go do something else for ten minutes before starting on the leeks. One evening, one of the other cooks put one, just one, teaspoon of ground chilli into the pot, causing a minor outbreak of coughing and eye-rubbing in the kitchen as the chilli vaporised, seeming to poison the air. Gradually, the dining floor staff began to splutter, and then the nearest diners; it was with a combination of horror and amusement that we listened to the seemingly contagious coughing move slowly through the dining room, right to the tables by the windows on to the street. It was 15 minutes before things returned to normal though – because there was no smell, nobody outside the kitchen fully realised that there was a single cause for the outbreak.

The cherry tomato-fennel salsa that I serve with the pancakes is another variation on what would be my favourite taste on most days – the heat of chillies with naturally sweet vegetables in warm olive oil. It's great with cheese dishes.

Serve two pancakes as a main course with the salsa, some potatoes or rice, and a simple green vegetable or salad.

120g fine maize meal
80g plain flour
pinch ground turmeric
pinch cayenne pepper
large pinch salt
3 eggs
450mls milk
olive oil

500g leeks
300g parsnips
1 tablespoon butter
3 cloves garlic, coarsely chopped
50mls white wine
1 teaspoon Dijon mustard
2 sprigs thyme
80mls cream
100g Gabriel cheese

1 small fennel bulb
1 fresh red chilli
2 cloves garlic, finely chopped
200g cherry tomatoes, halved
4 tablespoons olive oil
pinch salt

Sift the maize meal, flour, turmeric, cayenne and a large pinch of salt together. Whisk the eggs and milk together, then whisk them into the flour to get a smooth pouring batter. Heat a crêpe pan, brush it with olive oil and swirl in just enough batter to coat the pan. Cook the pancake for a minute or two and flip it over to cook the other side for a minute. The batter will make 12, but you need only eight (two each), so you have room for a few failed, stuck or burned pancakes.

Wash the leeks carefully, and cut them in half lengthways, then across into slices about 2cm thick. Peel the parsnips and grate them on the widest and thickest grater. Melt the butter in a large pan, and cook the leeks and garlic in it, over high heat, until the leeks are just tender but still bright green. Stir in the grated parsnip, cook for one minute, then add the wine, mustard and thyme, and cook on high for three minutes more, then add the cream and boil it for two minutes. Pour the leeks into a wide bowl to cool. If the heat is high enough and you have worked quickly, the leeks should be quite dry.

Grate the Gabriel cheese and stir it into the cooled leeks.

Place a pancake on a work surface, best-looking side down, and cut a slice off the bottom, about 2.5cm up, and a similar slice from the top. Place two tablespoons of the leek filling along the bottom edge and roll up the pancake tightly, pressing the filling as you go so that it fills the full length of the tube you are forming from the pancake. Repeat with the rest of the pancakes, then place the filled pancakes on an oven tray, lined with baking parchment. Brush them with olive oil and bake them in the oven at 190°C/375°F for ten minutes, until the pancakes are crisp.

Save any green fronds in good condition from the top of the fennel bulb, discard any stringy or discoloured leaves of the bulb and cut out the thick core. Chop the rest of the fennel into very thin, short slivers. Halve the chilli lengthways, then slice it thinly. Put the fennel, chilli, garlic and tomatoes in a small pan with the four tablespoons of olive oil and a pinch of salt. Bring it to a boil and simmer for one minute. Chop the fronds of fennel herb, and stir them into the salsa just before you serve it.

Serve two pancakes per portion, with some warm salsa spooned over each.

Risotto of leeks, butternut squash and sage with pumpkinseed oil and braised lentils

Butternut squash risotto is becoming quite a common dish on restaurant menus, but what interests me about this recipe is the way it uses the white and green parts of the leeks in different ways. The whites are finely chopped and used in the role usually played by onions at the start of the cooking of the risotto; the green tops of the leeks are stewed in olive oil and added to the risotto at the end of cooking, as a featured vegetable. The presence of sage and braised lentils rounds off the warm, autumnal feel of the dish, both being flavours that I often use with pumpkins and squashes.

When writing this recipe, I had just rediscovered a toasted pumpkinseed oil I had lost track of over a year previously. Having struggled on manfully, occasionally using an insipid French oil instead, I was moaning one day about the lost oil to a class I was giving. A woman in the class went off and came back with a few tablespoons of the oil in a little jar and, more importantly, the address of the makers. Turns out it was an Austrian oil, which I could never have remembered, and it was exactly as it had been in my hazy memory – an intense toasty flavour and the most amazing shade of green, which seems almost black except when thinly spread on a white plate. I wrote to the makers explaining my plight and they posted six large bottles, without payment upfront. Such trust, but so much oil! So, now I'm in the pumpkinseed oil business, if anyone's interested.

FOR FOUR:

400g peeled butternut squash

olive oil

1 large leek

1400mls vegetable stock (see page 276)

60g puy lentils

4 cloves garlic, chopped

1 sprig thyme

rind of 1 lemon

salt and black pepper, to season

60g butter

60mls olive oil

320g risotto rice, such as arborio or carnaroli

120mls dry white wine

6 leaves sage, chopped

60g Parmesan, grated

2 tablespoons toasted pumpkinseed oil

Chop the squash into 2cm dice, toss them in a little olive oil and roast them in a moderate oven until tender and lightly coloured.

Slice the leeks in half lengthways, wash them carefully and chop off the white ends. Slice the green tops of the leek about 1cm thick, and the whites much finer.

Bring the stock to a boil in a pot and keep it at a very low simmer.

Heat a tablespoon of olive oil in a pan and cook the lentils and two cloves of garlic together for two minutes. Add the thyme, lemon rind and stock, bring it to a boil and cook at a lively simmer until the lentils are just tender. There should be a little juice left, formed by the mingling of the olive oil and 200mls of the stock; if not, or if the stock boils off before the lentils are quite done, simply add a few spoons of stock at the end or at any stage of the cooking. Season the lentils with salt and black pepper.

Melt one tablespoon of the butter with one spoon of the olive oil, and cook the white of the leek for a minute. Add the rice and two cloves of garlic, and stir well to coat the grains with oil. Cook the rice gently for ten

minutes, stirring often, then pour in the wine, bring it to a boil quickly, and simmer until the wine is absorbed. Now add a ladle or cup of the stock, and continue to simmer, stirring often until it is all but absorbed. Add another cup of stock, and carry on absorbing, stirring and adding stock until the rice is almost cooked. Take care that the stock going into the rice pot is at a boil and not, therefore, interrupting the cooking of the rice.

While the risotto is cooking, stew the leek greens for about ten minutes in a tablespoon of olive oil until just tender but still green.

Test individual grains of rice – they should be cooked through but firm, while the stock has become a little creamy and is almost completely absorbed. When the risotto reaches this stage, stir in the leek greens, roasted squash, chopped sage leaves, the remaining butter and olive oil, and the grated Parmesan. Season well with salt and pepper.

Serve the risotto with a little pumpkinseed oil drizzled over, some lentils in their juice scattered around each portion, and some Parmesan on the side, either finely grated or in a chunk to be shaved.

Roasted leeks with a lemon, ginger and pinenut marinade

Although leeks roast very well – in that they become soft, succulent and sweet – I've never been completely confident about the process because I've never found a way to do it that doesn't leave at least the outer leaves tough to slice through. There's something about the texture of a roasted leek that makes it tricky for a table knife. I've even tried out recipes from other people's books and they turn out the same. In my most recent attempts, I came up with this absolutely delicious version, which involves slicing the leeks in half lengthways into pieces about 10cm long. We ate the leeks with grilled haloumi, which always needs some lemon and olive oil, and roasted pumpkin. The leeks in their marinade did away with the need for a sauce for the haloumi, and set me thinking that the combination could be turned into an elegant starter. Then it went to the back of my mind and I haven't done it yet. Maybe someone else will, perhaps at a fabulous dinner party that I'll get invited to…

I put ginger in the marinade simply because I love ginger with leeks, but if you're worried that ginger will clash with the rest of your harmoniously balanced meal, change the marinade. Think of the marinade as essentially a lemon and olive oil combination, and then any herb or spice that goes well with leeks can be added to it – basil, thyme, garlic, chillies, fennel and rosemary are all good.

Roasting leeks this way also works very well with the baby leeks that appear occasionally in the summer, though the outer leaves will still be a little stubborn to table knives.

FOR FOUR:

4 medium leeks
drizzle of olive oil
salt
splash of water or stock
1 tablespoon pinenuts
1 lemon
1 tablespoon fresh ginger, grated
2 tablespoons olive oil

Cut the green tops from the leeks and save them for another dish. Slice the white parts in half lengthways and check carefully for dirt – wash the leeks if necessary, being careful not to break them up. Arrange the leek pieces in an oven dish with olive oil and a little salt, and roast them in a moderate oven for 15 to 20 minutes. Sprinkle a little stock or water over occasionally, to help the leeks cook without burning.

Lightly toast the pinenuts in the oven, then place them in a small pan with the rind of the lemon, the juice from half of it, the ginger and two tablespoons of olive oil. When the leeks are tender, heat the marinade and pour it over them. If you are transferring the leeks to a serving dish, do that before you pour the marinade over.

Winter

cauliflower

winter greens

pears

roots

potatoes

clementines

pineapple

store

blood oranges

Cauliflower and beetroot tempura with ginger-soya dip

There are vegetables that are good as tempura and vegetables that are not. Of those that are, some are actually improved by the cooking method, as though it reveals something in the character of the vegetable that wasn't obvious before. This is the best that cooking can achieve, and it is why I love tempura. So much of the time cooks who are lucky enough to have good produce strive to preserve the vegetables' qualities and to present them intact at the table. Sometimes, by the magic of cooking, hidden qualities are teased out. Some of the best vegetables to cook as tempura are pumpkin, broccoli, carrot, aubergine, oyster mushrooms and asparagus, but this pair – cauliflower and beetroot – is my favourite. They certainly look good together, but beetroot would look good anywhere, and its earthy sweetness is a nice contrast to the more elusive flavour of cauliflower.

I have carried out experiments on my children, cauliflower-haters to a man, on the matter of tempura and vegetables. Presented with a platter of vegetable tempura, they will avoid the aubergines and mushrooms because they don't like the vegetables and tempura hasn't changed them; they will eat the carrots and broccoli because they like carrots and broccoli; they will eat the beetroot grudgingly, admitting its nicer than they expected, but they will eat the cauliflower because it makes the best tempura. And this isn't a case of children eating anything deep-fried because it all tastes the same; tempura batter is too thin to hide the nature of the food it coats.

Naturally, these experiments were carried out under gentle, caring conditions and no children were hurt or injured in the process.

It is essential to cut slices of even thickness from the cauliflower, even when this seems to involve cutting cross-sections from the rounded florets, which may seem wasteful. However, frying rounded slices of cauliflower, or any vegetable, in tempura will result in uneven cooking and undercooked centres. This is especially true of both cauliflower and broccoli, the loose florets of which can hold half-cooked batter, which is particularly nasty to eat.

The beetroot must be sliced thinner than the cauliflower so that it will be cooked through in the short time it takes the batter to crisp.

FOR FOUR:

150mls soy sauce
2 tablespoons saki or sherry
1 tablespoon grated ginger
100mls water

half a medium cauliflower
1 largish beetroot

225g plain flour
2 egg yolks
375mls iced water

Stir together in a jug the soy sauce, saki, ginger and water.

Break the cauliflower into large pieces, keeping the florets intact. Use a sharp knife to cut flat slices 5–6mm thick.

Wash the beetroot and, without peeling it, slice it into thin rounds or half-rounds, no more than 2mm thick.

Heat a deep fryer to 190°C/375°F.
Put the flour in a bowl and add the egg yolks, then whisk in the cold water to make a thin batter.

Drop some of the cauliflower and beetroot pieces into the batter. Lift one slice out, gently shaking the batter from it so it has just a thin coating, then carefully slide it into the hot oil. Put in as many slices as will comfortably fit in the fryer without overcrowding. Turn each slice once with tongs, and lift the slices out on to absorbent paper when they are crisp and very lightly coloured. If you need to do a second batch, leave the first on the paper until the second is just about cooked, then toss the first lot back into the fryer for the last few seconds of cooking. Serve the tempura immediately, either on individual plates or a communal platter, with separate bowls of the dip.

Cauliflower soup with green peppercorns and avocado oil

The flavour of raw cauliflower can sometimes be so robust, even spicy in a peppery way, that it is often shocking how that flavour can disappear in even the gentlest of cooking, especially in water. Cauliflower soup that involves quite long cooking in water can easily end up tasting of the support flavours and not at all of the cauliflower. With this in mind, I have tried to come up with a way to prepare cauliflower soup that tastes primarily of cauliflower, without being merely a purée of cauliflower. The cauliflower is braised briefly and blended with a potato-thickened stock. To add complexity without drowning the cauliflower, I add other flavours at the table. This version uses green peppercorns and avocado oil; herbs such as chives and fennel are good, as are nut oils, especially hazelnut.

FOR FOUR:

100g floury potato

1 small onion, chopped

2 cloves garlic, finely chopped

1 sprig thyme

800mls vegetable stock (see page 276)

1 large cauliflower, about 450g net weight

120mls white wine

salt, to season

2 teaspoons freeze-dried green peppercorns

1 tablespoon avocado oil

Peel the potato, chop it and put it in a pan with the onion, garlic cloves, thyme and stock. Bring the stock to a boil and simmer until the potato is soft and breaking up. Remove the thyme sprig and blend the rest to get a smooth, slightly thickened, liquid.

Chop the cauliflower into small pieces, put it in a pan with the wine, over low heat. Cover and braise the cauliflower for about five minutes until it is tender but not too soft. Add the potato stock, bring it to a boil and simmer for one minute. Blend the soup to a smooth purée and season with a little salt.

To serve, ladle the soup into bowls, crack some green peppercorns between your fingers and sprinkle them over the soup, then drizzle a little avocado oil on top.

Savoy cabbage dolmas of wild rice, leek and eggs in truffle oil

As best I can remember it, this came about from a brief and uncharacteristic obsession with hard-boiled eggs. Once you've gone there, it's a short step to eggs with truffle oil. The filling has a very loose texture, with nothing to bind it, so I cook the wild rice so that the grains soften and open up, which is more than if I was serving it as a grain in its own right.

Savoy cabbage isn't the most obvious leaf to use as a wrapping. With its crinkled texture, it can easily end up being a more substantial part of the dish than the filling. Even so, it's the one I like to use for this dish, for its flavour of course, but also because for a time in winter it's the best cabbage there is. So we persevere. First, we make sure the leaf is fully cooked in boiling water, not merely blanched; then the stem is trimmed to the thickness of the leaf; and finally the leaf is pressed completely flat. The leaf is now a suitable wrapping material, but there's more: as the leaf is rolled around the filling, any excess pieces are trimmed away. All of this seemingly laborious process is to get a parcel that is well sealed and contained, but that has only a thin layer of cabbage all around.

I don't usually serve a sauce with the dolmas. In Café Paradiso, we serve them cooked wet with the braised cannellini beans on page 252, wet so that they double as vegetable and sauce, and some parsnip chips. If you do want to serve a sauce, make a light cream sauce flavoured with fennel perhaps, or dill and a little mustard.

FOR FOUR:

60g wild rice
300g leeks
tablespoon butter
olive oil
2 cloves garlic, finely chopped
50mls white wine
1 sprig fresh thyme
1 sprig fresh fennel
50mls cream
4 hard-boiled eggs
12 savoy cabbage leaves
salt and pepper, to season
white truffle oil
a little vegetable stock (see page 276)

Cook the wild rice in boiling water until tender and the grains have opened a little, then drain it in a colander or sieve.

Chop the leek in half lengthways, wash it and chop it into thin slices. Melt a tablespoon of butter with a little olive oil in a wide pan and cook the leek and garlic over high heat for five minutes, then add the wine, the thyme leaves and the fennel, and cook for two minutes more. Pour in the cream and boil it for one minute, then add the wild rice, take the pan off the heat and transfer the cooked filling to a dish. When the filling has cooled, chop the hard-boiled eggs and stir them in. Season with salt and pepper.

Trim the stalks of the cabbage leaves with a sharp knife or vegetable peeler, to make them as thin as the leaves, and take a slice off the base to give a flat edge there. Bring a pot of water to a boil and drop in the cabbage leaves to cook for five minutes or so until fully tender, then drop the leaves into cold water to cool.

Lay a cabbage leaf on your work surface and flatten it with a rolling pin. Put a tablespoon of filling at the base, shaped to form a tube 8cm long. Sprinkle a few drops of truffle oil over the filling. Cut the corners off the leaf just outside this shape, about 6cm up into the leaf. Leaving a 4cm-long section in the centre at full length, repeat the cutting at the top of the leaf, to leave a cross-shaped leaf. Roll the leaf up around the filling from the base, fold over the side flaps of leaf and continue rolling, keeping the parcel as tight as possible. Cut off the end of the leaf when the parcel has been rolled one full turn after the middle.

Repeat this process with the rest of the leaves, then place the rolled parcels in an oven dish that has been brushed with olive oil. Brush the tops of the dolmas generously with more olive oil and sprinkle over some stock, enough to just cover the base of the dish. Loosely cover the dish with foil or baking parchment and place it in an oven at 190°C/375°F for 20 minutes, then remove the cover and cook for five minutes more.

Thai cabbage and onion soup with coconut, lime and coriander

This is about as basic as it gets, really: cabbage and onion soup. Every culture that has a cabbage or two has a cabbage soup. Whether a bread-thickened stew from the Mediterranean or a thin, spiced broth stretching a few leaves into a meal, cabbage soup is usually a way to feed whatever number of stomachs are present with the cheapest, possibly only, ingredients to hand. Food from the last ingredients in the kitchen or the only ones in the garden. You could say that, if you don't have some cabbage and onions left in the kitchen, then you're in bad shape. Well, you could, except that with the familiar becoming increasingly unfashionable you are now very likely to find a kitchen without cabbage while still well stocked with out-of-season asparagus and the ubiquitous broccoli. We are indeed out of sorts.

I called this a 'Thai' soup when I first put it on the Café Paradiso menu. Thai food was very fashionable, and still is. The word 'Thai' on a menu suggests certain flavours – coconut, citrus, chillies and fresh coriander being some – so the customers weren't disappointed; in fact, there was one who needed to be contacted when the soup was made. But the recipe is not derived from any authentic source, nor is it inspired by a dish eaten or seen. I mean that it is 'Thai' only in the widest sense; it is cooking in the general area of a style, not an attempt at authenticity. This brings together two potentially contradictory aspects of how I like to cook: working with local produce in its best season, and using flavours, methods and styles from all over the world. The second is a very common phenomenon these days; combining it with the first can bring out surprising characteristics in familiar ingredients, even give them a new lease of life. To me, this seems like much more fun than chasing down authentic ingredients to duplicate dishes out of context.

The onion and cabbage in the soup are cooked until just tender and the broth is heavily spiced and sweet, making the dish quite refreshing and invigorating. This freshness, by the way, makes it difficult to maintain on a restaurant menu because making a large batch (and restaurants love to make large vats of soup) will give you refreshing soup for an hour and stodgy soup for a day or two. Serve it fresh. Any leftovers will be fine tomorrow as a more comforting soup – try adding some beans, noodles or rice to make a substantial lunch of it.

FOR FOUR:

500g white onions
250g savoy cabbage
2–4 fresh green chillies
olive oil
4 cloves garlic, sliced
4cm piece ginger, finely chopped
1 tablespoon coriander seeds, ground
800mls vegetable stock (see page 276)
400mls coconut milk
1 bunch fresh coriander, chopped
large pinch salt
1 lime

Chop the onions in half, then into thin slices. Shred the cabbage leaves into similar slices. Slice the chillies into thin rounds.

Heat a little oil in a large pan, put in the onion and cabbage together and cook them over medium heat for three minutes before adding the chillies, garlic, ginger and coriander seeds. Continue cooking for about 15 minutes, stirring often, until the onion and cabbage are tender but not soft. Bring the stock to a boil in a separate pan, then add it to the vegetables and simmer for five minutes.

Add the coconut milk, half the fresh coriander, and a large pinch of salt, and bring the soup back to the boil.

Serve the soup in deep bowls with a scattering of extra coriander leaves and a generous sprinkling of lime juice.

Braised cabbage with fennel, tomato and chickpeas

Cabbage has historically been boiled, and well boiled at that, until the house took on and gave out the horrid smell. Digby Law, in his *Vegetable Book*, recommends to those who 'insist on boiling the hell out of cabbage' that adding a slice of bread soaks up the smell, almost accepting that it was a cultural battle that could never be won. How things change – now it would be easier to find someone to admit to having ever voted for Margaret Thatcher than to being a practising cabbage-boiler. We're all stir-frying and wilting these days. Me included. But, hey, here is a way to get lovely, soft buttery cabbage without stinking the house out. You can use any green cabbage. The recipe came about on one of those evenings when the only certainties for dinner were that it would involve cabbage and that there would probably be more people than currently present in the kitchen. To buy time, I started cooking the cabbage while trying to think of what to do next. I'm a very slow thinker in a domestic kitchen; in fact, Bridget usually has to give me clues like peeled potatoes and cracked eggs, or some spring roll pastry and a few carrots left on the bench. The cabbage was compulsory because it was my son Oscar's pride and joy – on a visit to the country that afternoon he had climbed a ditch and traipsed through a few rows of turnips to pick it out of a farmer's field with the permission of the farmer's next-door neighbour. Nice neighbours, eh? It wasn't the kind of cabbage I would usually give much attention to – a few huge tough green leaves wrapped around a tight head of smooth crisp leaves, which were a very pale green. Half an hour of cooking showed it to be sweet and delicious. We ate it with mashed potatoes, egg frittata and boiled turnips – yes, Oscar had also secured a huge turnip from the same field.

In dishes like this, which call for a small quantity of chickpeas, it is invariably too late to start cooking dried chickpeas, unless you are practised with a pressure cooker. I usually use tinned ones; it's a good idea to keep a few tins of organic chickpeas in the cupboard.

FOR FOUR:

300g cabbage

1 onion

1 small bulb fennel

2 tablespoons olive oil

2 tomatoes

4 tablespoons cooked chickpeas

100mls white wine

2 tablespoons butter

salt and pepper, to season

Quarter the cabbage and cut the core from the pieces you are using. Wrap any cabbage not being used in paper and keep it in the fridge or any cool place. Chop the cabbage into slices about 1cm thick. Chop the onion in half and then into slices half as thick as the cabbage. Halve the fennel bulb and slice it as thickly as the onion, discarding any stringy parts and the core.

Heat two tablespoons of olive oil in a large wide pan, and toss in the cabbage, onion and fennel. Cook over a medium heat, stirring often, for five minutes or more until the vegetables have softened a little. Chop the tomatoes into large dice and add them to the pan with the chickpeas and the wine. When everything is hot and bubbling again, turn the heat down to low, cover the pan and simmer for 20 minutes. Lift the lid occasionally to check that the vegetables aren't sticking, and add a splash of water or stock if necessary. Season well with salt and pepper before serving.

Wilted kale with garlic, puy lentils and thyme

Kale – common curly kale – is the king of winter greens, higher in my estimation even than savoy cabbage. Through the cold months I use kale in the way that I would ordinarily use spinach – in gratins, crêpes, pastries and so on. My favourite recipe of autumn and early winter is a gratin of gingered kale and pumpkin (from *The Café Paradiso Cookbook.*)

Mostly, however, I like to just wilt some kale in olive oil. There are a number of ways to dress up the basic model of wilted greens. Among my favourites are adding chickpeas, lemon and cumin, or a few tablespoons of cooked wild rice and red onions. In this recipe the kale uses the lentils as a flavouring, along with garlic and thyme, rather than a dish of lentils with some greens stirred in. Puy lentils are certainly substantial enough to be the main element of a dish but they are also intense enough in flavour to be a supporting element. This characteristic also makes them good scattered through pasta dishes, around risotto and in salsas.

FOR FOUR:

2 tablespoons puy lentils

2 tablespoons olive oil

1 onion, thinly sliced

4 cloves garlic, thinly sliced

2 large handfuls kale, roughly chopped

2 tomatoes, diced

2 small sprigs of thyme, leaves only

salt and pepper, to season

Boil the puy lentils in plenty of boiling water until just tender (about 12 minutes).

Heat a tablespoon of olive oil in a wide pan and cook the onion for one minute over medium heat. Add the garlic and kale, increase the heat and cook for two minutes until the kale has wilted and turned a dark glossy green. Add the tomatoes to the pan with the cooked lentils and the thyme. Continue cooking, stirring often and adding a splash of water occasionally, until the tomatoes are soft and the kale is tender. Add another tablespoon of olive oil at the end, along with salt and pepper to season.

Brussels sprouts with tomato, ginger and coriander

To many of us, Brussels sprouts are known only as neat little net sacks of vegetables on shop shelves at Christmas time. If only we could see them as the extraordinary vegetables they are: tight mini-cabbages sprouting along a tall brassica stalk with rampant greens at the top, like a cabbage gone crazy. I recently saw sprouts for sale at an American city market, the entire two-foot-long stalks laid out on trestle tables. They were so beautiful and striking that all passing shoppers and tourists were drawn to them, and you would think it was indeed a rare and exotic luxury that was for sale. I watched the sprouts sell like hot cakes and you can be sure they were lovingly cooked that evening, treated as the wonderful vegetables they are.

Brussels sprouts are available for a much longer season than the two weeks of glory usually granted them, but they are hopelessly linked with the annual feast. Any vegetarian who puts his head over the parapet – or indeed people of minority religions and those who go for solitary walks on 25 December – will be asked once or twice what he or she will be eating for Christmas dinner while the 'rest of us' are dining on tradition and nostalgia. Suggesting that Brussels sprouts are a pleasure can cause a mixture of rage and pity.

They divide people into lovers and haters as only fiercely individual vegetables can, and the lovers are further divided into those who like their sprouts cooked soft and those who like them crunchy. I take no sides here: I like them boiled soft or firm, puréed, fried, spiced and cold from the fridge at 3am. Whatever one's personal preference, it is undeniable that such a strongly flavoured vegetable can tolerate more robust cooking than plain boiling. Like most cabbages, sprouts are great with tomatoes, ginger and soy sauce. So this recipe is really nothing like as shocking as it might seem to annual sprout-boilers. Excellent as a side dish, it can also be made into a pilaf by adding some cooked rice, fresh coriander and maybe some toasted cashews.

FOR FOUR:

400g Brussels sprouts

4 tomatoes

1 tablespoon olive oil

1 red onion, thinly sliced

2 cloves garlic, thinly sliced

1 fresh chilli, thinly sliced

1 tablespoon coriander seeds, crushed

1 tablespoon fresh ginger, sliced

1 tablespoon soy sauce

Peel the outer leaves from the sprouts and slice the larger ones in half. Bring a pot of water to a boil and drop the sprouts in for just half a minute before removing them again.

Chop the tomatoes in half, then into thickish slices.

Heat a tablespoon of olive oil in a wide pan and add the sprouts and the red onion. Cook over a medium-high heat for two minutes, stirring, before adding the garlic, chilli, coriander and ginger. After another two minutes, add the tomatoes and soy sauce, and cook on a medium heat for five minutes more. Add a splash of water if the dish seems to be drying out – it should be moist when finished.

Vanilla-poached pears with cinnamon ice cream

I love the quote from Edward Bunyard in Alan Davidson's *Companion to Food* that, while it is the 'duty of an apple to be crisp and crunchable, a pear should have such a texture as leads to silent consumption'. Mind you, eating a very ripe and juicy pear can be a cacophony of slurping and sloshing, so either he is referring to a firm pear or he had very refined eating manners. More than apples, pears last well into the winter because they can be picked a little under-ripe and left to ripen in a cool place. Pears that are ripe but firm are perfect for poaching, in that they hold their shape and colour while absorbing the flavours of the poaching liquid. There are a few timeless flavours that complement pears, and vanilla and cinnamon are two of the best. Chocolate is almost universally accepted as another, though the case doesn't seem to be completely closed on that one yet. If you like chocolate with pears, a thin chocolate sauce would go very well with this dessert.

FOR FOUR:

FOR THE PEARS:
600g sugar
800mls water
2 vanilla pods
6 pears

Bring the sugar, water and vanilla pods to a boil in a small deep pan. Peel the pears and put them into the syrup. Simmer very gently for 20 or 30 minutes until the pears are just tender, then leave them to cool in the syrup. Serve at room temperature, with the cinnamon ice cream.

FOR THE ICE CREAM:
300mls milk
2 cinnamon sticks
3 egg yolks
140g light muscovado sugar
300mls cream

Put the milk and cinnamon sticks in a pan and heat slowly, almost to boiling. Whisk the egg yolks and sugar together until they are pale and thick. Pour the warm milk through a sieve into the sugar and egg, still whisking. Return this custard to the pan and heat gently until thickened a little. Strain this through a sieve into a bowl and leave it to cool. Add the cream and freeze in an ice cream machine.

Roasted roots and some uses for them

Although not a new idea, roasting roots has become very common and popular in the last decade or so. And for good reason, because the roasting transforms what are often perceived to be dull vegetables into sweet treats. It's not magic, rather that cooking by roasting draws out the natural sweetness of vegetables, and roots contain quite a bit of sugar, especially carrots and parsnips, but turnips too. Celeriac and salsify are relatively low in sugar and don't benefit much from roasting, though they can be worth including in a mix of roots for their distinctive flavours. Beetroots are, of course, very sweet and roast beautifully, but should always be cooked separately if you want to avoid a purple mess. While one type of root alone makes a nice roast, I think a pair is a little more interesting, and the best combination is the classic trio of carrots, parsnips and turnips. That last is the large yellow-fleshed turnip sometimes called a swede, as distinct from the little white summer turnips beloved of many restaurants. I don't understand the fuss about those at all, and have never found anything useful or tasty to do with them that couldn't be achieved by sucking on a golf ball. The swede turnip, or simply 'turnip' as it shall be called from here on, can have a wonderfully rich, sweet flavour. The colour of the flesh is a good indicator of quality, much as is the case with pumpkins: the yellower and denser the flesh, the better the flavour will be.

One evening in the Paradiso kitchen we tried, as an experiment, eating that other great root of the Irish countryside, the sugar beet. It was a quiet night and these little games get us through. We boiled a few slices and roasted some chunks, then gathered round sheepishly. It was one of the vilest things I've ever tasted, a nauseating combination of a kind of sickly sweetness, an earthiness that seemed to be from very deep down in a filthy field and a quality that I can only call oldness; it was like eating something from thousands of years ago. The taste, even from a small bite, wouldn't go away all evening and I suspect the memory never will.

You can roast roots in olive oil, clarified butter (see page 60) or a combination, as I like to do, simply because I like the taste of both butter and olive oil on roots. Garlic is excellent with roots, as are some herbs (the hardier ones such as rosemary, thyme or sage). Some red onion is good too, especially if you are going to use the roots in a pilaf or stew later (see below).

Although you can roast roots from raw, I think this can dry them out too much, so I like to boil them for a minute or two first. That way you get a crisp outside and a moist inside. To cook similar-sized pieces of different roots, it's a good idea to boil the longer-cooking roots for a few minutes more than the others and then roast them all together.

You will get the perfect balance of sweetness if the roots are roasted until the outsides begin to caramelise – beyond this point, the roots can easily burn and become bitter instead of sweet.

1kg roots (carrots, parsnips, turnips)

1 head garlic

4 sprigs rosemary, thyme or sage

Peel the roots, chopping medium-sized carrots and parsnips in half and bigger ones into large pieces. Chop the turnip into pieces of a similar size to the other roots. Bring a pot of water to a boil and drop in the turnip pieces to cook for two minutes before adding the carrots. Cook for one minute more, then add the parsnips and cook another minute. Drain the vegetables and toss them in an oven dish in just enough olive oil and/or clarified butter to coat them. Be careful not to use too much or the vegetables may fry instead of roasting. Peel the garlic cloves and toss them with the herbs through the vegetables. Roast the roots in a hot oven, about 200°C/400°F, for 30 minutes or so, until the roots are beginning to caramelise on the outside and are tender inside. Turn the roots a few times during the cooking.

Couscous pilaf

Fry some sliced red onion and chillies, cumin and fennel seeds in a generous amount of olive oil and add them to the roasted roots, with some soaked couscous, just less than the volume of roots. Serve the pilaf with fresh coriander scattered over and some accompaniments such as marinated feta, spiced chickpeas, toasted almonds, green beans with tomato and herbs, deep-fried felafel or other fritters.

Roasted roots gratin

Chop the roots into smallish dice rather than large pieces and use them instead of pumpkin in the recipe on page 189.

Roasted roots soup

Cook some onions until soft; add the roasted roots, a little chopped potato and some stock. Cook until the potato is soft, then purée the soup. Serve quite thick with some soured cream or yoghurt swirled on top.

Roasted roots mash

Mashed roots is a favourite food from my childhood, so it was inevitable that I would eventually try mashing some roasted roots. It's wonderful, but be careful not to roast the vegetables too much or their outsides will be too tough to mash. Boil about a quarter as much potato as you have roasted roots and mash it with plenty of butter. Blend the roots in a food processor, in short pulses, until the roots are very finely chopped but just short of puréed. Transfer them to a pot, stir in the potato and reheat to serve.

Coconut curry of roasted roots

Make a simple curry sauce by putting equal quantities of cream and coconut milk in a pan with some toasted and ground cumin, coriander and fennel seeds, turmeric, sliced green chillies and the rind of a lime. Heat gently and simmer for a few minutes until the sauce is slightly thickened, then add the roasted roots and some fresh coriander.

Risotto of parsnip, salsify and sage with beetroot crisps

When I first got a supply of salsify a few years ago, I thought I was in roots heaven, pleased with myself for having access to large quantities of an obscure root, a small team of cooks to prepare the things and time to play with ways to cook it. I enjoyed being generous with it. By all accounts, it's not easy to grow and it needs a good depth of soil to accommodate its length, which can be up to 40cm or more. In the stony soil of most of Ireland that would guarantee you some pretty weird, gnarly shapes, but in parts of Europe it thrives. It is hell to prepare too: it must be peeled without washing, preferably over an expanse of old newspapers, and quickly immersed in water with lemon juice added to prevent discolouring. No matter how fast you go, it makes a fierce mess and gives off a sticky sap that causes all the loose dirt from the outer skin to stick to your hands and the lovely creamy inner flesh that you're trying to keep from discolouring. Or so the boys tell me – I avoid the chore if I can. However, I still admire salsify's unique, subtle flavour and the vegetable's admirable persistence in surviving in these times of convenience when awkward species are dying off at an alarming rate. I have learned to buy small quantities of salsify and to use it sparingly, as in this risotto, where it is paired with parsnip, another root with a fine individual character.

Roast parsnip is delicious in risotto but salsify doesn't roast well, so rather than cook the roots in two different ways, we compromise and fry them together in butter until lightly browned.

Beetroot crisps are delicious and fun, both to make and to eat. Because the crisps shrink a bit in the cooking, you need a fine big beet to cut slices off, and you will probably need a mandolin slicer to cut uniformly thin slices. The ideal thickness is the second thinnest setting on the mandolin, which I'm afraid I can't translate into millimetres. The slices need to be kept separate from each other in the fryer, and if you do this quite busily you will get some lovely chaotically curved crisps. The crisps will keep for a few days in a tightly sealed container.

FOR FOUR:

FOR THE CRISPS:
1 large beetroot
salt and pepper, to season

Slice the beetroot into very thin slices, as large as possible, using a mandolin slicer if you've got one. Heat a deep fryer to 170°C/340°F and put in a batch of the beetroot slices. Stir frequently to encourage even cooking and prevent sticking, until the oil becomes calm and the beetroot appears cooked. Tip out the slices on to kitchen paper, season with salt and pepper and leave them in a warm part of the kitchen to become crisp.

FOR THE ROOTS:
200g salsify
juice of half a lemon
200g parsnip
1 medium leek
1 tablespoon butter
1 tablespoon olive oil
4 cloves garlic, chopped
6–8 sage leaves

Peel the salsify with a vegetable peeler and drop the pieces into cold water with lemon juice added to prevent discolouring. Peel the parsnips, chop out and discard the core. Chop the flesh of both roots into small pieces. Bring a pot of water to a boil and cook the parsnip until almost tender, then remove it and cook the salsify to the same stage.

While the risotto is cooking (see below), wash and chop the leek. Melt a tablespoon of butter and a tablespoon of olive oil in a pan and cook the salsify, parsnip, leek and garlic over moderate heat for ten minutes, stirring often. Tear the sage leaves, add them to the pan and cook for a few minutes more until the roots are tender and lightly coloured.

FOR THE RISOTTO:

1200mls vegetable stock (see page 276)

60g butter

60mls olive oil

320g risotto rice, such as arborio or carnaroli

120mls dry white wine

60g Parmesan, grated

Bring the stock to a boil in a pot and keep it at a very low simmer. Meanwhile, melt one tablespoon of the butter with one tablespoon of the olive oil, and toast the rice in it for eight to ten minutes, stirring often. Pour in the wine, bring it to a boil quickly, then simmer until the wine is absorbed. Now add a ladle or cup of the stock, about 150mls, and continue to simmer, stirring often until that is all but absorbed. Add another cup of stock, and carry on absorbing, stirring and adding stock until the rice is almost cooked. Take care that the stock going into the rice pot is at a boil and so not interrupting the cooking of the rice. Test individual grains – the rice

should be cooked through but firm, while the stock has become a little creamy and is almost completely absorbed.

When the risotto reaches this stage, stir in the cooked roots and leek, take the risotto off the heat and stir in the remaining butter and olive oil, and the grated Parmesan. Add a little stock to the pan that the roots were cooked in and bring it to a boil. Serve the risotto with these pan juices poured over each portion, some beetroot crisps on the side and some more Parmesan to sprinkle or shave on to the risotto.

Carrot and chestnut cannelloni with watercress cream

Like most people, we use carrots all year round. Carrots go into stocks and soups, in the Monday-night stir-fries when you can't decide whose turn it is to cook, in fritters for the children, and in pasta dishes when pasta is only an excuse to make them eat all the vegetables in the fridge. And carrots are the best all-round multi-purpose side dish: a bowl of cooked carrots, however dressed, will be welcome on any table, no matter what the main dish. Some people will swear that carrots are best eaten raw and no amount of cooking will improve on that. Others insist that only baby carrots are worth any special attention, and they certainly do make a lovely sweet contribution to salads and other dishes in the summer. But when I want carrots that really taste intensely of that sweet and rich flavour of carrot, I look for the really big ones with a deep orange colour. Carrots grown to maturity in comfortably yielding soil. Some vegetables seem very Catholic in their need for a bit of stress and hardship in their lives; they may like a touch of frost or thin, undernourished soil. Not carrots. Carrots are guilt-free hedonists and thrive only if you pamper and pleasure them.

This cannelloni recipe is not the classic way of making the famous pasta dish. Instead of baking the filled tubes in a sauce, the cannelloni are only heated through in the oven as they are already warm inside and out, and the sauce is added on the plate.

When buying chestnuts, try to ensure they are fresh and in good condition. Not only will they taste better, but they will also peel more easily which is no small matter.

500g carrots
1 tablespoon butter
1 small onion, chopped
3 cloves garlic
2 sprigs thyme, leaves only
120g fresh chestnuts
80g cream cheese
salt and pepper, to season

80g watercress
olive oil
200mls cream
20g Parmesan, finely grated

100cm sheet of fresh pasta, 10–12cm wide

Peel the carrots, chop them into chunks and put them into a pan with the butter, onion, garlic and thyme leaves, and enough stock or water to almost cover the carrots. Bring this to a boil, cover and simmer for 20 minutes or so until the carrots are tender. Remove the lid and boil off any liquid remaining. Put everything from the pan into a food processor and blend in short bursts to get a coarse mash.

Peel the chestnuts and boil or roast them until tender. Break or chop the cooked chestnuts into small pieces; crumble the cream cheese and stir both into the carrot. Season with salt and pepper.

Put the watercress in the food processor with a tablespoon of olive oil and blend to a smooth purée, adding a few tablespoons of water if necessary. Put the purée in a pan with the cream and Parmesan and, just before you serve the cannelloni, simmer the sauce for one minute. Season with salt and pepper.

Slice the pasta into pieces 10cm long and cook them in boiling water for a few minutes until tender. While the pasta is cooking, warm the carrot filling in a pan over low heat.

Drop the cooked pasta sheets into a bowl of cold water for a few seconds to cool them just enough to handle, then remove them to another bowl and toss them in a little olive oil. Place a few sheets on your worktop and put a heaped tablespoon of carrot filling on each. Roll the pasta around the carrot filling to form well-packed tubes. Place the filled tubes in an oven dish brushed with olive oil. Brush the tubes with more olive oil and sprinkle them with a few tablespoons of hot stock or water. Cover the dish loosely with foil and put it in the oven at 160°C/320°F, for ten minutes or so until the cannelloni are warmed through.

Heat the watercress cream. Serve the cannelloni with the watercress cream poured over.

Carrot and cabbage spring rolls with a pomegranate, mint and yoghurt sauce

First, I must admit that I changed the sauce in this recipe while reading Diana Henry's book, *Crazy Water, Pickled Lemons,* during the late stages of finishing the text of this book. Good thing it didn't come out sooner because I think, if I had read it earlier, there would have been pomegranates and all sorts of other exotic fruits, scents and flavours all over my recipes. It's a very inspiring book – if you haven't got it, go straight back to the shop and get a copy.

Carrots and cabbage are surely at the other end of the scale of exotica from pomegranates, but they make great spring rolls. Texture is equally important as taste in a spring roll, so to keep the filling crisp the vegetables are sliced very thinly and hardly cooked at all. I use the inner heart of savoy or a smooth green cabbage.

This is another recipe that needs fine big richly flavoured carrots to carry the spicing in the dish. The flavours are a variation on what I think of as North African spicing – a combination of hot, sweet and aromatic spices.

1 large onion

4 cloves garlic

400g carrots

100g cabbage, white or the heart of green cabbage

1 tablespoon olive oil

2 teaspoons black mustard seeds

4 bird's eye chillies, ground

1 teaspoon fennel seeds, ground

2 teaspoons cumin seeds, ground

large pinch cinnamon

large pinch nutmeg

rind of 1 orange

salt, to season

8 large spring roll pastry sheets

2 cloves garlic

1 handful mint leaves

400mls thick yoghurt

1 pomegranate

Chop the onion and garlic into very thin slices. Peel the carrots and grate them on the widest grater blade. Chop the cabbage into very thin slices.

Heat a tablespoon of olive oil in a large pan, and cook the onion and garlic for one minute. Add the spices and cook for one minute more, then add the carrot, cabbage and orange rind. Cook one more minute, stirring to combine everything, then immediately remove the pan from the heat. Season with salt.

Lay a spring roll sheet on a work surface, with a corner pointing towards you. About 4cm up from the bottom point, spread a heaped tablespoon of the filling into a 12–15cm-long shape. Fold the bottom point of the pastry over the filling and roll the pastry up tightly until just past the widest points in the middle. Fold the sides in, brush the remaining edges lightly with water and continue rolling the pastry to the end. Repeat this process with the rest of the pastry sheets.

To make the sauce, crush the garlic, chop the mint leaves and stir both into the yoghurt. Slice the pomegranate in half horizontally and use a teaspoon to scoop the seeds into a bowl. Stir four tablespoons of the seeds and their juice into the yoghurt sauce.

In a large frying pan, heat 2cm of oil to a medium temperature. Fry the spring rolls in the oil, turning once, until the pastry is crisp and lightly browned.

Serve the spring rolls with the yoghurt sauce, either as a dip or poured over the rolls.

Beetroot soup with cabbage and vodka

Big stored winter beetroots aren't best suited to roasting individually, so I tend to make them into dishes that use puréed, mashed, grated or chopped beetroot. The beetroot mousse in *The Café Paradiso Cookbook* is the one I love most, and it still greatly amuses diners in the restaurant. Beetroot also makes great risotto that looks shocking, in the best sense, and tastes wonderful. *The Paradiso Cookbook* also had a recipe for a chilled summer beetroot soup, and in a way this is a winter cousin of that recipe. Where the chilled soup had cucumber and soured cream, this robust winter version has fried cabbage and vodka for a warming kick. The vodka element I took from a beautiful meal served in the now-defunct Stepping Stone restaurant in Kerry. This was no delicate drizzle of alcohol over the soup, it was more like someone had formed a shot glass in the thick soup and poured in a generous measure of vodka – good vodka too. The effect is like having your aperitif and starter at the same time. Conversation moves along at a lively hop after that.

FOR SIX TO EIGHT:

800g beetroot

3 onions

6 cloves garlic

half a bulb of fennel or 1 stick celery

olive oil

100g potato

1500mls vegetable stock (see page 276)

1 tablespoon fresh dill, fennel or lovage

large pinch cayenne pepper

1 tablespoon balsamic vinegar

salt and pepper, to season

2 leaves savoy cabbage

vodka, to serve

cream or soured cream, to serve

Cook the beetroot in boiling water until tender, then peel under cold running water and chop coarsely.

Meanwhile, chop the onions, garlic and fennel or celery, heat some olive oil in a pot, and cook them until the onions are soft. Chop the potato and add it to the onions along with the beetroot, the stock and your chosen herb. Bring this to a boil and simmer, covered for thirty minutes or so until the potato breaks down. Add the cayenne pepper and balsamic vinegar, and simmer for one minute more. Blend the soup to a smooth purée, season well with salt and pepper, and reheat to serve.

Chop the cabbage into short, thin slices and fry them in olive oil over medium heat for a few minutes, until the cabbage is tender but not quite soft.

Pour the soup into bowls and place a little cabbage sitting in the centre on top of each. Put a teaspoon or two of vodka into each soup, in just one or two places rather than scattered thinly. Finally, if you like, drizzle a little cream or soured cream over the soup.

Potatoes

Potatoes… mmm… if I start on potatoes I might go on forever. Indeed, I wouldn't be the first. There are a few wonderful books written about potatoes, most notably *The Potato: How the Humble Spud Rescued the Western World* by Larry Zuckerman, which traces the history of the potato and the social effects of its rise from a mistrusted, potentially poisonous fodder to the staple of so many countries and cultures. He is brilliant on Ireland and the potato's role in the social structures before, during and after the famines of the nineteenth century. The potato is still a very loaded symbol in Ireland, and our relationship with it a little uneasy. Oh, we love our spuds, no doubt about that, especially those who are comfortable with being of rural stock. But we are also naturally uncomfortable with the idea of being dependent on potatoes. As a modern, wealthy and almost-civilised nation, we are pleased to have replaced potatoes with other less volatile staples like pasta. With good reason. It is well documented that the potato is a near-perfect food, capable of maintaining life for longer than any other crop. The awful irony, the awful shortcoming, of the potato as a near-perfect staple food is that it is great for only 10 or 11 months. The stress caused by the fear that the stock won't last the full year would make anyone want to liberate themselves from dependency. It's a miracle that, having loosened the potato's grip, our love for them survives. Now we eat them purely for pleasure.

The pattern of dinner in my childhood was for everyone to scoff, first, and in a cursory manner, the protein (with sauce on Fridays and Sundays), then the vegetables (carrots, turnips, parsnips and cabbage), and then to devote serious attention to the potatoes, taking first two from the piled plate in the centre of the table, followed by one more at a time, up to seven or eight, until the spuds were all gone. The condition of the protein might be acknowledged, but the potatoes would be discussed in great detail: their age, how they were holding up, their flouriness, size, dirtiness, availability and their anticipated storage life; the character of the man who dug and sold them would be admired or castigated. To this day my mother asks where I get my spuds from, never where I get the artichokes, pumpkins or asparagus.

There was only one ideal potato then: large, floury and unblemished, cheap, local and of guaranteed supply. Only rarely would we hit a vein of such perfection, of course, but the search was eternal and absorbing. Now we seem to need a lot of different potatoes, depending on whether they are to be used in mash or salads, steamed or roasted, in gratins, fried cakes or tortilla. I can't always remember the names of the ones I want. So I end up asking for things like 'some more of those fat, thin-skinned, medium-floury ones I used for tortilla last year'. It is the mark of a good wholesaler to be able to translate such vague gibberish into top-class vegetable delivery. Now then, there I am discussing the character of the potato man! Some things never change, and we become our mothers even against our steely determination.

There are so many potatoes out there at any one time – old reliables and new hybrids – and they all have their time and their dish. There is no point in trying to mash potatoes with little starch and we've all met those delicatessen potato salads made with mashing potatoes – comfort food gone too far west, I think. Until someone comes up with a scale identifying the starch content of different potatoes, we will have to go on learning by practice: the daily, weekly and seasonal routines. Try to learn about the potatoes available in your area. From what is available locally

to you, decide what is good for salad, baking, mashing and so on. Ask about variety names and remember them. All that I can do here is tell you the ones I use, but there is little point in me insisting on potato varieties you can't get. You may well already have access to perfectly good potatoes and you don't need me to tell you to switch allegiance.

I recently came across a new variety, ancient but new to me – 'pink fir apples'. I thought they were extraordinary, richly flavoured dense and heavy, yet firm in texture. Others weren't so keen, including the grower who says they're too much trouble for the yield. Almost half those who tried them said that they were "alright", an Irish euphemism for "don't do that again" – as in reply to "how was that?" "Alright".

Potato, sweet onion and basil tortilla with green chilli aioli

For tortilla, you need what the Spaniards consider a floury potato, but which is in reality about halfway on the virtual scale of flouriness, maybe a bit more. It must be just firm enough to hold its shape while frying, while leaking enough starch to make a cake of the tortilla rather than an omelette with potatoes in it. In my tiny enclave, I find Rooster and Nicola perfect for tortilla. If these names mean nothing to you, you want a potato that makes decent but slightly wet and disappointing mash – I'm sure you've come across those!

This tortilla recipe is for a very large heavy frying pan, with a 24cm base and shallow, sloped sides. It will feed six to eight people as a meal and even more as a snack or finger food. I like to serve it with some greens in tomato sauce, or the aubergine relish on page 162, but as a snack I like to eat it with aioli, all the better if it's spiced like this green chilli one. When Bridget turns up her nose at eating an egg dish with eggy sauce, I remind her of the classic egg mayonnaise, a dish that only went downhill when people started to make it from crappy eggs and cheap factory mayonnaise.

FOR FOUR:

FOR THE TORTILLA:

3 large white onions

olive oil

1kg potatoes, such as roosters or Nicola

12 eggs

large handful basil leaves

salt and pepper, to season

Chop the onions in half, then into thin slices. Heat two tablespoons of olive oil in a pan and cook the onion at a moderate temperature for half an hour or so, until it is very soft and sweet but not browned.

Meanwhile, peel the potatoes and chop them into thin chips – classic Belgian chips, that is. Heat a 2cm depth of olive oil in a large frying pan, and cook the potato chips at a fairly high temperature, stirring often to keep them separate, until the potato is cooked through and lightly coloured. At the same time, beat the eggs well, tear the basil leaves and add them to the eggs. Drain the potatoes, saving the oil to use again. Add both the potatoes and onions to the eggs while they are still hot, stirring them in quickly. This will help the egg to start cooking, making it easier to cook through to the centre of the tortilla.

Season very well with salt and pepper.

Quickly wipe the pan clean, brush it lightly with olive oil and set it over a low wide heat. Tip in the tortilla mix. Smooth down the edges quickly, then leave the tortilla to cook slowly. In ten minutes, run a spatula under the edges of the tortilla to loosen it. Slide the tortilla on to a large plate, invert the pan over it and flip it over. If you like, you can firm up the top of the tortilla a little by putting the pan under a grill before turning. Put the pan back on the heat and leave it to cook for five minutes more. The tortilla should be firm to the touch. Turn off the heat and leave the pan where it is for five minutes more.

Slide the tortilla on to a plate before cutting it into wedges. Serve it warm or at room temperature.

FOR THE AIOLI:

5 cloves garlic

1 or 2 mild fresh green chillies

1 egg

1 teaspoon smooth mustard

250mls olive oil

salt, to season

squeeze of lemon juice

Roast the garlic cloves in a low oven until soft, then squeeze the garlic from its skin. Chop the chillies and put them into a food processor with the garlic, the egg and mustard. Blend for a minute, then slowly pour in the olive oil in a thin stream, until the aioli thickens. If it becomes too thick for your liking, dilute with a few drops of hot water. Season with salt, and a squeeze of lemon juice to your taste.

Celeriac, leek and potato gratin with capers and thyme

When our family is in need of calming comfort food, Bridget cooks and I keep my advice to myself. This recipe is a variation on one of her classics: potato, leeks and garlic baked slowly in cream. Changing the focus from potatoes to celeriac makes the dish more interesting, possibly a little less like comfort food. Celeriac has a very upfront flavour, very much that of celery, as its name suggests, with a touch of the earthiness inevitable in roots. Try to buy medium-sized ones of about 600–800g. Because celeriac can be a bit gnarly, and peeling them involves slicing off the skin and roots, the smaller ones give a very poor yield; much larger celeriac can often be overblown and have a hollow centre.

Celeriac is quite a versatile root, making wonderful soup and fritters, recipes for both of which I included in *The Café Paradiso Cookbook*. The combination in this gratin recipe of potato and celeriac also makes great mash, though celeriac doesn't have enough starch to make mash on its own. The best way to make potato and celeriac mash is to make potato mash in the usual way and then to add celeriac that has been puréed in a food processor.

1 medium celeriac

600g potatoes (Nicola, Roosters or similar)

2 medium leeks

10 cloves garlic

3 sprigs thyme, leaves only

100mls white wine

2 tablespoons small capers

butter

salt and pepper, to season

300mls cream

Use a knife to slice the skin off the celeriac, then chop it into slices 5mm thick. Cook the slices in boiling water for three minutes. Wash the potatoes, slice them to the same thickness and cook them for three minutes too. Peel the potatoes only if the skin doesn't appeal to you.

Slice the leeks in half lengthways, wash them and chop them into slices about 2cm thick. Slice the garlic. Melt a tablespoon of butter in a pan and cook the leeks, garlic and thyme for five minutes over a fairly high heat. Pour in the wine and cook on high for one minute more. Off the heat stir in the capers.

Heat the oven to 170°C/325°F. Butter an oven dish and line the base with overlapping celeriac and potato slices. Season with salt and pepper, then cover with a thin layer of leeks, then another of celeriac and potato; repeat until the vegetables are all used up. Pour over the cream and press down gently on the vegetables. Bake for 30 to 40 minutes until the roots are tender.

Grilled potato and kale gnocchi in a hazelnut and rosemary cream

Potatoes and kale are soulmates, though usually in much more robust combinations like colcannon or soup. It wasn't my idea to somehow get kale into tiny gnocchi, it was Johan's – so I left him to figure out how to do it. He did too, bless him. The crucial part is not to overcook the kale, to preserve its flavour; and then to squeeze the living daylights out of it so that it is not bringing water to the dough, which would make it tough. After that, keep a cool head and you'll get the most refined variation of potatoes and kale ever.

As always with gnocchi, you need the most floury, starchy potato you can get, bearing in mind that the flourier the potato, the less wheat flour you will need to make a dough, and the better your gnocchi will be. In Ireland, that probably means the old reliables like Kerr's pink, queens or golden wonders.

The sauce is a basic cream sauce flavoured with the lovely warming flavours of rosemary and hazelnuts. If you can get fresh hazelnuts, it will raise the sauce to a very classy level, but quality dried hazelnuts are always very good. The sauce is lovely with pasta too, especially long fresh strands like spaghetti or linguini.

FOR FOUR:

150g hazelnuts
2 tablespoons olive oil
300mls cream
2 sprigs rosemary
2 cloves garlic

600g floury potatoes
150g kale
120g Parmesan, grated
salt and pepper, to season
120g plain white flour

Roast the hazelnuts in a moderate oven for ten minutes, then place them in a tea towel and rub them to loosen the skins. Sieve out the skin and chop the nuts finely in a food processor. Add the olive oil and blend for a few seconds to get a paste. Put the cream in a pan with the whole rosemary sprigs and cloves of garlic, and bring it to a boil. Simmer for two minutes, then leave it to infuse for 15 or 20 minutes.

Peel and steam the potatoes, then gently mash the cooked potato flesh, or pass it through a sieve. Cook the kale in boiling water for five minutes, then cool it in cold water. Squeeze out all of the water and chop the kale very finely – it is best to do this in a food processor. Stir the kale into the potato mash, add 80g of the Parmesan, and season well with salt and pepper. Add the flour and quickly work it into the potato. If the dough feels like it's not too sticky to roll out, nick off a small piece, roll it into a ball and drop it into boiling water to test. If it holds its shape firmly, without falling apart or getting gloopy on the outside, it's fine – don't add any more flour to the dough. If in any doubt, add some flour and test again. When you've got a dough you trust, tear off a piece and use your hands to roll it into a long tubular shape,

about the thickness of your finger, and cut off pieces 2–3cm long. Drop the gnocchi into a large pot of boiling water, but don't over-crowd them – do a second batch if necessary.

The gnocchi are done when they float to the top. Remove the cooked gnocchi with a slotted spoon.

While the gnocchi are cooking, take the rosemary and garlic out of the cream you prepared earlier, whisk in the hazelnut paste and gently reheat the sauce, whisking all the time. Just before you serve, whisk in the remaining 40g of Parmesan and some salt and pepper. Place the gnocchi on four small plates, or one large one, drizzle the sauce over and cook them under a hot grill for a few minutes until the sauce bubbles.

Chocolate pecan pie, whiskey ice cream and darling clementines

Few people would see this dish as being an orange one. The chocolate pecan pie will push the buttons of chocolate lovers and the whiskey ice cream will complement the pie perfectly while raising a few eyebrows; and so the clementines must be a garnish, right? I don't do garnishes, so you will have to believe me when I say that we put the dish together the other way around, adding the ice cream and the tart to create an attractive package to entice people to buy the clementines. They, after all, are the one ingredient I bought enthusiastically from a man who himself bought them because he thought they were delicious and would be a pleasure to sell; they are in the height of their season and at their juicy best. Chocolate and ice cream I can sell any day, the things that I really deal in are vegetables and fruit. There are a few people who think I did the dish just to use the corny name. As if…

Any good sweet oranges are lovely poached in this way, but around the end of December we get wonderful organic clementines, a variety of tangerine, from Spain or North Africa, very sweet and with deep-orange flesh. When serving the clementines with other accompaniments, I would often use brandy instead of whiskey. However, it is not a token thing to write 'Irish' whiskey in the recipe. Irish whiskey is very smooth and clean, mainly due to the double and triple distilling, whereas American is very sweet and decent Scottish will give your oranges a taste of the bog – not a pleasant thought.

FOR FOUR:

FOR THE PIE:

175g light muscovado sugar

150g maple syrup

3 eggs

1 egg yolk

1 tablespoon cream

half teaspoon vanilla extract

70g dark chocolate

250g pecan halves

1 pastry case, blind-baked (as in the recipe on page 194)

Gently heat the sugar and maple syrup until dissolved. Boil for two minutes, then leave it to cool a little. Beat the eggs, egg yolk, cream and vanilla gently, then beat in the syrup mixture. Melt the chocolate and stir it in.

Roughly chop two-thirds of the pecans and scatter them over the base of the prepared pastry case. Pour the custard over and arrange the remaining pecans on top. Bake at 200°C/400°F for ten minutes, then at 175°C/340°F for 30 minutes until the centre is just set. Leave the tart to cool before slicing.

FOR THE ICE CREAM:

400mls milk

5 egg yolks

125g caster sugar

2 tablespoons Irish whiskey

200mls cream

Heat the milk until almost boiling. Whisk the egg yolk and sugar until the mixture is thick and pale. Pour the milk on to the egg and sugar while still whisking, then return this custard to the pan. Heat gently, stirring, until the custard has thickened a little. Stir in the whiskey and leave the custard to cool before adding the cream and freezing in an ice cream machine.

FOR THE CLEMENTINES:

12 clementines

500g sugar

500mls water

2 cinnamon sticks

2 tablespoons Irish whiskey

Peel the clementines, slice each one into three horizontal slices and put them in a bowl.

Heat the sugar, water, cinnamon and whiskey together until boiling, then simmer for three minutes. Pour this syrup over the clementines and leave them to cool to room temperature before serving.

Baked organic pineapple with rum and spices, a lime tuille and coconut ice cream

Pineapple is an extraordinary fruit. Think about it for a minute. Try to imagine having only ever seen apples and pears, an orange once in a fancy shop, and hedge berries. Now take your first pineapple into your hands. Press it. Smell it. Slice it open. Fainted yet? It's easy to forget that extraordinariness because pineapples are always there, propping up the supermarket shelves, fresh and canned, and it pops up in the most peculiar places, like on your pizza, for god's sake! Pineapple is one of those unfortunate fruits that can't ripen by even the tiniest degree after picking, which is the second reason we have been blinded to its qualities: most pineapples in shops are very ordinary because they have been picked too soon. They can't be picked too close to ripeness for export, so the matter of when to pick becomes something of a gamble. The safe and lazy way out is to pick too soon and to hell with the flavour.

To have any hope of regaining pineapple's magic, can I suggest that you eat them only when you find one of irresistible quality? You will eat less pineapple, but enjoy it to a degree otherwise not available to you. There are three things to look, or sense, for: the skin should be predominantly orange with no green; the pineapple should give off a sweet, aromatic smell of ripeness without a hint of fermentation; the central leaves at the top should slip out easily when pulled, showing as pale yellow in colour at their base. It's a good idea to buy organic pineapples, not only for the chemical safety of it but because the people who grow organically almost always hold the final quality of the fruit as a higher priority than other producers. This is true of all foods and is probably the real reason organic food is usually so much fresher and better in flavour. It is grown to be eaten, not stacked on shelves.

Pineapple is a tropical fruit and, therefore, not really seasonal. We use it in winter to brighten up the long dark days. This recipe is almost a caricature of the flavours of the West Indies, where Columbus first came across the fruit, what with the rum, coconut and spices. Try to imagine you're lying on a beach of white sand… Okay, these things can go too far… let it go.

FOR FOUR:

FOR THE PINEAPPLE:
100mls rum
100g butter
80g dark muscovado sugar
juice of 1 lemon
half a teaspoon each cinnamon, nutmeg, ginger
1 large pineapple

Put the rum, butter, sugar, lemon and spices in a pan and heat gently until they become a bubbling syrup. Peel the pineapple and chop the flesh into large slices 2cm thick. Place them in an oven dish and pour the syrup over. Bake in an oven at 180°C/350°F for 15 minutes.

FOR THE ICE CREAM:

400mls coconut milk

100mls milk

6 egg yolks

125g sugar

125mls cream

Bring the coconut milk and milk gently to a boil. Whisk together the egg yolks and sugar until the mixture is pale and thick. Pour the milks over the egg and sugar while still whisking. Return this custard to the pan and heat gently, stirring, until the custard has thickened to coat the back of a spoon. Leave it to cool before stirring in the cream and freezing in an ice cream machine.

FOR THE TUILLE:

2 egg whites

85g caster sugar

3 tablespoons plain flour

1 tablespoon cornflour

50g melted butter

4 teaspoonfuls ground almonds

rind of 2 limes, finely grated

Beat egg whites until stiff, then beat in the sugar until glossy. Add the flour and corn-flour (through a sieve), the melted butter, almonds and lime rind. Fold gently to get a smooth, thick batter.

Line baking trays with parchment and heat an oven to 200°C/400°F. Drop teaspoonfuls of the batter on to the trays, using the back of the spoon to spread the batter into a very thin circle of 8–9cm diameter. Do just one tray at a time. Bake for four to six minutes until the tuilles are lightly coloured. Lift them from the trays carefully and drape them over a wooden spoon, an inverted cup or the side of a long glass, depending on how you want to shape them. Remember, they are very flexible, but only for a short time – in half a minute they will be crisp.

Serve a few slices of hot pineapple in their syrup, with coconut ice cream and a tuille.

Tortellini of Cashel blue cheese and sundried tomato with nutmeg spinach and an artichoke cream

Tortellini are fun to make when you get the hang of them and they give the dish an element of structure – 'height', in other words – that ravioli can't do. If it won't come together for you, serve the pasta as flat parcels, it won't taste any different.

Sometimes dishes like this can seem daunting until you break them down. Don't try to do everything in a flurry when your guests are in the hallway. Follow the example of the restaurant kitchen approach, which makes a simple job of a potentially chaotic one without compromising the quality or your sanity. The tortellini can be stored, tossed in rice flour, in the fridge for a few hours, or longer in the freezer. The sauce can be made ahead up to the point of adding cream. Then, all that's required to cook this spectacular starter is to boil the pasta, wilt some spinach and simmer a cream sauce. You can probably do that while sipping a fine sherry, holding two conversations and minding the main course in the oven. My cooks can, anyway – yak, yak, yak, all evening.

FOR FOUR:

150 Cashel blue cheese

50 sundried tomatoes, soaked

50g fine breadcrumbs

16 x 60cm sheet of fresh pasta, or equivalent

2 tinned artichokes, rinsed

2 cloves garlic

150mls vegetable stock (see page 276)

100mls white wine

400mls cream

salt and pepper, to season

1 teaspoon chopped chives

400g spinach

olive oil

salt and pepper, to season

1 large pinch grated nutmeg

Crumble the blue cheese, chop the sundried tomatoes finely and mix them with the breadcrumbs. Cut circles of 8cm from the pasta – you will need 12 for four portions but try to make a few spares to allow for accidents. Leaving an edge of 1cm, put a teaspoon of filling on one half only of each circle. Moisten the edge, fold over the empty half and press it firmly to seal the edges, making sure that you leave no air pockets inside. Holding the two unfilled corners, pull them to bring them together underneath the filled middle, which should fold away from the corners in the process. Press the corners together.

To cook the tortellini, bring a large pot of water to a boil and drop in the tortellini. Cook them at a gentle rolling boil for four or five minutes until tender.

Make the sauce when the tortellini are made but not cooked, and simmer it to thicken while the pasta cooks. Chop the artichokes and garlic, put them in a pan with the stock and wine, and simmer for five minutes. Blend to a purée in a food processor and pass the purée through a sieve. Return the purée to the pan with the cream and simmer for a few minutes until the sauce thickens to a nice pasta-coating consistency – try some on the back of a wooden spoon to get an idea. Season carefully with salt and pepper. Add the chopped chives just before you serve.

While the tortellini are cooking, wilt the spinach in a pan with some olive oil, then season it with salt and pepper and the nutmeg.

Place a little spinach on each plate and sit three or four tortellini on top. Pour some cream around.

Sweet chilli-fried tofu with leeks in coconut and lemongrass broth

Sambal oelek, the Indonesian chilli sauce, makes a great base for the marinade here because of its sweet and hot flavour, of course, but also because its slightly thickened texture helps the marinade to coat the tofu. The marinade is quite hot and, if it coats the tofu successfully, the tofu has quite a kick too, which is why I like to serve it with a cooling coconut dish.

The coconut broth is very simple, to act as a cooling foil to the hot tofu. To use it on its own as a sauce for a noodle dish, you might want to add more ginger and some other spices. As well as the coconut milk, I use a little coconut cream from one of those concentrated blocks to help thicken the broth a little. Any greens, western cabbage or Asian choi are good in the broth instead of, or with, the leeks.

If you feel the need for some carbohydrates with this, and I usually do, serve some noodles sitting underneath the leeks. Flat rice noodles are especially nice here.

FOR FOUR:

3 tablespoons sambal oelek

6 tablespoons soy sauce

2 tablespoons sugar

juice of 1 lime

600g tofu

olive oil

300mls vegetable stock (see page 276)

4 stalks lemongrass

1 tablespoon grated ginger

1 handful each basil and coriander leaves

2 medium leeks

600mls coconut milk

50g coconut cream

pinch salt

Stir together the sambal oelek, soy sauce, sugar and lime juice in a shallow bowl. Add two tablespoons of water. Chop the tofu into 12 thick slices and put them in the marinade for 15 minutes.

Heat a large frying pan and brush it with oil. Put in the tofu to fry briefly over medium heat for a minute on both sides, then pour a spoonful of marinade on to each side. Continue cooking, swirling the pan, until the marinade has been absorbed by the tofu. Turn the tofu slices once during this cooking, spooning a little more marinade over them just before the turning. You can cook the tofu in two batches and keep the first warm in an oven.

To make the coconut broth, bring the stock to a boil in a pot, drop in the lemongrass, ginger and herbs and simmer for five minutes. Remove the lemongrass and herbs. Trim the coarsest green parts from the leeks, then slice the rest into diagonal slices, wash them and put them in the stock. Simmer gently for ten minutes or so until the leeks are tender. Pour in the coconut milk, coconut cream and a pinch of salt, and simmer for one minute before serving.

Serve the tofu sitting on the leeks in a generous pool of coconut broth.

Black bean, aubergine and leek chilli with polenta gnocchi and lime soured cream

Having spent years shaking off the stodgy, wholefood associations of vegetarian food, and practically refusing to cook pulses at all except for my beloved chickpeas, I was a bit nervous about putting this simple chilli on the Paradiso lunch menu. It's been a big hit – partly, I think, because it is rich rather than heavy, and partly because we managed to make it look pretty – no mean feat with a dish that's packed with beans. The black turtle beans, small and dense, are essential to this richness, as is the aubergine. Although I vary the third vegetable in the chilli according to moods and seasons, I never cook it without aubergine. The aubergine is roasted in quite a lot of olive oil and this gives the dish a rich, oily lusciousness. Hey, I never said it was diet food! Low-fat bean stews are monotonously dull and starchy to wade through and, anyway, I don't believe that olive oil-rich food is unhealthy.

This chilli is hot. That's why it's called a chilli. Occasionally, a faint-hearted cook will leave out some of the chillies, removing the essential character of the dish. Usually by the time I find out, the cook and the bemused customers have gone home. It's a pet hate of mine: restaurant food that advertises itself as something that couldn't be detected in a blind tasting. Sometimes it's caused by meanness on the part of the kitchen or the kitchen's accountant; sometimes it's a timid belief that subtle and bland are more or less the same. If you buy something because its description includes the names of tastes you lust for but the food tastes politely of nothing, you're left with a screaming sense of frustration... or at least some mild disappointment because, well, you've become used to this happening. Chilli should taste of chilli, and if you don't like hot chillies, order a dish that doesn't include them.

The base of the chilli is a simple tomato sauce, heavily laced with the holy triumvirate of spices: chillies, cumin and coriander seeds. I don't think chilli needs a complicated spicing, but it does need a good balance. It is for simplicity and balance that I only ever use three vegetables: the beans, aubergines and one green vegetable. Any more and the dish will become too confusing to be interesting.

FOR FOUR:

FOR THE CHILLI:

200g dried black turtle beans

olive oil

2 onions, finely chopped

3 cloves garlic, finely chopped

1 tablespoon coriander seeds, ground

1 tablespoon cumin seeds, ground

8 dried bird's eye chillies, ground

500g tinned tomatoes

1 tablespoon tomato purée

salt, to season

400g aubergines

1 large leek

1 bunch fresh coriander

Soak the turtle beans for two hours or more in cold water, then cook them in lots of boiling water until tender (about an hour).

Heat a little olive oil in a large pan and cook the onions until soft. Add the garlic and spices, and cook for two minutes before adding the tomatoes and the tomato purée. Bring the sauce to a boil and simmer for 15 minutes. Season with salt and check the spice levels – the sauce needs to be very strongly spiced at this point, as the beans and vegetables will dilute its power considerably.

While the sauce is cooking, chop the aubergine into large chunks, toss them in olive oil and roast them in a hot oven until browned and softened. Turn and toss the aubergines once or twice as they cook.

Chop the leeks into chunks and wash them. It's best to wash unsliced leek pieces in a large container in a few changes of water. Heat two tablespoons of olive oil in a wide pan and cook the leeks in it until just tender, stirring often.

Add the cooked turtle beans, aubergines and leeks to the sauce and simmer for ten minutes. Stir in the fresh coriander, and check the seasoning and spicing again before serving.

FOR THE LIME SOURED CREAM:

rind and juice of 1 lime

200mls soured cream or crème fraîche

Stir the lime rind and juice into the soured cream.

FOR THE GNOCCHI:

1200mls vegetable stock (see page 276)

250g coarse maize

1 teaspoon salt

60g cream cheese

1 tablespoon chives, finely chopped

Bring the stock to a boil in a large pot, then whisk in the maize and the salt over high heat until the stock comes back to the boil, then quickly turn the heat to a very low setting and replace the whisk with a wooden spoon. Cook the polenta for 15 to 20 minutes, stirring frequently, until the grains are soft. Stir in the cream cheese and chives, and tip the polenta out on to an oiled tray. Try to keep the polenta at a height of about 2cm, which may mean not using the full tray to spread the wet polenta on. Spread the polenta evenly and quickly, using your hands dampened with cold water or a spatula. In about 20 minutes, the polenta will be ready to cut, but leave it longer if you can. (In fact, the polenta can be made up to a day in advance.) Use a circular cutter to cut small circles from the polenta. About five minutes before serving, toss the polenta pieces in olive oil and roast them in a hot oven until crisped on the outside

Serve the chilli surrounded by some of the polenta gnocchi and soured cream.

Rigatoni with winter greens, artichokes, dried tomatoes, chillies and capers

This combination of cupboard ingredients and fresh winter vegetables sounds like a mouthful to say, never mind to eat, but it's just pasta and vegetables with two strong flavours I use together a lot at home – chillies and capers. Put this on a restaurant menu and half the people who order it will ask for one or more of these ingredients to be left out. At home, you can do the same to adjust the dish to your likes and dislikes, and without upsetting any fragile cheffy egos.

Kale and cabbage are surprisingly good in pasta, though they do cook differently. Kale, and smoother cabbages and spring greens, will cook down to a softly chewy finish while tougher cabbages like savoy will hold their essential character more, but in a way that is completely compatible with the strong flavours of this dish.

FOR FOUR:

1 small leek
200g kale or cabbage
6 large tinned artichokes
500g rigatoni
3 tablespoons olive oil
3 cloves garlic, thinly sliced
8 halves of sundried tomatoes, thinly sliced
4 dried bird's eye chillies, chopped
1 tablespoon small capers
pinch salt
Parmesan, finely grated, to serve

Halve the leek lengthways, wash and chop it into thin diagonal slices. Chop the greens into similar slices. Drain the artichokes and rinse them very well under lots of running cold water.

Bring a pot of water to a boil and cook the rigatoni until just tender.

At the same time, heat three tablespoons of olive oil in a pan, and cook the leeks and greens together for five minutes, then add the garlic, artichokes, dried tomatoes and chillies. Cook for a few minutes more until the cabbage is tender, then add the capers and a pinch of salt.

Drain the pasta and stir it into the vegetables. Serve with some finely grated Parmesan to sprinkle over.

Pistachio, cardamom and basmati rice cake with coconut greens and gingered mango salsa

Although this recipe gives instructions for cooking basmati rice, this is more of a recipe for leftover rice, or at least rice cooked much earlier on in the day. It could be seen as a way to serve rice and greens in a pretty and structured way in a restaurant, but there is more than aesthetics to it. As much as the shaping into a cake is for appearance, it also gives a texture that is vastly different from scooping up a plate of rice. There should be just enough egg in the mix to hold the cake together without making a too-solid mass. The dish is very fine in itself but will find a perfect balance if you also serve a simple tomato-based curry of green beans, squash or broccoli.

In her beautiful book *Crazy Water, Pickled Lemons,* Diana Henry says there should always seem to be just too little cardamom, leaving an element of tease. This was a revelation to me, so I checked this and some other cardamom recipes to see if I was hitting people over the head where I might have been better off teasing. Let's just say, I'll be saving some money on the cardamom seeds in future.

FOR FOUR:

olive oil
500g basmati rice
500mls boiling water
large pinch salt
60g pistachio nuts
8 cardamom pods
1 small leek, white part only
butter
2 eggs

half a mango
1 sweet ginger nut in syrup
juice of 1 lime

1 red onion
kale, spinach or green cabbage
400mls coconut milk

Heat a little oil in a pan and gently toast the basmati in it for a few minutes, then pour in the boiling water and a large pinch of salt. Simmer, covered, over very low heat for ten minutes, then turn off the heat and leave the pan for five minutes. Turn the rice out into a wide bowl and leave it to cool.

Toast the pistachios lightly in an oven, then chop them coarsely. Crack the cardamom pods, remove the seeds and discard the pods. Chop the leek finely. Melt a little butter in a pan and cook the leek, pistachio and cardamom for two minutes, then stir this into the rice. When the rice is cool, or just before you cook the cakes, stir in the eggs.

Dice the mango flesh and the ginger, and stir them together with the lime juice and a teaspoon of the ginger syrup.

Heat four rings 10cm in diameter by 2cm high in a wide shallow pan over low heat, brush them lightly with olive oil and fill them with the rice mix, pressing it in to get an even finish. Cook the cakes for five minutes before flipping them over to cook the other sides. Cook until both sides are lightly coloured and the cakes are just set. If you don't have a pan big enough to hold all four, the cooked cakes will keep warm in a low oven while you do a second batch.

As the cakes are cooking, slice the red onion thinly and tear the greens. Cook them together in a little olive oil over high heat until the greens are wilted, then pour in the coconut milk and take the pan off the heat.

Serve each rice cake sitting on some greens, with a little dollop of mango salsa on top.

Tagliolini with lemon, olive oil, chickpeas, flat leaf parsley and pecorino

Bridget made this one evening when we were huddled in front of the television watching a video. We were tired, in need of a family night in with the curtains drawn and a fire in the grate. Maybe I should lie and say it was a winter's evening, but the truth is that it was in the early stages of that dreadful summer of rain, and the dish came about for the not very seasonal reason that the cupboard was bare, as were the fridge and pantry. Like the cobbler's barefoot children, I'm afraid a professional cook's pantry is often a neglected thing. Well, it wasn't quite bare, because Bridget knocked up this simple but stunning combination. It distracted me from the plot of the movie and my ranting about the perfect simplicity and simple perfection of the meal distracted everyone else to the point that we abandoned the telly for a friendly but vicious game of cards. The power of food, eh?

The whole thing can be cooked in less time than the argument about whose turn it is to cook, especially if you have fresh pasta to hand and you use tinned chickpeas. It is my natural inclination to meddle with recipes, add a few more ingredients, make things a little more complex, sometimes just keeping one element and ending up with another dish entirely. So I have thought of altering this, and I do believe it will stand a little meddling and personalising, but I decided to write down the classic version and let the rest of you get on with your own meddling. Some things that would definitely work would be the addition of garlic and/or chillies, using rocket instead of parsley or tinned artichokes instead of chickpeas. Always, when confronted by something new, whether a dish or a vegetable, it's best to try it straight first and then the possibilities will open up.

I have suggested pecorino, a hard sheep's cheese, here because the dish seems to have a southern Italian or eastern Mediterranean character, and sheep's cheese fits into that picture. However, if you can't get, or don't like, sheep's cheese, then Parmesan or any hard cheese will be fine.

FOR FOUR:

120mls olive oil

rind of 2 lemons

juice of half a lemon

200g cooked chickpeas

large handful flat leaf parsley

500g fresh tagliolini pasta, or similar

salt and black pepper, to season

100g pecorino or other hard cheese, finely grated

Put the olive oil, lemon rind and juice and chickpeas into a pan large enough to hold the cooked pasta. Tear the parsley leaves from their stalks and finely chop any stalk tender enough to use, then add the parsley to the pan.

Bring a pot of water to a boil and drop in the pasta to cook for two or three minutes until just tender. While the pasta is cooking, cook the sauce ingredients over a medium heat for two minutes. Drain the pasta and stir it into the sauce with a generous seasoning of salt and black pepper, and half of the grated cheese. Serve the pasta with more cheese scattered over.

Braised cannellini beans

Variations on this bean dish have become a staple on Paradiso menus since I first made it a few years back. As well as its primary function as an intensely flavoured accompaniment to many dishes such as the cabbage dolma on page 209, gratins, crêpes and so on, it is a good base for a stew or pasta dish.

The beans are cooked in two stages: first in water and then in the sauce in the oven. Be careful to get them out of the water before they are fully cooked or they will turn to mush in the second cooking.

Don't think of all dried beans as the same – as with any product, it is worth buying from someone who you know buys good produce and has a good turnover of stock. Age is a crucial factor in beans. Dried beans should be from the previous harvest or, at worst, the one before, but there are beans on the market much older than that. Usually you can tell by the skin – any wrinkling or discolouring is a dead giveaway, but check the 'use by' date too.

FOR FOUR:

400g dried cannellini beans
150mls olive oil
150mls white wine
200mls vegetable stock (see page 276)
3 sprigs thyme
1 sprig rosemary
4 cloves garlic
4 sundried tomatoes
salt and pepper, to season

Soak the beans in cold water for at least two hours, then cook them in boiling water for 30 to 60 minutes, depending on their age and quality, until the beans are almost but not quite tender. Strain the beans and put them back in the pot with the olive oil, wine, stock, thyme and rosemary. Slice the garlic thinly and chop the sundried tomatoes into small dice, then stir both into the beans. Season with salt and pepper. Bring the beans to a boil and transfer them to an oven dish. Cover the dish loosely with a sheet of baking parchment and place it in the oven, at 180°C/350°F. Check the beans after half an hour, and every 20 minutes or so after that. You may need to add some more liquid. The beans should be cooked after an hour but it may take longer, and remember that the longer and slower the cooking the more the beans will have absorbed the flavours around them. When done, the beans will be tender and the liquids will have come together and reduced to a moist, well-flavoured background sauce.

Blood orange and fennel sorbet with marinated blood oranges

We get organic blood oranges from Sicily late in winter, just as spring is about to, well, spring. They're not exactly a sign of spring, but you know you're almost there and that, before the oranges are all gone, there will be greens sprouting furiously. At the creeping onset of every winter I have a sense of dread about the vegetables we gradually lose as we go deeper into the cold season. Coming out the other end, the excitement of the new year ahead is always accompanied by a sense of reassessment, and I think that, yeah, that wasn't so bad, we had some nice food in there, in the deep dark recesses; it always turns out okay and winter has its own enjoyable challenges. Then I pull myself together, shut the winter away and get on with the good things in life. As a last throw of the season, blood oranges are a class act and certainly no novelty. At their best, they have a very fine, intense flavour, as perfectly balanced between sweet and acid as an orange gets. We poach them and serve them with puddings and cheesecakes, or with a sorbet of the same flavours, as here. The aniseedy flavour of fennel is excellent with oranges, in savoury cooking as in desserts. Make a decent batch of sorbet and before it's gone there will be daffodils in the garden.

FOR FOUR:

750g caster sugar
450mls water
handful of fennel herb
12 large blood oranges
1 egg white

Make a fennel syrup by bringing the sugar, water and fennel to a boil; simmer for five minutes and leave to cool for an hour. Grate the rind of six blood oranges finely, squeeze the juice from them and add them to 600mls of the syrup. Whisk the egg white briefly, fold it into the syrup and freeze in an ice cream machine.

Peel the remaining oranges with a knife, slicing off the skin and the outer white pith. Slice each orange horizontally into three or four thick slices. Heat the remaining syrup to just below boiling, pour it over the oranges and leave to cool.

Serve the sorbet with some marinated blood oranges.

Early Spring

spring greens

purple sprouting
broccoli

watercress

Spring cabbage timbale of roasted aubergine and Gabriel cheese with a plum tomato-basil sauce

The outer leaves of spring cabbage are soft, dark and very supple when cooked, and they make a wonderful material for parcels of all sorts. In this recipe the inside leaves of the cabbage form the bulk of the parcel filling too. So in a way the cabbage is put back together, though in a very formal reconstruction and not at all in a way that its mammy would recognise. Although there is a bit of fiddly preparation and construction involved in these timbales, it is quite rewarding if you like that kind of work. Also, the construction is very solid, more packing than delicate arrangement, and there are no tricky cooking techniques involved at all. You will, however, need individual metal rings to hold the timbales together as they cook in the oven. The fundamental idea of the dish – constructing a drum-like timbale from cabbage leaves – will accommodate a wide range of variations on the filling, whether they use the inner cabbage leaves or not. This is the first version I did, and I'm still very fond of it. Okay, it's not the most certifiably seasonal version of the timbale, but equally it's important not to get too hung up on absolutes when dealing with food – down that road lies nothing but paranoia and self-flagellation. When I did the timbale without the aubergines, it missed them more than I could bear. Equally, the plum tomato sauce I originally used, and include here, is out of season unless you use tinned tomatoes (and they would do very nicely if you drain them carefully), but it's just so perfect… Serve the timbales with some steamed or roast potato. Later in the season some grilled asparagus will give the dish a luxurious finish.

FOR FOUR:

4 plum tomatoes
1 bunch basil leaves
150mls olive oil
salt and pepper, to season
2 heads spring cabbage
1 leek, chopped
4 cloves garlic, chopped
100g Gabriel cheese
1 small bunch chives
2 aubergines
splash of water or stock

The tomato sauce can be prepared at any time during the timbale preparation. Cut a little cross into the base of the tomatoes and drop them into boiling water for a few seconds. Remove the tomatoes to cold water and peel off the skins. Cut the tomatoes in half and scoop out the seeds. Chop the flesh into dice. Put the basil in a jug with the olive oil and use a hand blender to make a basil oil. Put the tomatoes in a small pan with enough of the oil to give a wet consistency. Season with salt and pepper. When you are ready to serve the timbales, heat the sauce for one minute.

Separate the outer leaves from the cabbage heads. You will need one or two leaves per portion, depending on their size. Trim any thick stalk to the thickness of the leaf. Bring a pot of water to a boil, drop in the leaves and cook them until tender, about five minutes. Lift the leaves out of the pot and put them in a bowl of cold water to stop the cooking. Wash the leek, slice it in half lengthways and chop it into thin slices. Chop the remaining cabbage in the same way and mix it with the leek and the garlic. Heat some oil in a wide pan and cook the cabbage and leek until just

beginning to soften. Move it to a bowl to cool, then stir in the cheese and the chives. Season with a little salt and pepper.

Cut the aubergine into rounds of 1cm thickness, brush them with olive oil on both sides and roast them in a hot oven, 200°C/400°F, until browned and fully cooked.

Take a metal ring of 7 or 8cm diameter.
Brush the inside lightly with olive oil and
push a cabbage leaf into the ring, ideally to
cover over half of the base, half of the side
and with some leaf overhanging. It may take
one more leaf, or two to three leaves or
pieces of leaves, to give a full single-layer
covering of the base and the sides, each piece
overhanging the top of the ring. Cover the
base with a layer of aubergine slices, then a
thick layer of the cabbage and cheese mix, to
just short of the top, followed by another
layer of aubergine slices. Fold over the overhanging cabbage leaves and trim them so
that they cover the top adequately but not
too thickly. Brush the top with olive oil.
Repeat the process to get four timbales. Place
the timbales in an oven dish brushed with
olive oil and sprinkle a little stock or water
over them. Cook the timbales in an oven at
180°C/350°F, sprinkling a little water over
occasionally to stop the timbales drying out
or the cabbage burning. After ten minutes,
flip over the timbales to cook both sides
evenly, and cook them for a further five
minutes.

Serve the timbales sitting in a pool of the
tomato-basil sauce, with some grilled asparagus spears and steamed potato.

Braised spring cabbage and tomato pesto rolls

All cabbages seem to love the sweetness of tomatoes, and the lovely fresh cabbage of early spring is no different, though locating a nice sweet tomato in early spring can be tricky. Which is why, in winter and spring, I often use dried tomatoes or roasted tomatoes from the freezer. These little stubby cabbage rolls are an attempt to dress the first greens of the year up for dinner but without over-elaborating or making the filling the focus. Served in their juice, they are fantastic with a rich risotto, say with blue cheese and spring onions or wild garlic, or they can help to make a fine dinner of a simple potato gratin. In the Paradiso kitchen, they are a good-humoured pick-me-up for flagging cooks.

FOR FOUR:

2 tablespoons pinenuts

3 tablespoons thick tomato pesto (see page 32)

1 head spring cabbage

olive oil

200–300mls vegetable stock (see page 276)

Lightly toast the pinenuts in a heavy pan over low heat, or on a tray in the oven, until very lightly coloured. Tip them on to a chopping board and chop them roughly with a knife, then stir them into the tomato pesto.

Cut the base off the cabbage and separate the leaves. Bring a pot of water to a boil, drop in the leaves, giving the dark outer ones a head start of a minute or two, and cook them until tender, about six to eight minutes. Remove the leaves to a bowl of cold water to stop the cooking while preserving their lovely colour. Lay the leaves flat on a work surface and spread a thin layer of the pinenuts in pesto on each one. Fold a third of a large leaf over on itself, then fold again. Starting at a short end, roll the leaf, reasonably tightly but not so the

pesto squirts out. You should have something that resembles a green cigar stub. Repeat this with the rest of the leaves, bearing in mind that smaller leaves will possibly take just one initial fold. Cut the larger stubs in half but leave the smaller ones – an inch (3mm) is a nice size. Place them in a small oven dish, brush them generously with a good olive oil and spoon over enough stock to just cover the bottom of the dish. Place the dish in a moderate oven, about 180°C/350°F, for 12 to 15 minutes. Ideally the oils from the brushing and the pesto will have mingled perfectly with the stock to give a sweet rich gravy to serve the rolls in.

Spring greens and potato colcannon

You can make colcannon out of potato and greens at any time of year, so this version differs from a winter one only in the taste of the greens. But if you accept, as I do, that the fresh greens of a season offer its most defining flavours, then this colcannon will be as different to a winter one made with kale or savoy cabbage as a miserable, cold and wet day in early December is to a bright, slightly-chilly-but-getting-there day in early March. Spring cabbage, fast-growing, soft and bursting with life, tastes of its time, and indeed even bringing it home from the market instead of that hoary old, frostbitten last-of-the-winter cabbage can put a spring in your step and make the year seem full of promise. Honest.

FOR FOUR:

1 kg floury potatoes
half head spring cabbage
4 spring onions, chopped finely
4 cloves garlic, chopped finely
2 tablespoons olive oil
200mls milk
60g butter
salt and pepper, to season

Peel the potatoes and steam them until soft. Chop the cabbage and cook it in boiling water until tender, then drain and chop it quite finely. Fry the onion and garlic in the olive oil for two minutes. Add the cabbage and cook for one minute more. Warm the milk and butter together in a large pot, then add the potatoes and mash them until you have a smooth mash. Nothing will cause more derision in an Irish household, even in the twenty-first century, than lumpy mash, so do go at it with some energy, but don't ever be tempted to put it in the blender – that's called thick soup. Stir in the cabbage and season well with salt and black pepper, though white pepper would be more, strictly traditionally, correct.

Spring greens with coriander seeds, chillies and ginger

A simple fried cabbage recipe that I use as a side dish to liven up many dinners at home. If dinner is in the child-friendly and comfort-food zone, a side dish with a little fire and the freshness of greens is a nice option. Ginger, chilli and coriander are all great cabbage spices, separately or together, but the coriander seeds shine here, the cracked seeds bursting with aromatic flavour. At least they do if you buy fresh seeds in good condition. It really is important with dried spices to hunt down a good source, and an organic one too if you can.

FOR FOUR:

1 head spring cabbage
4 spring onions
2 teaspoons coriander seeds
1 fresh chilli, sliced
olive oil
2 teaspoons fresh ginger, grated
2 tomatoes, sliced
1 teaspoon soy sauce

Cut the base off the cabbage and slice the leaves in half lengthways, then across in pieces about 1mm wide. Trim the spring onions and slice them diagonally in long pieces. Crush the coriander seeds with the back of a knife or a rolling pin – they should split or just open.

Heat some olive oil in a wok or wide pan and toss in the cabbage. Cook over a medium heat for a minute, then add the spring onions and the spices. Fry for another few minutes, stirring and turning the cabbage constantly, until the cabbage is tender. Finally, add the sliced tomato and the soy sauce, and heat through for one minute more.

Warm salad of purple sprouting broccoli with radishes, Parmesan polenta and avocado oil

Purple sprouting broccoli is often the first local fresh greens we get after the long winter up to our elbows in roots – not that I don't love my roots too, but I do drop them like discarded peelings when the ground thaws and something beautiful and green pushes its head up. Sprouting broccoli has a shortish season, but if you can convince different growers to grow early and late crops it can stretch for up to eight weeks, thus carrying you through from late winter to the end of spring. It still hasn't made an impact in the shops, and seems to be grown only by dedicated growers who appreciate it for itself. Although there are some interesting hybrids of broccoli with thinner, tender stalks appearing in supermarkets, they don't come near the real thing for taste. I have come to accept that the only way sprouting broccoli will become more widely available is for the public and producers alike to accept that it is a luxury vegetable with a market value similar to, say, asparagus.

If you grow your own, you know how to prepare it. If you are lucky to have access to it in a farmers' market, it should be sold more or less in a ready-to-use state – thin, single shoots about three to four inches long, the edible leaves attached. The most you should have to do is trim a little off the ends. Any sprouting broccoli sold in heads will have up to 80 per cent waste by weight, and should have an appropriately lower price.

This recipe is really a loose sketch, a prototype of endless variations, the essence of which is some purple sprouting broccoli wilted in good olive oil and served at room temperature with a little carbohydrate, polenta, crostini, potato maybe. Without the carbs, it can just as easily be a side dish, part of a main course or a little something to suck on just because you feel like it. Sprouting broccoli seems to give as much to olive oil in the cooking as it takes from it, and, to be honest, I rarely cook it any other way .

The only decent avocado oil I have ever found is from New Zealand, where avocado cultivation has been perfected – it is just appearing outside New Zealand as I write, and if it hasn't found its way into every foodie home by publication date I'll… I'll… well, I'll sell my shares.

FOR FOUR:

1 litre vegetable stock
(see page 276)

200g coarse maize

1 teaspoon salt

60g Parmesan grated

2 tablespoons parsley,
finely chopped

black pepper, to season

2 tablespoons avocado oil

4 handfuls sprouting
broccoli

splash of water or stock

1 small red onion, thinly
sliced

1 bunch radishes, thickly
sliced

First make the polenta. Bring the stock to a boil in a large pot, then whisk in the maize and the salt, whisking over high heat until the stock comes back to the boil, then quickly turn the heat to a very low setting and replace the whisk with a wooden spoon. Cook the polenta for about 20 minutes, stirring frequently, until the grains are soft. Stir in the Parmesan, herbs and a generous sprinkling of black pepper, then tip the polenta out on to a work surface or into an oiled tray – a tray or dish about 25cm square will give a good thickness of polenta, but a little thinner is fine; using an open work surface will give the polenta that rustic cooking feeling you may very well be after. Either way, spread the polenta evenly and quickly, using your hands dampened with cold water or a spatula. Work quickly – the polenta sets fast. In about 20 minutes, it will be ready to cut, but leave it longer if you can. In fact the polenta can be made up to a day in advance.

Cut the polenta into small wedges. Heat a grill, lightly brush the wedges with olive oil and place them under the grill on a tray, turning once to brown both sides. Or you can cook them in the same way on a griddle pan.

At the same time, heat one tablespoon of avocado oil in a pan and toss in the sprouting broccoli. Cook it over a medium to high heat for about five or six minutes, turning and stirring almost constantly, and occasionally splashing in a little stock to keep the broccoli wilting and stop it from frying. Add the red onion slices and cook for one minute more, and then stir in the radish slices to heat through.

Pile the salad on to plates, tuck the freshly grilled polenta wedges in under the salad, and drizzle some avocado oil hither and thither.

Purple sprouting broccoli with dried tomatoes and garlic on a corn pancake of leeks and puy lentils, with a rosemary cream

It surprised me when I sat down to write out this recipe that it seems an elaborate dish of many parts and much labour. In the restaurant, it seems a simple one – some briefly cooked vegetables on a simple pancake – and with elements of it being made by different people at different times, it doesn't seem much trouble to any particular person in the process, especially the one who finishes it by cooking the broccoli and the sauce: me. The thing is that I really wanted to make an impressive main course with the sprouting broccoli, but everything I looked at that involved lots of cooking, chopping or processing of the vegetable, only reminded me that, although it can deal with many flavours, strong and robust ones too, the broccoli itself is always best left whole and briefly cooked. So, how to make an impressive main course out of that? In a sense, I just plonked it on top of what is already a main course looking for a vegetable, and inverted the way it might read on the menu. I don't mean that to seem devious, rather that what I want to get across is that the star element of the dish, the part I want the customer to be attracted to, is the purple sprouting broccoli. The dishes I focus most attention on in Paradiso are the ones that are designed to draw attention to a particular vegetable in the prime of its season, and even if there are more expensive elements in the dish, or more intensely flavoured ones, they are subordinate, present only to enhance and support the star vegetable and the customers' pleasure in it.

The quantities in the pancake recipe are tiny – it will make five pancakes if you're good and have no accidents. I would suggest that, for peace of mind, you make a double batch and have the spares for breakfast tomorrow.

FOR FIVE:

FOR THE PANCAKES:

50g fine cornmeal

20g plain flour

large pinch each paprika and turmeric

quarter teaspoon salt

1 egg

140mls milk

50g puy lentils

800g leeks

olive oil

2 cloves garlic, finely chopped

1 teaspoon Dijon mustard or similar

small sprig thyme

50mls white wine

100mls cream

salt and pepper, to season

50g Gabriel or other hard cheese, finely grated

Sift the flours and seasonings together. Whisk the egg with the milk, then whisk this into the flour mix. Use this batter to make thin pancakes, taking care to whisk up the batter each time, as the corn tends to sink, causing the pancakes to stick.

Cook the lentils in boiling water until just tender, then drain them.

Slice the leeks in half lengthways, wash them well, then chop the lengths across into short slices. Heat a pan, large enough to hold the leeks, to a high temperature, pour in a little olive oil and immediately toss in the leeks and garlic. Cook on high heat, stirring often, until the leeks soften. Add in the mustard, thyme and white wine, cook for one minute, then add the cream. Keep the heat high, boiling the cream and, hopefully, reducing the liquid from the leeks, to give a dryish, creamy finish. If you end up with a very wet mixture at this point, don't keep boiling to evaporate the liquid or you will overcook the leeks. Instead, drain the leeks, saving the liquid, then reduce the liquid on its own and pour it back into the leeks. Finally, stir in the lentils and season with salt and pepper.

Lay a pancake on the bench, prettiest side down. Place a rectangular thin layer of the leek and lentils in the centre of the pancake, sprinkle a little cheese over it, then fold up the rest of the pancake, short sides first, then the long sides, to form a closed parcel, and brush the top with olive oil. When you need to cook the pancakes, they need 10 to 15 minutes in a moderate oven, 180–190°C/350–375°F.

FOR THE ROSEMARY
CREAM:

*100mls vegetable stock
(see page 276)*

200mls cream

*50mls rosemary oil (see
page 18)*

*large pinch Gabriel
cheese or similar*

Bring the stock to a boil in a small pan and
simmer until there is just a tablespoon left.
Add the cream and simmer again for two
minutes, then whisk in the rosemary oil and
cheese. Season lightly. The sauce should
really be made at the last minute but, if
you're anxious, you can get it done a little
before and add a splash of stock or water
before heating it through to serve.

FOR THE BROCCOLI:

*4 handfuls purple
sprouting broccoli*

6 cloves garlic

*100g semi-sundried
tomatoes*

Heat some of the rosemary oil in a wide pan,
toss in the broccoli and cook over a fairly
high heat, stirring constantly for two
minutes. Add in the garlic and the tomatoes,
and continue cooking for a further three to
four minutes, adding an occasional splash of
stock or water to prevent burning or sticking.
In any case, finish with a splash of stock
before removing from the heat so that the
dish finishes just a little moist with juice.

To serve, place a pancake on each plate
(check the bottom side, sometimes it's better-
looking and always a flatter surface). Pile a
mound of broccoli and tomatoes on top and
pour the rosemary cream around. Finish
with some small, peeled and steamed potatoes dotted around in the cream.

Stir-fried sprouting broccoli, carrots and almonds in a hot-and-sour black bean sauce

Despite my fondness for sprouting broccoli with olive oil, the vegetable has more than enough character to be used with Asian-style flavourings, whether simply seasoned with ginger and sesame oil or with this very robust sauce. I've been using this sauce since the early days of Café Paradiso, and I would guess that, for everyone who gets a kick out of it, there's another who finds it shocking. Come to think of it, I haven't used it at all this past year – hope I'm not losing my nerve. Maybe it's the staff – for all their fine qualities of subtlety and finesse, I do find it a bit tricky working with cooks who don't like chilli – everyone's insecure to some extent and having someone go 'oh, yeucch' or roaring in pain behind you will wear you down eventually. The sauce is very hot and quite sour, but a little goes a long way, and it is great fun to eat if you're into those things, certainly more than its Chinese restaurant cousin, the 'sweet and sour', which is usually more one than the other and not a lot of anything. Serve this with noodles or rice, though be warned that rice will absorb the sauce more than noodles.

The recipe for the sauce will make more than you need at one time. It is impossible to make smaller quantities than these; so, if you get to like it, I suggest you make a bigger quantity, as it keeps for a week or more in a sealed jar in the fridge.

FOR FOUR:

75g salted black beans

4 cloves garlic, finely chopped

1 tablespoon ginger, grated

1 teaspoon dried chillies, ground

250mls hot water

100mls rice or white wine vinegar

25mls sherry or sake

25mls soy sauce

1 teaspoon sugar

PER PERSON, TO STIR FRY:

half a small onion, thinly sliced

1 handful purple sprouting broccoli

2 baby carrots, halved, or 1 medium carrot, sliced

1 dessertspoon sliced almonds, lightly toasted

Put half of the salted beans in a food processor with the garlic, ginger and chillies and pulse them to get a very coarse mash. Transfer this to a jug, add the rest of the beans, the liquids and the sugar, and leave for two hours to soak. Taste a little of this sauce before you use it, so you know what you're dealing with. Remember that it will be merely coating the vegetables, but also that while the sauce is not thickened it will be reduced and intensified in the pan.

Heat some oil to a fairly high temperature in a wok, and drop in the onion, broccoli and carrots together. Cook over a high heat, stirring all the time, occasionally splashing in some water to add a little steam to the process, but not so much that it slows the cooking. Just as you sense the vegetables are almost done, no more than five minutes, add a ladle of the black bean sauce – try 50mls per person the first time and adjust that to your taste next time – and cook for a further minute at high heat to boil off some of the liquid. Add the almonds just before serving.

Goats' cheese crottin and caramelised red onion in a hazelnut tartlet with watercress pesto

The first batch of watercress arrives. You feel, or imagine, just a hint of warmth in the air, and it seems like a good time to lighten the food a little. Watercress has a vibrant, peppery flavour that adds sparkle to salads and makes great sauces and soups. Watercress pesto retains the peppery sharpness of the raw leaves and is a fantastic sauce for pasta or eggs. The flavour does fade, however, so use it within two days to get the best out of it.

Crottins, the miniature whole cheeses of goats' milk, are used in these little tartlets in preference to using, say, a slice of a large log of goats' cheese. The very youngest crottins are essentially tiny logs of fresh cheese, but they mature very quickly as the surface mould grows all round the relatively small surface. Thus a crottin that is about two weeks' old is perfect here, as it will have a thin skin to help it keep its shape in the pastry case, but will still have that mild, fresh flavour that is in keeping with spring cheeses. You can, of course, get more mature crottins with a thick skin and intense flavour. If that's your thing, go right ahead; they make a fine snack with crackers and a hearty bottle of red, but don't use them in these delicate little tartlets.

FOR SIX TARTLETS:

40g hazelnuts
150g plain flour
large pinch of salt
75g cold butter
40mls cold water

400g red onions
4 tablespoons brown sugar
4 tablespoons balsamic vinegar

140g watercress
1 clove garlic
40g walnuts
200–250mls olive oil
40g Parmesan, finely grated
3 goats' cheese crottins, 80g each

If you can get good-quality blanched hazelnuts… well, lucky you. Otherwise, roast the hazelnuts for about 20 minutes in a low to medium oven, then remove their skins by wrapping the nuts in a towel or cloth and rubbing them. Grind the skinned hazelnuts as finely as possible, then sift them with the flour and salt. Cut in the butter. A food processor does this very efficiently, but remove the pastry to a bowl before stirring in the water with a few quick strokes. Shape the pastry into a ball with your hands, flatten it gently and chill for at least half an hour. Roll the pastry and cut out circles to fit six small tartlet cases of about 7cm diameter. Prick the pastry cases all over with a fork and chill them again for 30 minutes; then bake them for eight to ten minutes at 180°C/350°F until crisp. Check after five minutes in case the pastry has puffed up in places; if it has, press it gently back in place while it is still soft. Slice the red onions in half, then into thin slices. Cook the onion in a little olive oil, stirring often, until the onions are fully cooked and beginning to caramelise. Add the sugar and balsamic vinegar, and continue to cook for a further 20 minutes or so until the onions are very soft and the liquid is syrupy. Leave to cool.

Put 100g of the watercress, the garlic and walnuts in a food processor and chop to a coarse purée. Add 200mls of olive oil and blend briefly to get a thick sauce. Add more oil if the pesto seems too thick, then stir in the Parmesan. Check the seasoning, and add salt and pepper if needed.

Put a tablespoon of caramelised red onion in each pastry case. Cut the crottins in half across the centre and place a half in each pastry case, skin side up. Bake the tartlets at 190°C/375°F until heated through, and the cheese has coloured a little and started to melt. Chop the remaining watercress coarsely and serve the tartlets sitting on a little of it, with the watercress pesto spooned around.

Grilled watercress and potato gnocchi with wild garlic and a roasted tomato cream

My neighbours, and anyone else who calls round, will tell you that I'm not the most enthusiastic gardener. I can dig a hole if Bridget points me at the spot, and I'm quite good at chopping down an unloved, oversized bush that has decided to become a tree in late life. There are two plants I guard carefully, however. One is the lemon verbena that wafts an incredible scent around the back door and gives a strong hint of childhood sherbet to desserts in Paradiso. The other is the white-flowered grass-like cousin of bluebells that we call wild garlic. During the early growth of spring, no mowing is allowed anywhere near it, and this year it is halfway across the 'lawn' because Bridget is away in New Zealand testing the sea temperatures in the Bay of Plenty. I am told by one who affects to know these things that what I have is a wild leek, and another similar plant with a wider leaf has been produced to make mine feel like a counterfeit. Both plants are hedge dwellers, the flowers of both are as edible as the stems, and both spread merrily if encouraged – so if you can get hold of either, give it a home at the base of your hedge or fence and don't mow quite so close to the edge in the spring. Some very finely sliced young spring onions and/or chives will be just lovely in this recipe while you wait for next spring to come round.

If you want to learn more about the hundreds of plants known as wild garlic, check out Alan Davidson's *Oxford Companion to Food*; in fact if you want to find out anything about anything, get a copy. My current favourite item in the book is the disgusting sea cucumber and the worm that lives off its, er, delicacies – look it up for the full horror. And no, it's not a vegetable.

The weights and measurements in this recipe need to be taken as guidelines only. So much depends on the flouriness of the potatoes you use, and the moisture content of the cress. You simply have to do it, get a feel for it, and do it often enough not to forget what that feels like. That might only be a few times a year if you have a good tactile memory. When these, or any other gnocchi, are on the menu in Paradiso, one person is put in charge of making it for the time it stays on the menu. Once they get it right and know what 'right' feels like, the small adjustments caused by potato types and so on are a doddle to adapt to. What you are trying to achieve is this: get a good balance of potato and watercress, lots of cress, in a lightish, soft dough, and flavour it very well with Parmesan, salt and pepper. The potato will give a nice soft texture to the gnocchi but won't quite hold it together. So you add flour to help make a dough. The wetter your potato, the more flour you need. And the more flour you add, the more out of balance your dough becomes, and then you have to backtrack and add a little more of everything again. Also, I think it's true to say that, the more flour you add, the tougher the dough – and your gnocchi – will be. So, use a fine floury potato – 'balls of flour' as our Irish mammies used to call them – and your gnocchi will have a fine start in life. The quantity of flour given is a minimum amount – it should be safe to add that much in one go.

1kg tomatoes
6 cloves garlic
1 sprig rosemary
1 sprig thyme
olive oil, to cover

600g floury potatoes
150g watercress
100g Parmesan, grated
salt and pepper, to season
120g plain white flour

300mls cream
small bunch wild garlic,
chopped

To make the tomato sauce, chop the tomatoes coarsely and put them in an oven tray with the garlic and herb sprigs, and add a coating of olive oil. Roast in a hot oven until the tomatoes are well coloured and broken down. Take out the rosemary and thyme sprigs, purée the tomatoes in their juices and pass the purée through a sieve to remove the skins.

Peel and steam, or boil and peel, the potatoes, according to your beliefs. Indeed, baking them in the oven and scooping out the cooked flesh is an excellent way to get the driest possible potato flesh. Either way, gently mash the cooked potato flesh, or pass it through a sieve. Chop the watercress very finely, put it in a clean cloth and squeeze out any moisture. Stir the watercress into the potato mash, add 80g of the Parmesan, and season well with salt and pepper. Add the flour and quickly work it into the potato. If the dough feels like it's not too sticky to roll out, nick off a small piece, roll it into a ball and drop it into boiling water to test. If it holds its shape firmly, without falling apart or getting gloopy on the outside, it's fine – don't add any more flour to the dough. If in

any doubt, add some flour and test again. When you've got a dough you trust, tear off a piece and use your hands to roll it into a long tubular shape about the thickness of your finger (or slightly thicker if you've got very elegant hands), and cut off pieces 2–3cm long. Drop the gnocchi into a large pot of boiling water, but don't overcrowd them – do a second batch separately if necessary.

While the gnocchi are cooking, put four tablespoons of the tomato sauce in a wide pan, add the cream, bring it to a boil and keep it at a very low simmer. The gnocchi are done when they float to the top. Remove the cooked gnocchi with a slotted spoon. If you are cooking two or more batches of the gnocchi, drop the cooked ones into the sauce to wait for the final batch. Then spoon the gnocchi on to plates or dishes just wide enough to hold them without crowding and pour over enough sauce to cover the surface of the plate. Scatter the chopped garlic leaves and the remaining Parmesan liberally over the gnocchi and finish the dish briefly under a hot grill, or in a hot fan oven.

Watercress, pear and walnut salad with blue cheese

Without the blue cheese, this is essentially a very simple, refreshing salad with clean flavours, and that is how I would use it most often – usually as a garnish for rich starters or as a salad with dinner at home. The cheese adds a sharp edge to the salad, and dresses it up enough to be a starter in its own right. I use mature Cashel blue here, though other semi-soft blues like Gorgonzola would be lovely too.

FOR FOUR:

200g watercress
60g walnut halves
60g mature blue cheese
1 pear
1 tablespoon walnut oil
3 tablespoons olive oil
juice of half a lemon

Pick over the watercress, discarding any less than perfect leaves and very thick stalks. Tear it into fairly big pieces – this won't be necessary if you bought the cress in prepared portions in a supermarket. Lightly toast the walnut halves. Break the cheese into a rough, large crumble. Slice the pear into thin wedges, then put everything in a bowl. Shake or whisk the oils and lemon juice together, add them to the bowl and toss the mixture gently. Now divide the salad on to plates, making sure each gets a nice proportion of cress to the other stuff.

A basic stock

A basic stock

Not all dishes need a stock. Indeed, as a younger cook I was interested only in the flavours of the main ingredients of dishes and almost never used stocks. If I felt a dish needed some complexity I put more ingredients in, spices, herbs, oils and so on. What I've come to like about using stock is the layering of flavours that can be achieved. The stock holds a balanced collection of flavours, as one, in the background as a support to the upfront primary flavours of the dish, given by the main ingredients. Think of stock as the bass tone, the element which holds the mood while the main ingredients amuse and entertain. This is important in dishes like risotto, soups and stews.

The title to this recipe doesn't lie. This is the basic model. The ingredients given here will make an acceptable, multi-purpose stock, and they are usually all present in the stocks we use in Paradiso. However, on any given day, it is likely that there will be a few extra seasonal twists. While I don't subscribe to the practice of throwing every spare piece of vegetable matter into the stockpot and boiling overnight, I do use appropriate pieces of cut-offs, leaves and stems of seasonal vegetables. In spring, for example, the asparagus stems are either added to the stockpot, or the water the asparagus is cooked in is also used to cook broad beans, green beans and spinach, and then reduced to a fraction of its volume and added to the stock; or it is used as the starting water for a stock. In winter, I prefer to use celeriac instead of celery, as it has the essential flavour of celery with an earthy tone which is very welcome in winter dishes. Other roots can be used too, though parsnips will add a sweetness you may want to make allowance for. I love tomatoes in a stock for their lovely sweet but sharp nature, but they will colour the stock, so use them only if a slightly orange tint doesn't matter. Most vegetables in their season will contribute a little something to stock, with some exceptions, such as aubergines. Bitter greens and cabbages will dominate a stock too easily, and if you do want to use them, they should only be cooked very briefly.

Herbs play a vital role in deciding the tone of the stock. As well as the basic thyme and parsley, which I would think of as staple winter herbs and use in greater amounts then, a stock in spring will often have fennel and dill herb because I like their airy, heady tone, and in later spring a little of the summer herbs. Basil and, to a lesser extent, oregano speak of the summer and should be used abundantly through the season. Tarragon and sage are powerful but deep herbs that should be used in small doses. I never use rosemary in stock because I feel it is too aromatic and overpowering, but I concede that may be a personal thing, and it's not that I don't love rosemary.

Finally, keep a very good stock powder, or bouillon, handy. I don't like it on its own, but sometimes, if a stock is lacking in depth and dimensions, if you don't have enough ingredients or herbs, add a careful pinch of a very high-quality stock powder and boil the stock for one more minute. The Swiss brand, Marigold, is excellent.

3 litres water
3 onions
8 cloves garlic
4 sticks celery
3 carrots
1 sprig thyme
1 bunch parsley
1 teaspoon peppercorns
1 teaspoons salt

To make the stock, bring the water to a boil in a large pot and drop in the rest of the ingredients. Bring it back to a boil and simmer for thirty minutes. Take the pot off the heat and leave it to rest for thirty minutes more, then drain the stock through a fine sieve to remove all the solids.

Vegetables, by and large, give up their flavour easily and long cooking can cause some to become bitter and old-tasting. A half-hour's simmering and a further half hour resting is enough to draw out the flavour of vegetables, herbs and spices. If you feel you need the stock to be stronger or more intense, you can simmer it again to reduce the volume after discarding the solids. Vegetable stocks need to be fresh, and to somehow retain something of the fresh qualities of the ingredients in them. Don't make stock from vegetables that would otherwise be destined for the compost; your stock, like everything else you cook, will taste of what you make it from.

Acknowledgements

I can't think of enough ways to say how lucky I am to have Sara Wilbourne as a publisher. I can't properly think of one way, actually. Sara teased and coaxed the book into being; when we lacked courage she pushed us on; other times she was the support that propped up our swaggering but flimsy confidence. She gave the book its genesis, its backbone and its sense of possibility.

The designer of the book, John Foley, is a good friend and I know him well enough, but even so I am still gobsmacked by the unique imagination he brings to his work. This is very much John's creation; only the words are mine. And yet, the best thing I can say is that working with him is great fun, especially the photography sessions. Jörg Köster's photography in *The Café Paradiso Cookbook* was beautiful, and I think it is even better this time. If I ever do another book it will probably be because I miss them.

Eoin Kelly has changed careers and flown away to London since he did the installation that became the cover of *The Café Paradiso Cookbook* but he took a step back in time to give us another beautiful composition for this cover.

This time around, I had the luxury of writing while working only part-time in the restaurant. I don't leave my kitchen easily, and I didn't until I was sure there was a crew there who could keep the standards up. Big thanks to all the staff, inside and outside the kitchen, but especially Tamzin, Mags and Johan, whose attention to detail in running the kitchen gave me the peace of mind to tune out for days on end. Outside the kitchen, Bridget picked up all the extra chores I opted out of. The more I dropped, the more she picked up; but then the more she picked up, the more I dropped. Sorry, Bridge, and thanks!

The inspiration for the food in Café Paradiso and in these recipes comes from the constantly shifting seasonal supply of vegetables. The motivation to move on and change comes from the pressure to react to what comes in next. I love vegetable growers. I love their energy, passion and ferocious optimism. Being a little bit of a control freak, I don't think I could stand it myself, having my proud work constantly at the mercy of the cruel elements, but I am in awe of those who do. Special thanks to Simon and Colette at Hollyhill Farm, Marc O'Mahony of the Organic Shop and the new boy on the block, Ultan Walsh.

Vegetable growers practically make cheese-makers seem sane, but only just. We're blessed to have some world class cheese makers within a couple of hours slow driving, making cheeses I would fly across the world to eat, including Bill Hogan's Gabriel, Wolfgang and Agnes Schliebitz' Knockalara, Dick Willems' Coolea, Rochus and Rose's Mature Oisín.

There are other people whose produce and dedication to excellence makes sure we always have the best of everything, especially the Iago folk for pasta and emergency cheese supplies, Toby and his gang for olives, olive oil and all sorts of delicious things, and Fran and Jim for the oyster mushrooms.

I mustn't forget to thank my mother, for a great many things of course, but especially for a few sensible words, also known as a gentle kick up the arse, when I was in the process of talking myself out of doing the book.

Finally, and most importantly, my family: Bridget, Tom and Oscar. There is a cliché often spoken and written by which the producer of a piece of work thanks his/her family for all the selfless support without which the work could not have been completed. It conjures up images of devoted angels tip-toeing around the house, a tray of tea and muffins left outside the great one's closed study door every few hours and announced by a barely audible tap; every little need of the creative one guessed at and delivered seconds before it even arises. I have come to understand the true meaning of self-less support; and so… I want to thank my wonderful family for almost always biting their tongues, rarely losing their tempers and ultimately not throwing out or killing the totally self-obsessed and terminally distracted person who clogged up the dining room and kitchen with papers and books, cooked only 'experiments' and never 'dinner', spread an atmosphere of mildly threatening tension and was of next to no use around the house for the best part of a year. Is there any greater expression of love and support?

Index

roasted globe artichoke with sheep's cheese and pinenuts, wilted greens and tomato pesto, 32

roasted green beans and shallots with couscous and marinated feta, 85

roasted roots gratin, 220

roast pumpkin, onion and feta tart in walnut filo pastry, 186–7

rocket salad with avocado, spring onion, garlic croûtons and pecorino, 11

spinach ravioli of pumpkin, basil and Gabriel cheese with lemon and black peppercorn butter, 180

spring cabbage timbale of roasted aubergine and Gabriel cheese with a plum tomato-basil sauce, 258

spring vegetable and herb soup with a fresh goats' cheese ravioli, 47

tagliolini with lemon, olive oil, chickpeas, flat leaf parsley and pecorino, 251

tomato, saffron ricotta and olive tart, 100

tortellini of Cashel blue cheese and sundried tomato with nutmeg spinach and an artichoke cream, 241

watercress, pear and walnut salad with blue cheese, 274

watermelon and feta salad with lime, pumpkinseed oil, toasted pumpkin seeds and green peppercorns, 89

cherries in kirsch with chocolate-olive oil mousse, 52

chestnut and carrot cannelloni with watercress cream, 224

chickpeas

braised cabbage with fennel, tomato and chickpeas, 211

chickpea, leek and rosemary soup with a hot pepper salsa, 192–3

roasted butternut squash with chickpeas and cumin, 179

tagliolini with lemon, olive oil, chickpeas, flat leaf parsley and pecorino, 251

chillies

aubergine, potato and fennel stew with red wine, thyme and chillies, 166–7

black bean, aubergine and leek chilli, 245–6

and black kale, plum tomatoes, olive oil and garlic, 57–8

fresh green chilli pesto, 135

green chilli aioli, 232

green chilli, pistachio and coconut chutney, 143

hot pepper salsa, 192–3

lemon chilli oil, 14

Parmesan and chilli polenta, 138

rigatoni with winter greens, artichokes, dried tomatoes, chillies and capers, 247

spring greens with coriander seeds, chillies and ginger, 262

sweet chilli-fried tofu, 242

sweet and hot pepper chutney, 143

chives

chive and mustard cream, 25

mint and chives in risotto of fresh peas, 87

chocolate

chocolate-olive oil mousse, 52

chocolate pecan pie, whiskey ice cream and darling clementines, 236

ciabatta with goats' cheese, 104

cinnamon ice cream, 216

clementines *see oranges*

coconut

coconut curry of roasted roots, 220

coconut greens, 248

coconut ice cream, 238–9

coconut-peanut relish, 183

coconut satay, 132

green chilli, pistachio and coconut chutney, 143

spiced beetroot in coconut pancake, 7, 75–6

in summer squash salad, 70

sweet chilli-fried tofu with leeks in coconut and lemongrass broth, 242

Thai cabbage and onion soup with coconut, lime and coriander, 210

colcannon of spring greens and potato, 262

Coolea cheese

in aubergine wraps with spinach and pinenuts, 164–5

grilled sandwiches of artichoke paste, spinach and, 140

coriander

Brussels sprouts with tomato, ginger and coriander, 215

spring greens with coriander seeds, chillies and ginger, 262

in summer squash salad, 70

Thai cabbage and onion soup with coconut, lime and coriander, 210

corn-crusted aubergine fritters with tamarillo chutney, 130

corn pancakes

with leek, parsnip and Gabriel cheese, 197–8

with leeks and puy lentils, 266–7

courgette flowers, poached, with herbed ricotta stuffing in a tomato and basil broth, 68

courgettes

barbecued, 126

pan-fried, with cherry tomatoes, basil and garlic, on a new-potato tortilla, 65–6

couscous

pan-fried couscous cake of red onion, feta cheese and pinenuts, 107–8

pilaf, 220

with roasted green beans, shallots and marinated feta, 85

crispbreads, 35–6

croûtons *see garlic*

cucumber and yoghurt sauce, 186–7

cumin with roasted butternut squash and chickpeas, 179

currants and Knockalara sheep's cheese ravioli in a lemon-thyme cream, with spinach and sundried tomato, 42

dark chocolate tart with raspberry sorbet and fresh raspberries, 82

desserts

baked organic pineapple with rum and spices, a lime tuille and coconut ice cream, 238–9

blackberry tart with Calvados ice cream, 148–9

blood orange and fennel sorbet with marinated blood oranges, 255

cardamom and orange-roasted figs with amaretto semi-freddo, 172

charentais melon sorbet with honey and rosewater baklava, 94–5

cherries in kirsch with chocolate-olive oil mousse, 52

chocolate-olive oil mousse, 52

chocolate pecan pie, whiskey ice cream and darling clementines, 236

dark chocolate tart with raspberry sorbet and fresh raspberries, 82

gooseberry fool with gingered sponge fingers, 51

lemon verbena, ricotta and white chocolate pudding with blueberry compote, 147

tortellini of Cashel blue cheese and sundried tomato with nutmeg spinach and an artichoke cream, 241

pastry, 20, 194

almond, 44–6

hazelnut, 270

see also **tarts**

peaches, 2, 6

oven-roasted, with lavender and honey ice cream and pistachio biscotti, 91–2

peanut-coconut relish, 183

pears

vanilla-poached pears with cinnamon ice cream, 216

watercress, pear and walnut salad with blue cheese, 274

peas

fresh pasta in a sweet pepper cream with mangetout, aubergine, spring onions and basil, 110

and oyster mushroom ravioli with a truffled lovage cream, 154

risotto of fresh peas, mangetout and sugar snaps with mascarpone, mint and chives, 87

summer stew of sweet peppers, new potatoes and sugar snaps with basil, garlic and olives, and goats' cheese ciabatta, 104

pecans

and baked portobello mushroom, Cashel blue cheese and sage, 153

chocolate pecan pie, whiskey ice cream and darling clementines, 236

glazed, in rhubarb crumble with a gingered rhubarb syrup, 26–7

salad of grilled figs with pecans, rocket and watercress, mascarpone and a vanilla-citrus dressing, 171

pecorino

with rocket salad, avocado, spring onion and garlic croûtons, 11

with tagliolini, lemon, olive oil, chickpeas, flat leaf parsley, 251

peppers, 2, 6

grilled artichoke with roasted pepper and basil aioli, 29

hot pepper salsa, 192–3

pan-fried couscous cake of red onion, feta cheese and pinenuts with green olive tapenade and spiced roast peppers with spinach, 107–8

roasted pepper and garlic oil, 61

roasted pepper rolls of black kale and pinenuts, 129

spiced red pepper and tomato jam, 62–3

summer stew of sweet peppers, new potatoes and sugar snaps with basil, garlic and olives, and goats' cheese ciabatta, 104

sweet and hot pepper chutney, 143

sweet pepper cream, 110

Turkish pepper sauce, 168–9

pesto

fresh green chilli, 135

tomato, 32, 261

watercress, 270

pineapple, baked organic, with rum and spices, a lime tuille and coconut ice cream, 238–9

pinenuts, 11

in aubergine wraps with spinach and Coolea cheese, 164–5

pan-fried couscous cake of red onion, feta cheese and pinenuts, 107–8

in ravioli, with currants and Knockalara sheep's cheese in a lemon-thyme cream, with spinach and sundried tomato, 42

and roasted globe artichoke with sheep's cheese, wilted greens and tomato pesto, 32

roasted leeks with a lemon, ginger and pinenut marinade, 200

roasted pepper rolls of black kale and pinenuts, 129

pistachios

biscotti, 91–2

green chilli, pistachio and coconut chutney, 143

pistachio, cardamom and basmati rice cake with coconut greens and gingered mango salsa, 248

scallion and pistachio cream, 75–6

poached courgette flowers with herbed ricotta stuffing in a tomato and basil broth, 68

polenta

gnocchi, 245–6

lemon and almond polenta cake, 54

Parmesan and chilli polenta, 138

Parmesan polenta, 264–5

pomegranate, mint and yoghurt sauce, 227

potatoes, 230–1

aubergine, potato and fennel stew with red wine, thyme and chillies, and goats' cheese gougères, 166–7

barbecued, 126

braised chard parcels of potato and lentil with spiced red pepper and tomato jam, 62–3

celeriac, leek and potato gratin with capers and thyme, 234

crushed, in almond pastry galette with wilted spinach, Knockalara sheep's cheese and tomato-cardamom relish, 44–6

grilled potato and kale gnocchi in a hazelnut and rosemary cream, 235

grilled watercress and potato gnocchi with wild garlic and a roasted tomato cream, 272–3

new-potato tortilla, 65–6

and parsnip and wild rice cake, 156–7

potato, sweet onion and basil tortilla with green chilli aioli, 232

spring greens and potato colcannon, 262

summer stew of sweet peppers, new potatoes and sugar snaps with basil, garlic and olives, and goats' cheese ciabatta, 104

pumpkins, 5, 175–7

baked pumpkin, cashew and yoghurt curry, 191

barbecued, 126

gratin of roast pumpkin, leeks, sweetcorn and hazelnuts with a Gabriel cheese cream, 189–90

pumpkin gnocchi with spinach in a roasted garlic cream, 181–2

roast pumpkin, onion and feta tart in walnut filo pastry with cucumber and yoghurt sauce, 186–7

spinach ravioli of pumpkin, basil and Gabriel cheese with lemon and black peppercorn butter, 180

see also **squash**

purple sprouting broccoli, 6

purple sprouting broccoli with dried tomatoes and garlic on a corn pancake of leeks and puy lentils, with a rosemary cream, 266–7

stir-fried sprouting broccoli, carrots and almonds in a hot-and-sour black bean sauce, 269

warm salad of purple sprouting broccoli with radishes, Parmesan polenta and avocado oil, 264–5

puy lentils

braised chard parcels of potato and lentil with spiced red pepper and tomato jam, 62–3

purple sprouting broccoli with dried tomatoes and garlic on a corn pancake of leeks and puy lentils, 266–7

risotto of leeks, butternut squash and sage with pumpkinseed oil and braised lentils, 199

wilted kale with garlic, puy lentils and thyme, 212

radishes, in warm salad of purple sprouting broccoli with Parmesan polenta and avocado oil, 264–5

raspberry sorbet, 82

ravioli

fresh goats' cheese in, 47

oyster mushroom ravioli with a truffled lovage cream and peas, 154

pinenuts, currants and Knockalara sheep's cheese in, 42

spinach ravioli of pumpkin, basil and Gabriel cheese with lemon and black peppercorn butter, 180

red onions

caramelised, aparagus and Knockalara sheep's cheese tart, 20

goats' cheese crottin and caramelised red onion in a hazelnut tartlet, 270

pan-fried couscous cake of red onion, feta cheese and pinenuts, 107–8

with rigatoni, chard and cannellini beans in a roasted pepper and garlic oil, 61

red peppers *see peppers*

rhubarb and glazed pecan crumble with a gingered rhubarb syrup, 26–7

rice cakes

pistachio, cardamom and basmati rice cakes, 248

wild rice, potato and parsnip cake, 156–7

ricotta

herbed ricotta stuffing, , 68

lemon verbena, ricotta and white chocolate pudding with blueberry compote, 147

tomato, saffron ricotta and olive tart, 100

rigatoni

with chard, red onions and cannellini beans in a roasted pepper and garlic oil, 61

with rocket, broad beans, cherry tomatoes, olives and fresh cheese, 12

with winter greens, artichokes, dried tomatoes, chillies and capers, 247

risotto

avocado and rocket, 14–15

fresh peas, mangetout and sugar snaps with mascarpone, mint and chives, 87

of leeks, butternut squash and sage with pumpkinseed oil and braised lentils, 199

of parsnip, salsify and sage with beetroot crisps, 222–3

roast beetroot with balsamic vinegar, caraway and wilted greens, 72

roasted aubergine rolls with sheep's cheese and almond stuffing, and a Turkish pepper sauce, 168–9

roasted butternut squash with chickpeas and cumin, 179

roasted green beans and shallots with couscous and marinated feta, 85

roasted leeks with a lemon, ginger and pinenut marinade, 200

roasted pepper and garlic oil, 61

roasted pepper rolls of black kale and pinenuts, 129

roasted roots and some uses for them, 218

roasted roots soup, 220

roast pumpkin, onion and feta tart in walnut filo pastry with cucumber and yoghurt sauce, 186–7

rocket

and broad beans, cherry tomatoes, olives and fresh cheese with rigatoni, 12

risotto with avocado, shavings of Oisín goats' cheese and a lemon chilli oil, 14–15

salad with avocado, spring onion, garlic croûtons and pecorino, 11

salad of grilled figs with pecans, rocket and watercress, mascarpone and a vanilla-citrus dressing, 171

root vegetables, roasted, 218–20

rosemary

aioli, 18

chickpea, leek and rosemary soup with a hot pepper salsa, 192–3

and hazelnut cream, 235

rosemary cream, 266–7

runner beans

barbecued, 126

green curry of cauliflower and beans, 184

sage

and baked portobello mushroom,

Cashel blue cheese and pecan crumbs, and smoked paprika aioli, 153

butter, 59–60

and cider cream with pan-fried mushrooms, 156–7

risotto of leeks, butternut squash and sage with pumpkinseed oil and braised lentils, 199

risotto of parsnip, salsify and sage with beetroot crisps, 222–3

salad of grilled figs with pecans, rocket and watercress, mascarpone and a vanilla-citrus dressing, 171

salsas and relishes

aubergine-tomato relish, 162

avocado-lime salsa, 184

beetroot relish, 156–7

cherry tomato-fennel salsa, 197–8

cherry tomato salsa, 21–2

coconut-peanut relish, 183

gingered mango salsa, 248

hot pepper salsa, 192–3

mango, lime and avocado salsa, 143

tomato-cardamom relish, 44–6

salsify, parsnip and sage risotto with beetroot crisps, 222–3

satay, coconut, 132

sauces, chutneys and syrups

artichoke cream, 241

balsamic-tomato emulsion, 159

chive and mustard cream, 25

cucumber and yoghurt sauce, 186–7

fresh tomato, thyme and caper sauce, 164–5

gingered rhubarb syrup, 26–7

hazelnut and rosemary cream, 235

hot-and-sour black bean sauce, 269

lemon-thyme cream, 42

lime soured cream, 245–6

plum tomato-basil sauce, 258

pomegranate, mint and yoghurt sauce, 227

roasted garlic cream, 181–2

roasted tomato cream, 272–3

rosemary cream, 266–7

sage and cider cream, 156–7

scallion and pistachio cream, 75–6

spiced red pepper and tomato jam, 62–3

star anise – citrus cream, 77

sweet and hot pepper chutney, 143

tomato – wild garlic concasse, 30–1

truffled lovage cream, 154

Turkish pepper sauce, 168–9

watercress cream, 224

watermelon and ginger sambal, 143

savoy cabbage dolmas of wild rice, leek and eggs in truffle oil, 209

scallions *see spring onions*

semi-freddo, amaretto, 172

shallots *see onions*

smoked paprika aioli, 153

sorbets

blood orange and fennel, 255

melon, 94–5

raspberry, 82

soups

beetroot soup with cabbage and vodka, 228

butternut squash soup with lime and a coconut-peanut relish, 183

cauliflower soup with green peppercorns and avocado oil, 206

chickpea, leek and rosemary soup with a hot pepper salsa, 192–3

roasted roots soup, 220

spring vegetable and herb soup with a fresh goats' cheese ravioli, 47

Thai cabbage and onion soup with coconut, lime and coriander, 210

tomato rasam, 98–9

spiced beetroot in coconut pancake, 7

spiced red pepper and tomato jam, 62–3

spinach, 6

in aubergine wraps with pinenuts and Coolea cheese, 164–5

grilled sandwiches of artichoke paste, spinach and Coolea cheese, 140

nutmeg spinach, 241

pan-fried couscous cake of red onion, feta cheese and pinenuts with green olive tapenade and spiced roast peppers with spinach, 107–8

pumpkin gnocchi with spinach in a roasted garlic cream, 181–2

and ravioli of pinenuts, currants and Knockalara sheep's cheese in a lemon-thyme cream, with sundried tomato, 42

spinach ravioli of pumpkin, basil and Gabriel cheese with lemon and black peppercorn butter, 180

wilted, in almond pastry galette with Knockalara sheep's cheese and

crushed potato with tomato-cardamom relish, 44–6

sponge fingers, gingered, 51

spring cabbage

braised spring cabbage and tomato pesto rolls, 261

spring cabbage timbale of roasted aubergine and Gabriel cheese with a plum tomato-basil sauce, 258

spring greens and potato colcannon, 262

spring greens with coriander seeds, chillies and ginger, 262

spring onions

barbecued, 126

fresh pasta in a sweet pepper cream with mangetout, aubergine, spring onions and basil, 110

in rocket salad, avocado, garlic croûtons and pecorino, 11

scallion and pistachio cream, 75–6

spring rolls of carrot and cabbage with a pomegranate, mint and yoghurt sauce, 227

spring vegetable and herb soup with a fresh goats' cheese ravioli, 47

squash

barbecued, 126

butternut squash, barbecued, 126

butternut squash soup with lime and a coconut-peanut relish, 183

grilled, with spiced coating, 136

honey-roasted butternut with avocado-lime salsa, and green curry of cauliflower and beans, 184

risotto of leeks, butternut squash and sage with pumpkinseed oil and braised lentils, 199

roasted butternut squash with chickpeas and cumin, 179

summer squash salad, 70

see also pumpkins

star anise – citrus cream, 77

stir-fried sprouting broccoli, carrots and almonds in a hot-and-sour black bean sauce, 269

stock, vegetable, 276–7

strawberries

and balsamic vinegar and Thai basil, 78

strawberry baked Alaska with summer berry compote, 81

summer berry compote, 81

summer squash salad with cashews, coconut, yoghurt,, lime, ginger and coriander, 70

summer stew of sweet peppers, new potatoes and sugar snaps with basil, garlic and olives, and goats' cheese ciabatta, 104

sweet chilli-fried tofu with leeks in coconut and lemongrass broth, 242

sweetcorn

barbecued, 126

barbecued, with basil and pepper-corn butter, 136

gratin of roast pumpkin, leeks, sweetcorn and hazelnuts with a Gabriel cheese cream, 189–90

sweet and hot pepper chutney, 143

sweet potato, tofu and shallot kebabs, ginger-glazed, 132

tagliolini with lemon, olive oil, chick-peas, flat leaf parsley and pecorino, 251

tamarillo chutney, 130

tapenade

green olive, 107–8

olive and caper, 138

tarts

aparagus, caramelised onion and Knockalara sheep's cheese tart, 20

blackberry tart with Calvados ice cream, 148–9

chocolate pecan pie, 236

dark chocolate tart, 82

goats' cheese crottin and caramelised red onion in a hazelnut tartlet, 270

leek and blue cheese tartlet with roasted cherry tomatoes, 194

roast pumpkin, onion and feta tart in walnut filo pastry, 186–7

tomato, saffron ricotta and olive tart, 100

tempura, cauliflower and beetroot, 204

Thai cabbage and onion soup with coconut, lime and coriander, 210

thyme

aubergine, potato and fennel stew with red wine, thyme and chillies, 166–7

celeriac, leek and potato gratin with capers and thyme, 234

fresh tomato, thyme and caper sauce, 164–5

lemon-thyme cream, 42